Praise for *Faith Alone*

"Dr. Schreiner has done a magnificent job of expounding the key doctrine of the Protestant Reformation, *sola fide*, which remains as vital for us today as when Martin Luther first proclaimed it. Schreiner's clear explanation of justification by faith alone will do much to strengthen the faith of a new generation and its witness to this timeless truth."

—GERALD BRAY, research professor of divinity, Beeson Divinity School

"The doctrine by which the church stands or falls—that's how Luther described the importance of justification by faith alone. Without the imputed righteousness of Christ received by faith alone, we are truly without hope before a holy God. Thomas Schreiner, one of the most clear-headed and biblically faithful New Testament scholars of our generation, has produced a compelling and careful defense of the doctrine of justification that readers will find both exegetically faithful and theologically enriching. This book will help the church in this generation to stand on solid ground."

—R. ALBERT MOHLER JR., president of the
Southern Baptist Theological Seminary

"As new ideas about justification have proliferated in recent years, the need for a clear analysis of these ideas and a better understanding of the traditional Reformation view has grown. Tom Schreiner's *Faith Alone* accomplishes both tasks admirably. Schreiner anchors his exposition of the key biblical themes in the history of the doctrine, and defends the Reformation view in light of the many current challenges. Comprehensive, readable, persuasive."

—DOUGLAS J. MOO, Wessner Chair of Biblical Studies, Wheaton
College; Chair, Committee on Bible Translation (NIV)

T0084342

Praise for the Five Solas Series

"The Protestant Reformation was driven by a renewed appreciation of the singular fullness of the triune God and his unique sovereignty in all of human life. But that profound reality expressed itself with regard to many questions and in a number of forms, ranging from facets of the liturgy to soteriological tenets and back again. I'm delighted to see this new series expositing the five most influential expressions of that God-centeredness, the pivotal *Solas* of the Protestant Reformation. By expounding the biblical reasoning behind them, I hope these volumes will invigorate a more profoundly theological vision of our lives and callings as Christians and churches."

—MICHAEL ALLEN, associate professor of systematic and historical theology, Reformed Theological Seminary

"The Reformation's five-hundredth anniversary will be celebrated as a significant historical event. However, the Five Solas series explores the contemporary relevance of this legacy for the global church. Superb evangelical scholars have been enlisted not only to summarize the 'solas,' but to engage each from historical, exegetical, and constructive perspectives. These volumes demonstrate that, far from being exhausted slogans, the Reformation's key themes need to be rediscovered for the church's existence and mission in the world."

—MICHAEL HORTON, J. Gresham Machen Professor of Systematic Theology and Apologetics, Westminster Seminary California

"I welcome this new series and its substantial engagement with the great themes of Reformation theology."

—TIMOTHY GEORGE, founding dean of Beeson Divinity School of Samford University and general editor of the Reformation Commentary on Scripture.

"A timely project—and not simply because the five-hundredth anniversary of the Reformation will soon be upon us. Much of 'who we are' is determined by 'where we have come from'; at a time when even so significant a part of our past as the Reformation is, for many, little more than a name, informed, accessible treatments of its basic principles are welcome indeed."

—STEPHEN WESTERHOLM, professor of early Christianity, McMaster University

Faith

ALONE

THE DOCTRINE OF
JUSTIFICATION

The Five Solas Series

Edited by Matthew Barrett

Books in Series:

THE **5 SOLAS** SERIES

Faith
ALONE

THE DOCTRINE OF JUSTIFICATION

What the Reformers Taught
... and Why It Still Matters

THOMAS SCHREINER

MATTHEW BARRETT, SERIES EDITOR

To my daughter, Anna.
Every day you bring me joy.

ZONDERVAN

Faith Alone — The Doctrine of Justification
Copyright © 2015 by Thomas R. Schreiner

This title is also available as a Zondervan ebook. Visit www.zondervan.com/ebooks.

Requests for information should be addressed to:
Zondervan, 3900 *Sparks Dr. SE, Grand Rapids, Michigan 49546*

Library of Congress Cataloging-in-Publication Data

Schreiner, Thomas R.
    Faith alone — the doctrine of justification : what the reformers taught and why it matters / Thomas R. Schreiner.
        pages   cm. - (The five solas series)
    Includes bibliographical references and index.
    ISBN 978-0-310-51578-4 (softcover)
    1. Justification (Christian theology) I. Title.
BT764.3.S37   2015
234.7 — dc23   2014044777

Cover design: Chris Tobias / Outerwear for Books
Interior design: Kait Lamphere

Printed in the United States of America

HB 03.12.2024

Contents

A Historical Tour of *Sola Fide*

A Biblical and Theological Tour of *Sola Fide*

Contemporary Challenges to *Sola Fide*

A Note from the Series Editor

What doctrines could be more foundational to what it means to be an evangelical Protestant than the five *solas* (or *solae*) of the Reformation? In my experience, however, many in evangelical churches today have never heard of *sola Scriptura* (by Scripture alone), *sola gratia* (by grace alone), *sola fide* (by faith alone), *solus Christus* (by Christ alone), and *soli Deo gloria* (glory to God alone).

Now it could be that they have never heard the labels but would recognize the doctrines once told what each *sola* means. At least I pray so. But my suspicion is that for many churchgoers, even the content of these five *solas* is foreign, or worse, offensive. We live in a day when Scripture's authority is questioned, the exclusivity of Christ as mediator, as well as the necessity of saving faith, is offensive to pluralistic ears, and the glory of God in vocation is diminished by cultural accommodation. The temptation is to think that these five *solas* are museum pieces of a bygone era with little relevance for today's church. We disagree. We need these *solas* just as much today as the Reformers needed them in the sixteenth century.

The year 2017 will mark the five hundredth anniversary of the Reformation. These five volumes, each written by some of today's best theologians, celebrate that anniversary. Our aim is not merely to look to the past but to the present, demonstrating that we must drink deeply from the wells of the five *solas* in order to recover our theological bearings and find spiritual refreshment.

Post tenebras lux

Matthew Barrett, series editor

Acknowledgments

As we look back to the early days of the Reformation, we give thanks for the recovery of the gospel. We see a similar recovery in our day for which we give praise to the God of the gospel. My hope is that this book will strengthen and comfort and challenge readers with the truth that salvation is of the Lord.

I would be remiss if I didn't express thanks for those who have helped me along the way. I am grateful to Matthew Barrett for his friendship, for inviting me to participate in this multivolume series on the five *solas*, and for his editorial work on the manuscript. Words can't capture the help I received from Aubrey Sequeira. Aubrey chased down books for me, copied articles, and helped me in countless ways, especially in the section on John Wesley. His indefatigable labors, which saved me hours and hours, have demonstrated his love to me.

I am also grateful to my dear friend Shawn Wright, who teaches church history at Southern and is one of my fellow elders at Clifton Baptist. Shawn took time out of his incredibly busy schedule to read and interact with what I wrote about *sola fide* in the history of the church. This is not to say, of course, that he would necessarily endorse what I have written or would put it the way I have. Still, the book would be worse off without his wise input.

Finally, I am grateful to Ryan Pazdur and Verlyn Verbrugge for their encouragement and for their excellent work in editing the final product. They both contributed significantly to the book being better than it would have been otherwise. As this book goes to press, I was saddened to hear of the death of Verlyn Verbrugge. Verlyn encouraged me greatly about this book, and I know he encouraged and strengthened so many by his faith in Christ and with his humility and love. Like Abel, though he has died, he still speaks to us through his faith (Heb. 11:4).

Thomas R. Schreiner

Foreword

Knowing from James 2:26 that there is such a thing as *dead* faith; and from James 2:19 that there is such a thing as *demonic* faith; and from 1 Corinthians 15:2 that it is possible to believe *in vain*; and from Luke 8:13 that one can "believe for a while, and in time of testing *fall away*"; and knowing that it is through faith that we are *born again* (1 John 5:1) and have *eternal life* (John 3:16, 36), therefore, surely we must conclude that the nature of faith, and its relationship to salvation, is of *infinite* importance.

I use the word *infinite* carefully. I mean that, if we don't have such faith, the consequences have infinite significance. *Eternal* life is an infinite thing. And thus the loss of it is an infinite thing. Therefore, any human concern that has only to do with this world, no matter how global, no matter how painful, no matter how enduring—if it has only to do with this world— compares to the importance of saving faith as a thimble to the ocean.

Which means, this book is dealing with treasures of immeasurable importance. Infinity cannot be measured. And infinite things are at stake. As Tom Schreiner says, the book "tackles one of the fundamental questions of our human condition: how can a person be right with God?"

The stunning Christian answer is: *sola fide* — faith alone. But be sure you hear this carefully and precisely: He says *right with God* by faith alone, not *attain heaven* by faith alone. There are other conditions for attaining heaven, but no others for entering a right relationship to God. In fact, one must already be in a right relationship with God by faith alone in order to meet the other conditions.

"We are justified by faith alone, but not by faith that is alone." Faith that is alone is not faith in union with Christ. Union with Christ makes his perfection and power ours through faith. And in union with Christ, faith is living and active with Christ's power.

Such faith always "works by love" and produces the "obedience of faith." And that obedience—imperfect as it is till the day we die—is not the "basis of justification, but ... a necessary evidence and fruit of justification." In this sense, love and obedience—inherent righteousness—is "required of believers, but not for justification"—that is, required for heaven, not for entering a right-standing with God.

Everything in this book is measured by the Scriptures. "We should hold to the tradition of *sola fide* because it accords with the Word of God." Therefore, thematically and structurally, the center of the book is biblical exegesis. "In this book I attempt to tour the *historical* teaching of the church, explain the *scriptural* teaching on justification, and provide some sense of *contemporary* relevance" (emphasis added).

But even in the historical and contemporary sections, Scripture remains the lodestar, guiding the ship of Schreiner's analysis. Thus the book is overwhelmingly constructive rather than merely polemical—and always careful, for when handling the most volatile issues, one must handle with care.

Schreiner is unusually careful in handling viewpoints that are different from his own. I have never read another author who states his challenger's viewpoint so fully and persuasively, that it seems so compelling, and then turns around and demolishes it one piece at a time with careful biblical observation and argumentation. It is a trait that awakens trust.

Schreiner does not play God. He does not render judgments about men's souls, only their doctrines. He follows John Owen in the gracious position that "men may be really saved by that grace which doctrinally they do deny; and they may be justified by the imputation of that righteousness, which, in opinion, they deny to be imputed."

His aim is not to defeat others or merely win arguments; his aim is the glory of God and the everlasting joy of people. "*Sola fide* gives all the glory to God, so that no one will boast in human beings (1 Cor. 1:31)." This is true not only because Christ is the sole ground of our right standing with God, but also because faith itself is a gift: "No one can boast about faith, for faith itself is a gift of God." Moreover, faith, by its very nature, "glorifies and honors God, for it confesses that God can do what he has promised."

And this faith is no mere mental assent, but a heartfelt embrace of Jesus Christ as its all-satisfying treasure. "Justification is by faith alone, for faith finds its *joy* in Christ alone, seeing him as the pearl of great price, the one who is more *desirable* than anything or anyone else" (emphasis added).

Thus Schreiner closes his book with a joyful testimony—and I rejoice to join him in it: "My confidence on the last day ... will not rest on my transformation. I have too far to go to put any confidence in what I have accomplished. Instead, I rest on Jesus Christ. He is my righteousness. He is the guarantor of my salvation. I am justified by faith alone, in Christ alone, to the glory of God alone."

John Piper
Founder and Teacher, desiringGod.org
Chancellor, Bethlehem College & Seminary

Abbreviations

AB	Anchor Bible
ABR	*Australian Biblical Review*
BECNT	Baker Exegetical Commentary on the New Testament
Bib	*Biblica*
BJRL	*Bulletin of the John Rylands University Library of Manchester*
CBQ	*Catholic Biblical Quarterly*
CH	*Church History*
CTQ	*Concordia Theological Quarterly*
DPL	*Dictionary of Paul and His Letters*
ESV	English Standard Version
ExpTim	*Expository Times*
FRLANT	Forschungen zur Religion und Literatur des Alten und Neuen Testaments
HCSB	Holman Christian Standard Version
HTR	*Harvard Theological Review*
IDB	*Interpreter's Dictionary of the Bible*
JBL	*Journal of Biblical Literature*
JEH	*Journal of Ecclesiastical History*
JETS	*Journal of the Evangelical Theological Society*
JSJ	*Journal for the Study of Judaism*
JSNT	*Journal for the Study of the New Testament*
JTS	*Journal of Theological Studies*
LCC	Library of Christian Classics
LNTS	Library of New Testament Studies
LXX	Septuagint
NAC	New American Commentaries
NIGTC	New International Greek Testament Commentary
NIV	New International Version
NovT	*Novum Testamentum*
NPNF	*Nicene and Post-Nicene Fathers*

NSBT   New Studies in Biblical Theology
NTAbh   Neutestamentliche Abhandlungen
NTS   *New Testament Studies*
Pillar   Pillar New Testament Commentary
ProEccl *Pro ecclesia*
SBLSP   Society of Biblical Literature Seminar Papers
SNTSMS   Society for New Testament Studies Monograph Series
TrinJ   *Trinity Journal*
TynBul *Tyndale Bulletin*
WA   *Weimarer Ausgabe*
WBC   Word Biblical Commentary
WTJ   *Westminster Theological Journal*
WUNT   Wissenschaftliche Untersuchungen zum Neuen Testament
ZECNT   Zondervan Exegetical Commentary on the New Testament
ZNW   *Zeitschrift für die neutestamentliche Wissenschaft und die Kunde der älteren Kirche*

Introduction

> "But when we rise to the heavenly tribunal and place before
> our eyes that supreme Judge ... then in an instant the vain
> confidence of men perishes and falls and conscience is
> compelled ... to confess that it has nothing upon which it
> can rely before God."   —*Francis Turretin*

O ne of the five rallying cries of the Reformation was the statement that
we are saved by faith alone—*sola fide!* These words declared that
salvation does not come from looking at our own works of righteousness,
but from looking outside ourselves to another, to the person and work of
Jesus Christ. This statement grew out of a desire to return to the biblical
text and to the teachings of the early church fathers, a cry to reform the
church and return it to biblical orthodoxy.

Centuries have passed since the Reformation, and we may wonder:
Does *sola fide* still matter today? Is the notion of justification by faith
alone just a relic of days gone by, reflecting a nostalgia for a previous time?
As will be evident throughout this book, I believe that the Reformation
cry of *sola fide* should continue to be taught and treasured today because it
summarizes biblical teaching, and God's Word never loses its transforming
power. The Word of God speaks in every era and in every place. While
some may hold on to *sola fide* to uphold tradition, I believe we should hold
on to the tradition of *sola fide* because it accords with the Word of God.
Justification by faith alone isn't the product of rigid and brittle orthodoxy.
It speaks to the minds and hearts of people all throughout history because
it tackles one of the fundamental questions of our human condition: How
can a person be right with God?

The words of Francis Turretin (1623–1687) testify to the pastoral
relevance of this truth that justification is by *faith alone*. He says we truly
understand "the controversy" on justification when we consider our own
standing, as individuals, before a holy and righteous God:

But when we rise to the heavenly tribunal and place before our eyes that supreme Judge ... by whose brightness the stars are darkened, at whose strength the mountains melt; by whose anger the earth is shaken; whose justice not even the angels are equal to bear; who does not make the guilty innocent; whose vengeance when once kindled penetrates even the lowest depths of hell ... then in an instant the vain confidence of men perishes and falls and conscience is compelled ... to confess that it has nothing upon which it can rely before God. And so it cries out with David, "Lord, if thou marked iniquity, who can stand?" ... When the mind is thoroughly terrified with the consciousness of sin and a sense of God's wrath, what is that thing on account of which he may be acquitted before God and be reckoned a righteous person? ... Is it righteousness inhering in us and inchoate holiness or the righteousness and obedience of Christ alone imputed to us?[1]

I will defend in due course the notion that *sola fide* is biblical, but we must never forget why its biblical truth matters to us today. While some may wish to talk about theology for the sake of theological disputation, the central issue, as Turretin points out, is personal. We are talking about standing before God on the last day, on the day of judgment, and *sola fide* answers that question: How will we stand before the Holy One of Israel?

Still, one might agree that how we stand at the final judgment is a crucial question and think at the same time that justification by faith alone should be abandoned. After all, *sola fide* is easily misunderstood, and because of this they believe that the slogan should be jettisoned. Why appeal to a slogan that needs to be qualified and explained carefully to avoid abuse? This objection, however, applies to every theological truth. We don't surrender the term Trinity, even though it is frequently misunderstood. Instead, what we mean by the word Trinity must be carefully explained and qualified. Theologians, scholars, and pastors must carefully unpack what that term means and what it doesn't mean, so that those who listen to them don't think Christians are tritheists. Yet despite these challenges, we don't abandon the word just because it is easily misinterpreted. Christians throughout history have believed that certain words and phrases are helpful in summarizing and enshrining crucial theological truths. We should not surrender a formula even though it is sometimes misunderstood or wrongly explicated, for the slogan expresses a vital theological truth, one that is worth cherishing and guarding.

---

1. Francis Turretin, *Institutes of Elenctic Theology* (trans. George Musgrave Giger; ed. James T. Dennison Jr.; Phillipsburg, NJ: Presbyterian & Reformed, 1994), 639–40.

Sometimes Reformed Christians are accused of focusing too much energy on guarding and protecting doctrines and traditions like justification by faith alone. Perhaps, at times, we are guilty of overemphasizing doctrinal fidelity to the neglect of cherishing the truth we confess. Yet guarding the faith is certainly a noble and biblical endeavor. Jude calls us to such in no uncertain terms (Jude 3), and both Galatians and 2 Timothy emphasize that we must guard the gospel and uphold it even when others deny it. Still, we must beware that our efforts at guarding the gospel do not become more important to us than cherishing the life-giving freedom and joy the gospel provides to us. We guard the truth *because* we cherish it, and we cherish the truth *because* it is our life. When we are alone and quiet before God, we remember our many sins and our great unworthiness. In such moments we see and sense the glory and beauty of *sola fide*; we confess "nothing in my hand I bring, simply to the cross I cling." We realize that we can enter boldly into God's presence only because of the grace of God, through faith in the righteousness of Christ alone.

Indeed, *sola fide* is important because it reminds us of the grace of the gospel, testifying that ultimately our salvation, our standing and acceptance before God, is entirely of the Lord. The works of human beings cannot accomplish salvation. Thus, *sola fide* gives all the glory to God, so that no one will boast in human beings (1 Cor 1:31). *Sola fide* reminds us that everything we have is a gift, that every benefit we enjoy is granted to us by God (4:7). The five *solas* of the Reformation are closely tied together, but when it comes to *sola fide* there is an especially close link with *sola gratia* and *solus Christus*. Faith looks to another for salvation, so that salvation is by grace alone and in Christ alone. It is my hope that this book will both guard and cherish the gospel so that we look to Christ as our only hope and give thanks daily for the grace that is our only source of strength.

A final word about the use of slogans and doctrines. Anthony Lane rightly says that doctrines are maps and models, not mathematical formulas.[2] We must avoid, then, relying on simplistic appeals to *sola fide*, or condemning without conversation or understanding those who reject the term. Instead, we must ask what those who reject *sola fide* intend when they question its adequacy. Perhaps those who reject it and those who affirm it are speaking past each other. The fears of those who reject *sola fide* may constitute legitimate objections to misunderstandings of the phrase. To be clear, I am not saying that all disagreements are merely misunderstandings.

---

2. Anthony N. S. Lane, *Justification by Faith in Catholic-Protestant Dialogue: An Evangelical Assessment* (London: T&T Clark, 2002), 128–32.

What I am saying is that we should be open to dialogue so that we don't too quickly assume that we disagree.

How important is "faith alone"—the doctrine of justification? I am not arguing that *sola fide* is the gospel, though I believe it is one element or entailment of the gospel.[3] Those who reject the motto aren't necessarily proclaiming a different gospel. It is possible, as I said above, that they are responding to a misunderstanding of the phrase or they have heard an inadequate presentation of what faith alone means, and they rightly disagree with the explanation they have heard. Slogans are helpful, for they summarize briefly our theology, but slogans can also be dangerous, for we may be in a conversation or a debate where we are unknowingly operating with different definitions and concepts. Before we indict someone else, we must be sure that we have heard what they are truly saying.

In this book I attempt to tour the historical teaching of the church, explain the scriptural teaching on justification, and provide some sense of contemporary relevance. At the outset, I should state that this book is not a technical investigation. It is truly a tour, visiting several destinations during the journey and meeting many interesting figures from the past and from today. Still, it is not intended to cover everything that has been or can be said on the topic of justification. Many significant figures in the discussion will be briefly summarized, and others will be passed over. Key periods and figures throughout history are touched upon so that readers gain a larger perspective.

As evangelicals we believe in *sola scriptura*, that the Bible alone is authoritative as God's Word, but it would be foolish to ignore the careful reflections of those who preceded us. It has often been pointed out that *sola scriptura* doesn't mean *nuda scriptura* (bare scripture).[4] With this in mind, my hope is that readers will be encouraged as a result of reflecting on justification by faith alone to stand in faith and to rejoice in faith and as a result give great glory to God.

---

3.   For the nature of the gospel, see especially D. A. Carson, "What Is the Gospel?—Revisited," in *For the Fame of God's Name: Essays in Honor of John Piper* (eds. Sam Storms and Justin Taylor; Wheaton, IL: Crossway, 2010), 147–70.

4.   See the forthcoming work by Matthew Barrett, *God's Word Alone—The Authority of Scripture* (Grand Rapids: Zondervan, 2016) in this series.

PART 1

A Historical Tour of *Sola Fide*

CHAPTER 1

Sola Fide in the Early Church

"O the sweet exchange, O the incomprehensible work of God, O the unexpected blessings, that the sinfulness of many should be hidden in one righteous man, while the righteousness of one should justify many sinners!"
— *The Epistle to Diognetus 9.5*

We begin our historical tour of the doctrine of justification by looking at the apostolic fathers and the patristic era. In doing so, we must acknowledge that our point of view affects how we read. At the outset we should say that the writings of the earliest Christians should be read with gratefulness and appreciation. When we read them, we recognize and affirm that they confessed the same faith we cherish. We resonate with their belief that Jesus is the Christ and that he fulfilled Old Testament prophecy, for they confessed that Christ is the center of their faith. Evangelical Protestants recognize that God guided the early church as it wrestled with the christological dimensions of the faith revealed to them. Protestants influenced by Reformation traditions affirm that the Nicean and Chalcedonian creeds capture the message of the NT. Nor do we limit our appreciation to christological matters, for we rejoice in their affirmation of the created world, their rejection of Gnosticism, and their concern for ethics proclaimed by Jesus Christ and the apostles.

The oft-repeated saying that we stand on the shoulders of those who precede us applies to the earliest theologians in the history of the church and indeed to all the saints and scholars before us. Protestants who ignore or despise the contributions of the earliest era of the church show their folly and arrogance, for we stand in debt to the church throughout the ages. By affirming *sola fide*, we are not saying that we believe the true church only arose in the sixteenth century, nor are we saying that the church was deeply flawed until the time of the Reformation. On the contrary, we stand in the deepest appreciation of believers who followed the

Lord before us, gratefully acknowledging their faith, wisdom, courage, and devotion. Luther himself acknowledged that there was much good in the church in the 1,500 years preceding him.[1] An observation like this doesn't mean that there weren't weaknesses in the church, nor should we assume that the church and its doctrines have always been biblical and healthy. The Reformation happened for a reason! Still, the danger for many Protestants is to assume that the church had little to no understanding of the Pauline gospel for its first 1,500 years. Such a judgment is a gross exaggeration.

This leads us to the question we first wish to consider: Is *sola fide* taught in the earliest period of church history? We know that the formula itself—"faith alone"—was confessionally adopted during the Reformation after the church had existed for nearly 1,500 years. This leads us to wonder: If the earliest Christians didn't espouse faith alone, should we do so today? Today, many evangelicals are returning to and recovering the voice of the early church fathers.[2] We recognize our debt to the early fathers, and there is now a fresh explosion of interest in their exegesis and theology.[3] We now recognize that the early fathers were careful interpreters of Scripture, and hence our interest in whether they confessed that salvation is by faith alone is piqued. Did Protestants during the time of the Reformation and subsequently perhaps overreact to Roman Catholics? Could there be a more balanced and biblical stance found in the earliest fathers, in those who lived and wrote before the controversies of the 1500s began?

I haven't said anything yet about the soteriology of the earliest Christians, for there is significant controversy in scholarship over whether they were, in fact, faithful to Paul's theology of grace. I can scarcely resolve the matter here, given the extensive debate on the topic. Still, I hope to provide a perspective for our study, and it will become apparent where I lean in the dispute over whether the earliest fathers were faithful to Paul. Some have argued, perhaps most famously Thomas Torrance, that those in the patristic era misunderstood the Pauline gospel and actually contradicted it.[4] Others claim that Torrance's conclusion isn't warranted, that a

---

1. Martin Luther, *Church and Ministry* II, in vol. 40 of *Luther's Works* (ed. Conrad Bergendorff; Philadelphia: Muhlenberg, 1958), 231.

2. This is evidenced by the movement known as the Theological Interpretation of Scripture.

3. The interest is witnessed in the multivolume Ancient Christian Commentary on Scripture and Ancient Christian Texts, both published by InterVarsity Press.

4. Thomas F. Torrance, *The Doctrine of Grace in the Apostolic Fathers* (Grand Rapids: Eerdmans, 1948). For a survey of those who think the earliest fathers misconstrued Paul and did not understand justification, see Thomas C. Oden, *The Justification Reader* (Grand Rapids: Eerdmans, 2002), 19–23. See also Louis Berkhof, who says that many of the earliest fathers did not understand justification by faith (*Systematic Theology* [Grand Rapids: Eerdmans, 1938], 511).

sympathetic examination of the theology of the earliest era shows that they affirmed Paul's gospel.[5] I incline more to the latter viewpoint, but before making that case, I should say another word about the matter of doctrinal clarity and precision.

To put it simply, we cannot expect the earliest Christians to have the same clarity on the issue of *sola fide* as the Reformers.[6] The emphasis we find among them on topics like good works and merit lacks the clarity of the later discussions, but a sympathetic reading doesn't posit a contradiction between them and the Reformers. True faith results in good works, and the term "merit" in the early fathers may designate the reward given instead of being interpreted to say that one earns salvation.[7] We must remember that the early believers were rightly concerned about antinomianism,[8] a misreading of Paul's theology of grace that supported a sinful lifestyle. The earliest fathers rightly opposed what Dietrich Bonhoeffer would later call "cheap grace," an abuse of the freedom of the gospel leading one to excuse sinful behavior.

The Reformers, unlike the church fathers, had the benefit of 1,500 years of Christian reflection in assessing justification and stood in debt to those who preceded them, especially to Augustine. The earliest church didn't encounter significant theological controversy over soteriology and the role of faith and works. They gladly affirmed that salvation was of the Lord. They also, in line with the Pauline witness, confessed that salvation was by faith instead of by works. At the same time they concluded that good works were necessary for final salvation. These affirmations need not be seen as contradictory. They accord with what the NT itself teaches,

---

He says that there is "an anti-Pauline strain of legalism" in the apostolic fathers (idem, *The History of Christian Doctrines* [Grand Rapids: Baker, 1937], 40–41). Later he says that both Irenaeus and Tertullian did not truly understand justification and were guilty of moralism (67–68). And the Alexandrian fathers "certainly did not have the Pauline conception of faith and justification" (74). Space is lacking to tackle all the fathers here, but for a different understanding of Irenaeus, see Mark W. Elliott, "The Triumph of Paulinism by the Mid-Third Century," in *Paul and the Second Century* (ed. Michael F. Bird and Joseph R. Dodson; LNTS 412 [New York: T&T Clark, 2011), 248.

5. E.g., Eric Osborne, "Origen and Justification," *ABR* 24 (1976): 18–29; D. E. H. Williams, "Justification by Faith: A Patristic Doctrine," *JEH* 57 (2006): 649–67 (though I do not concur with Williams's judgment that the view of the early fathers is a corrective to Reformation perspectives).

6. Nevertheless, Needham points out that the notion of faith, and even faith alone, was present in some of the early fathers, especially Chrysostom (Nick Needham, "Justification in the Early Church Fathers," in *Justification in Perspective: Historical Developments and Contemporary Challenges* [ed. Bruce L. McCormack; Grand Rapids: Baker, 2006], 38–42).

7. For this sympathetic reading, see ibid., 42–53.

8. So Robert B. Eno, "Some Patristic Views on the Relationship of Faith and Works in Justification," in *Recherches augustiniennes* 19 (1984): 4.

and thus they represent a faithful appropriation of the NT witness, even if some of the terms and expressions of the early fathers lacked the clarity and precision of later formulations. A faithful reception of the NT message shouldn't be equated with a full understanding of soteriology or with the precision that we find with the Reformers and their followers. But the vagueness of the early fathers isn't surprising, for controversy (as is evident with the early debates on the Trinity and Christology) is the furnace in which clearer theology is forged.

What we do not find in the patristic era, at least until Augustine, is a full discussion of the relationship between faith and works. That matter came to the forefront in Augustine's dispute with Pelagius. Before that time the church fathers were content with simply saying what we find in the NT: salvation is by faith and due to the grace of God, and those who experience God's grace should live a new life, for those who are not transformed will not receive an eternal reward. In that respect, the fathers faithfully captured the message of the NT. But we should not expect those in the patristic era to speak directly to issues that arose later in church history.

Some, lamenting the divisions between Roman Catholics and Protestants in the last five hundred years, may pine for the unity on soteriology we find in the early church and might wish that we could go back to that period. Such feelings represent nostalgia, a nostalgia that doesn't accord with historical realities. The truth is that every period of church history has been marked by doctrinal strife and dispute. Indeed, once the matter of faith and works came to the table in the dispute between Augustine and Pelagius, the matter was sharply controverted. Pastors were alerted in a fresh way to the issues at stake.

It is also nostalgic and sentimental to wish that we could discuss the matter of *sola fide* apart from the Reformation and the Counter Reformation, not to mention the four hundred plus years since. The controversy during the Reformation sharpened the debate and posed the issues with a clarity we don't find in the ancient church. Again, to say this is no criticism of the early fathers. We should not expect them to weigh in on issues that weren't debated in their time. We must be careful of an anachronistic criticism that judges theologians based on subsequent history. Nor can we go back to an earlier era to find the doctrinal purity and unity we long for. Instead, we must assess the question of justification in light of the entirety of church history and of the intensive debates and discussions that have arisen. Some may be satisfied with being Augustinian, but the discussion has moved past

Augustine. Such a statement doesn't mean that we ignore Augustine, for his contribution was vital and must be integrated into current discussions. Still, he did not give the final and decisive answer in the discussion, and the contribution of the Reformers and contemporary biblical scholarship must also be included in assessing the role of *sola fide* today.

Indeed, we should be grateful for the last five hundred years, for the debates and divisions and discussions have forced us to read the biblical text intensely and carefully. They prompt us to be like the Bereans, who examined the Scriptures to discern what they actually teach (Acts 17:11). Perhaps some theological formulations are more precise than Scripture warrants. Nevertheless, as the church has learned in christological controversies, it may be that the intense study on justification has led us to a more nuanced view, a view that does justice to the entirety of the scriptural witness. One reason we will engage in a tour of church history, despite the dangers of being selective and brief, is that it provides a taste of the depth and breadth of the work of those who have gone before us.

To sum up, as we consider the contributions of the apostolic fathers and the patristic era, we must not expect too much from them, nor too little.[9] We must not expect them to be conversant with the debates of the Reformation, for that would be anachronistic.[10] At the same time, we can be guilty of expecting too little as well, for if they are faithful to the apostolic witness, we will detect the gospel in what they have written.

Defining Key Terms

For those who may be new to these discussions or who are unfamiliar with the historic or contemporary debates on the subject of justification, it is important to gain familiarity with some of the key terms used. So, before we dive into the historical evidence for *sola fide*, let's consider some definitions.

Though I've used "justification" several times already and most readers will be familiar with what the term means, we can define it as being

---

9. Michael W. Holmes argues that Polycarp believed in both grace and human achievement and thus was synergistic in contrast to Paul ("Paul and Polycarp," in *Paul and the Second Century* [eds. Michael F. Bird and Joseph R. Dodson; LNTS 412; New York: T&T Clark, 2011], 66–69). For an even stronger indictment, see Torrance, *Doctrine of Grace in Apostolic Fathers*, 93–96. But in defense of the notion that Polycarp was closer to Paul than many have claimed, see Joel Willitts, "Paul and Jewish Christians in the Second Century," in *Paul and the Second Century*, 154–58.

10. Cf. Williams, "Justification by Faith: A Patristic Doctrine," 664–65. See also the comments by Andreas Lindemann, in *Trajectories through the New Testament and the Apostolic Fathers* (eds. Andrew F. Gregory and Christopher M. Tuckett; Oxford: Oxford University Press, 2005), 44.

right before God. Justification, then, refers to how we attain righteous-ness. *Forensic* understandings of justification see this as being declared righteous before God. By contrast, *transformative* understandings see it as being made righteous before God. Along with this, it is important that we grasp the distinction between an *imputed* righteousness and an *infused* righteousnes. *Imputed righteousness* means that we are declared to be in the right before God on the basis of the righteousness of Jesus Christ, which is given to us when we believe. *Infused righteousness* means that we are righteous before God because of our righteous behavior, because of the righteousness that transforms and changes us.

Historically, Roman Catholics have defended the notion that the righ-teousness that saves us on the day of judgment is infused, while Protestants have maintained that the righteousness that delivers us from God's wrath is imputed. I will argue in this book that the Protestant understanding is correct and that the Roman Catholic view deviates from the gospel of Jesus Christ. For those who are new to this discussion, know that we will unpack more of this in the chapters that follow. With these basic definitions in place, we can now turn to the historical evidence for *sola fide* in the early church.

Justification by Faith in *1 Clement*

In the writings of the earliest Christians we do not find many refer-ences to justification, but the evidence we do have supports the notion that most early church fathers understood justification forensically, and thus, as we will see, they stand in contrast to Augustine.[11] We begin with these fascinating words about justification in *1 Clem.* 32:3–4,[12] which most believe was written around AD 96.[13]

> All, therefore, were glorified and magnified, not through themselves or their own works or the righteous actions which they did, but through his will. And so we, having been called through his will in Christ Jesus, are not justified through ourselves or through our wisdom or understanding or piety or works, which we have done in holiness of heart, but through faith, by which the almighty God has justified all

---

11. See Needham, "Justification in the Early Church Fathers," 27–37. Clement of Alexandria is the other significant exception and seems to have understood the word to mean "make righteous."

12. All quotes from the apostolic fathers are from Michael W. Holmes, *The Apostolic Fathers: Greek Texts and English Translations of Their Writings* (2nd ed.; Grand Rapids: Baker, 1992).

13. Lindemann dates it in the late 90s AD (see "Paul's Influence on 'Clement' and Ignatius," in *Trajectories through the New Testament and the Apostolic Fathers* [eds. Andrew F. Gregory and Christopher M. Tuckett; Oxford: Oxford University Press, 2005], 9).

who have existed from the beginning, to whom be the glory for ever and ever. Amen.[14]

Clement clearly says that our works or holiness do not justify us. As Lindemann observes, Clement "shows quite clearly that he is not a teacher of 'justification by works.'"[15] He often emphasizes God's gracious work in believers.[16] Instead, justification is God's work and is granted to those who exercise faith. Such a notion accords with Clement's teaching on election (*1 Clem.* 32:3; 59:2), which features God's grace in salvation.[17] In Clement's emphasis on justification by faith (31:1–2), we have an early example of what would later be known as *sola fide.*[18] At the same time, Clement spends most of the letter exhorting his readers to live a virtuous life. Such an emphasis, however, does not mean that he denies what he wrote about justification.[19] We must consider the occasion and circumstances that called forth the document.[20] For Clement good works flow from faith (30:3) and are not the ground of justification. As Arnold says, good works in Clement "are the appropriate response to the work of salvation, not the foundation of justification."[21]

Clement doesn't tie justification to the person and work of Christ to the same degree Paul does. Even though we don't have the same kind of clarity that we find in Paul, the importance of Christ's blood is noted (7:4), and hence there are reasons to think that justification is due to what Christ has accomplished.[22]

Justification in Ignatius

Another early witness to justification by faith is Ignatius.[23] Ignatius emphasizes that believers live according to grace and center on Jesus

14. In support of the notion that 1 Clement doesn't deny grace, see Heikki Räisänen, "'Righteousness by Works': An Early Catholic Doctrine? Thoughts on 1 Clement," in *Jesus, Paul and Torah: Collected Essays* (trans. David E. Orton; Sheffield: Sheffield Academic, 1992), 202–24.

15. Andreas Lindemann, "Paul in the Writings of the Apostolic Fathers," in *Paul and the Legacies of Paul* (ed. William S. Babcock; Dallas: Southern Methodist University Press, 1990), 33.

16. Rightly Räisänen, "Righteousness by Works," 206–7.

17. Cf. Brian John Arnold, "Justification One Hundred Years after Paul" (Ph.D. diss., The Southern Baptist Theological Seminary, 2013), 43–44.

18. So ibid., 45–46.

19. For the contrary idea that Clement is legalistic, see Torrance, *Doctrine of Grace in Apostolic Fathers,* 49–50, 54.

20. So Lindemann, "Paul in the Writings of the Apostolic Fathers," 35; Räisänen, "Righteousness by Works," 205–6; Arnold, "Justification One Hundred Years after Paul," 41–42.

21. Arnold, "Justification One Hundred Years after Paul," 52.

22. Ibid., 53–54; Räisänen, "Righteousness by Works," 209.

23. My discussion of Ignatius is indebted to Arnold, "Justification One Hundred Years after Paul," 56–103, whom I largely follow here.

Christ (*Magn.* 8:1; *Phld.* 9:2). Even though he doesn't highlight the term justification, he features the content of the gospel and Jesus' death and resurrection (*Phld.* 9:2).[24] Those who center on Jesus Christ don't fall prey to Judaism (*Magn.* 10:3; *Phld.* 6:1). Instead, Ignatius calls on his readers to exercise faith and love (*Eph.* 1:14; *Magn.* 1). Justification for Ignatius centers on Jesus Christ (*Phld.* 8:2), and the atonement that comes through his blood (*Smyrn.* 6:1), so that Christ is understood as a substitute (*Rom.* 6:1; *Smyrn.* 6:2; *Trall.* 2:1; 9:2). Indeed, it seems that justification is apart from works of law since he rejects circumcision for salvation.[25] Ignatius recognizes his own imperfection and his need for mercy, finding rest in the death and resurrection of Jesus Christ, so that the gospel is his hope (*Phld.* 5:1–2; *Smyrn.* 11:1).[26]

Thomas Torrance thinks that faith and love in Ignatius mean that faith *and* works justify us.[27] But again we need to remember the situation and occasion that called forth the Ignatian letters. In this case, Ignatius was about to suffer martyrdom.[28] Still, he continued to emphasize the grace of God (*Magn.* 8:1; *Smyrn.* 6:2), and love should be construed as the consequence and fruit of faith.[29] Others see the emphasis on martyrdom in Ignatius to be opposed to justification by faith, as if he put his trust in his sacrifice. One could interpret his martyrdom in this way, but the necessity of martyrdom doesn't necessarily communicate works-righteousness, for the desire to be faithful accords with the Pauline teaching that one must endure to be saved.[30]

The Great Exchange in the *Epistle to Diognetus*

Sometimes scholars will say that the earliest fathers didn't understand substitution or grace, but the famous words of the *Epistle to Diognetus* 9:2–5 (written in the second century AD) show that such statements are off the mark.[31]

---

24. Ibid., 80–83.

25. Ibid., 85.

26. Ibid., 86–88.

27. Torrance, *Doctrine of Grace in Apostolic Fathers*, 60–61, 66–69.

28. For the circumstances that called forth what Ignatius wrote, see Lindemann, "Paul in the Writings of the Apostolic Fathers," 40–41.

29. Arnold, "Justification One Hundred Years after Paul," 96.

30. Ibid., 99–102.

31. See Brandon Crowe, "Oh Sweet Exchange!: The Soteriological Significance of Incarnation in the *Epistle to Diognetus*," ZNW 102 (2011): 96–109; Arnold, "Justification One Hundred Years after Paul," 104–36.

But when our unrighteousness was fulfilled, and it had been made perfectly clear that its wages—punishment and death—were to be expected, then the season arrived during which God had decided to reveal at last his goodness and power (oh, the surpassing kindness and love of God!). He did not hate us, or reject us, or bear a grudge against us; instead he was patient and forbearing; in his mercy he took upon himself our sins; he himself gave up his own Son as a ransom for us, the holy one for the lawless, the guiltless for the guilty, "the just for the unjust," the incorruptible for the corruptible, the immortal for the mortal. For what else but his righteousness could have covered our sins? In whom was it possible for us, the lawless and ungodly, to be justified, except in the Son of God alone? O the sweet exchange, O the incomprehensible work of God, O the unexpected blessings, that the sinfulness of many should be hidden in one righteous man, while the righteousness of one should justify many sinners!

Justification by grace and by the substitutionary work of Christ are clearly taught here, putting the burden of proof on those who claim that substitution is a modern or Western notion.[32] This text clearly teaches that the only hope of forgiveness and justification is the work of Jesus Christ on the cross, and thus there are reasons to conclude that he endorsed what we refer to as *sola fide*.[33] Brandon Crowe observes that chapter 9 of the *Epistle to Diognetus* contrasts the righteousness of God with the unrighteousness of humanity, showing "the impossibility of humanity to enter the Kingdom of God based on its own ability. Instead, human beings must rely on the power of God to be made worthy."[34] This is not to say that Diognetus is like Paul in every respect, for there are differences as well, but we do see the elements of Pauline soteriology here.[35]

Justification in the *Odes of Solomon*

Paul's understanding of justification doesn't vanish into the thin air after the first century. We also see a Pauline view of grace and faith in the *Odes of Solomon*.[36] In these writings, the grace of God is underscored by

---

32. Crowe goes beyond this and sees the positive imputation of the righteousness of Christ here, arguing that the author interprets Rom 5:18–19 this way ("Oh Sweet Exchange," 104–9).

33. Arnold, "Justification One Hundred Years after Paul," 134.

34. Crowe, "Oh Sweet Exchange," 101; so also Williams, "Justification by Faith: A Patristic Doctrine," 654.

35. See Michael F. Bird, "The Reception of Paul in *The Epistle to Diognetus*," in *Paul and the Second Century* (eds. Michael F. Bird and Joseph R. Dodson; LNTS 412; New York: T&T Clark, 2011), 85–88.

36. Arnold, "Justification One Hundred Years after Paul," 137–96. Again, I am indebted to Arnold for what follows.

the doctrine of election,[37] showing that salvation isn't attributed to the work of human beings (*Odes Sol.* 25.4). Justification is rooted in God's kindness and grace and is not based on human merit.[38] Arnold suggests that the grace of God is, in fact, the main theme of the *Odes*.[39] Justification is forensic and not transformative,[40] and perhaps the recognition of justification's forensic character is due to the writer being closer in time to the writings of the NT or to his knowledge of Greek, in contrast to Augustine, who, as we will see, believed justification was transformative. Indeed, it seems that the writer of the *Odes* believes in the imputation of righteousness in his conception of justification, which demonstrates that justification is a gift of God.[41] Arnold says, "For the Odist, imputation of the Spirit necessarily means the imputation of righteousness."[42] The writer celebrates the truth that justification is the Lord's work and is equivalent to imperishable salvation (17.1).[43] The centrality of Jesus is evident, for believers are united with Christ.[44] The author maintains that justification is by faith (29.5–6), which, when it is aligned with his views of grace, election, and imputation, suggest that justification is by faith alone.

Justification in Justin Martyr's *Dialogue with Trypho*

Though we cannot investigate the teaching of all the patristic writers on justification, the contribution of Justin Martyr in *The Dialogue with Trypho* is particularly fascinating and worth consideration.[45] The substance of the *Dialogue* lends credence to the notion that Justin knew Paul's theology and propagated it, even if there are differences. Trypho seems to be similar to Paul's opponents, for he insists that one must be circumcised and observe the other commands in the law to be saved (8.4; 10.1, 3–4).[46]

---

37. *Odes Sol.* 4.7; 8.13; 10.3; 12.3; 23.2–3; 41.9. In the past the *Odes* were often considered Jewish, but it is now acknowledged that they are Christian. See J. H. Charlesworth, "Odes of Solomon: A New Translation and Introduction," in *Old Testament Pseudepigrapha* (ed. J. H. Charlesworth; Garden City, NY: Doubleday, 1985), 2:725.

38. *Odes Sol.* 25.4, 12; 29.5.

39. Cf. *Odes Sol.* 4.13; 5.3; 23.2; 31.7; 34.6 (Arnold, "Justification One Hundred Years after Paul," 169–72).

40. *Odes Sol.* 17.1–17; 25.12; 29.1–11 (Arnold, "Justification One Hundred Years after Paul," 149, 154–56, 182–91).

41. *Odes Sol.* 25.7, 10; 33.12 (Arnold, "Justification One Hundred Years after Paul," 166, 175–78).

42. Arnold, "Justification One Hundred Years after Paul," 179.

43. Ibid., 154.

44. *Odes Sol.* 3.7; 17.13–17 (Arnold, "Justification One Hundred Years after Paul," 161–65).

45. See Arnold, "Justification One Hundred Years after Paul," 197–230.

46. See Graham Stanton, "The Law of Moses and the Law of Christ," in *Paul and the Mosaic Law* (ed. James D. G. Dunn; Tübingen: Mohr Siebeck, 1996), 102, 105–7.

On the other side, Justin, like Paul, stresses that justification is by faith, and hence circumcision is not needed for salvation (23.3–4; 92.2). After all, Abraham was justified by faith instead of his observance of the law (23.4; 92.3–4). Those who focus on circumcision and the law fall prey to works-righteousness (137.1–2), for the law doesn't save, but the death of Jesus accomplishes salvation instead (11.4–5; 137.1). The righteousness of believers is rooted in the cross of Christ, for he took upon himself the curse that believers deserve (95.1–3). Undoubtedly, Justin is teaching an understanding of substitutionary atonement.[47]

Other Witnesses in the Patristic Period

As we consider witnesses from the patristic period, we have to remember that the issue wasn't debated during this time and thus the theology isn't always integrated or consistent. While I include quotes that support the doctrine of justification by faith, I could also quote other statements in the period and from some of the same authors that seem to contradict justification by faith, especially justification by faith *alone*. The point made here is not that the early writers reached the same clarity as the Reformers. Instead, the early fathers often recognized what the NT said about justification by faith and proclaimed its truth in their teaching and preaching. Hence, the doctrine wasn't denied as we see in later Roman Catholicism. On the contrary, we see indications that justification by faith alone was embraced, even though the implications of the doctrine were not worked out thoroughly.

Origen (AD 185–254), for example, sees justification by faith in the thief on the cross and claims that faith is the foundation of our justification, so that righteousness isn't based on works of the law. Our obedience cannot justify since righteousness is by faith.[48] Origen regularly emphasizes that faith leads to good works, and in saying this he reflects a Pauline theme.[49] Origen's teaching on the matter is vague and imprecise at some points, but this is scarcely surprising, for he wasn't pressed to clarify the matter, and some of the same questions arise in reading Paul.[50] Yet there

---

47. I owe the reference to Needham ("Justification in the Early Church Fathers," 33–34).

48. Oden, *Justification Reader*, 45.

49. Cf. Williams, "Justification by Faith: A Patristic Doctrine," 655; Arnold, "Justification One Hundred Years after Paul," 655; Eno, "Some Patristic Views on the Relationship of Faith and Works in Justification," 6.

50. Cf. David M. Rylaarsdam, "Interpretations of Paul in the Early Church," in *Rereading Paul Together: Protestant and Catholic Perspectives on Justification* (Grand Rapids: Baker, 2006), 152–55.

are some statements in Origen that seem to contradict justification by faith, and hence he isn't the clearest witness.[51]

The fourth-century father Theodoret of Cyrrhus comments on Eph 2:8, "It is not of our own accord that we have believed … and even when we had come to believe, He did not require of us purity of life, but approving mere faith, God bestowed on us forgiveness of sins."[52] Chrysostom later in the same century understands Eph 2:8 similarly,[53] though he granted free will a role that would have been denied by Luther and Calvin. Still, Chrysostom insists that justification can't be given through works since God demands perfect obedience. Hence, the only way to be justified is through grace.[54] Chrysostom stoutly denies any notion of meritorious works[55] and sees good works as a consequence of faith.[56] Chrysostom's articulation of justification seems to be thoroughly Pauline.

Williams appeals to Marius Victorinus from the mid-fourth century, saying he taught "salvation by grace through faith. We are not saved by our own merits, as if by the works of the law, but only by the grace of God: 'it is by faith alone that brings justification and sanctification.'"[57] Victorinus also believes that good works are necessary, but in making this point he was faithful to the NT.[58] Williams especially highlights the writings of Hilary of Poitiers (fourth century), showing that he often used Pauline language of justification by faith in his commentary on Matthew, confirming that the Pauline understanding was deeply embedded in this thinking.[59] Hilary taught that the law can't bring justification on account of human sin.[60] He says in his commentary on Matthew that "salvation is entirely by faith,"[61] and emphasizes this theme repeatedly.[62] Hence, Abraham, the thief on the cross, and the eleventh hour workers in the vineyard (Matt.

---

51. See Eno, "Some Patristic Views on the Relationship of Faith and Works in Justification," 5.
52. Cited from Oden, *Justification Reader*, 45.
53. Ibid., 44–45.
54. John Chrysostom, *Homilies on Second Corinthians* 11.5 (*NPNF* 1, 12:334).
55. See Oden, *Justification Reader*, 76.
56. Rylaarsdam, "Interpretations of Paul in the Early Church," 160.
57. Williams, "Justification by Faith: A Patristic Doctrine," 655–56. The quotation is from Victorinus's commentary on Galatians, ii.15–16.
58. Cf. Eno, "Some Patristic Views on the Relationship of Faith and Works in Justification," 6–7 (though Eno raises questions about Victorinus's understanding of justification by faith, wondering if he was repeating Paul's wording without fully comprehending what Paul taught).
59. Williams, "Justification by Faith: A Patristic Doctrine," 657.
60. Ibid., 658.
61. Cited in ibid., 658. The quotation is from xi.10 of Hilary's Matthew commentary.
62. See Williams, "Justification by Faith: A Patristic Doctrine," 658–60.

20:1 – 16) are all justified by faith. Indeed, Hilary specifically declares that justification is by faith alone: "Because faith alone justifies … publicans and prostitutes will be the first in the kingdom of heaven."[63] Those who think that justification by faith alone is absent in the early fathers need to reckon with Hilary's clear words on the matter.

Ambrosiaster also taught that justification was by faith alone.[64] "By faith alone one is freely forgiven of all sins and the believer is no longer burdened by the Law for meriting good works. Our works, however, are demonstrative of our faith and will determine whether we are ultimately justified."[65] That sentence could have easily been written by Calvin or Luther. Nevertheless, Ambrosiaster lacked the clarity we find in the later Reformers, for he also wrote of meriting a final reward. In saying such, however, he called on another theme emphasized by virtually all early Christian writers, that is, the importance of good works.[66]

We could continue to cite others who made similar statements. Oden cites Prosper of Aquitaine, Ambrosiaster, Jerome, Augustine, and Marius Victorinus to demonstrate that justification by faith was a common teaching.[67] But we will conclude our brief tour of the early church with some comments on the most famous of the early church writers — Augustine.

Augustine

My goal in this section is not to investigate Augustine's entire theology of justification, for that would warrant a book in its own right. The purpose here is to sketch with some broad strokes his view of justification.[68] Augustine's understanding of justification is bound up with his mature view of predestination, so that God's grace secures the faith of human beings. He clearly thought that justification is due to grace. In this respect, he is close to the understanding of the Reformers, and it is scarcely surpris-

---

63. This citation taken from xxi.15 is again taken from Williams, "Justification by Faith: A Patristic Doctrine," 660.

64. Ambrosiaster wasn't the name of this fourth-century commentator on Paul's epistles. Originally, it was thought that these commentaries were written by Ambrose, but scholarship over the centuries has demonstrated that the author is unknown.

65. Williams, "Justification by Faith: A Patristic Doctrine," 662.

66. See Eno, "Some Patristic Views on the Relationship of Faith and Works in Justification," 8 – 10.

67. Oden, *Justification Reader*, 46 – 49.

68. Cf. Lane, *Justification by Faith in Catholic-Protestant Dialogue: An Evangelical Assessment* (London: T&T Clark, 2002), 45. See Augustine's discussion in "The Spirit and the Letter" in *Augustine: Later Works* (LCC; Philadelphia: Westminster, 1955), 193 – 250.

ing that Luther and Calvin often quote Augustine, for in his theology of grace and his view of predestination they found a kindred spirit. Augustine often proclaims, especially in his anti-Pelagian writings, that believers are saved by grace and not by works. Salvation is of the Lord, for believers cannot do anything apart from what they have received (1 Cor 4:7), a verse to which Augustine returned again and again in the Pelagian controversy.

Augustine differs from the Reformers, however, in that he understands the word "justify" to mean "make righteous" instead of "declare righteous."[69] Augustine believed that justification was more than merely an event; it was also a process, and thus he believed in *inherent* righteousness rather than *imputed* righteousness. Justification isn't a once-for-all declaration in his mind, for justification means that believers continue to be transformed and perfected. Augustine did not operate with the distinction between sanctification and justification, which is typical in Reformed and Lutheran thought. Since justification for Augustine means "to make righteous," the term includes within it what evangelical Protestants typically would call sanctification.[70]

So would Augustine have endorsed the Reformation teaching on *sola fide*? Aware that the question is anachronistic, Alister McGrath attempts to answer the question. He thinks not, given Augustine's emphasis on love. For Augustine faith is basically intellectual assent, and thus faith must be accompanied by love. Indeed, it works by love (Gal 5:6).[71] David Wright, however, criticizes McGrath for going beyond the evidence, for Augustine never says we are *justified* by love.[72] Perhaps different terminology and circumstances explain these differences between Augustine and the Reformers on the matter of faith alone. Wright says that in reading Augustine and the Reformers, it is easy to pass from the one to the other without noticing significant differences, for they breathe the same air theologically.[73] There is a sense, it seems then, in which Augustine would

---

69. This is the typical view of Augustine. See "Spirit and Letter," 208, 219, 228 (but see his comments on 229). See, e.g., Rylaarsdam, "Interpretations of Paul in the Early Church," 164. Wright, however, cautions that a declarative notion is present in Augustine as well (David F. Wright, "Justification in Augustine," in *Justification in Perspective: Historical Developments and Contemporary Challenges* [ed. Bruce L. McCormack; Grand Rapids: Baker, 2006], 55–72).

70. Lane notes that before the Reformation there wasn't a clear distinction drawn between justification and sanctification. But he insightfully remarks that this doesn't mean that the theological concept articulated in the distinction was absent, for a distinction was drawn between forgiveness of sins (status) and renewal of life (sanctification). Hence, we could overemphasize the difference between the Reformers and those who preceded them on this matter (*Justification by Faith in Catholic-Protestant Dialogue*, 139–40).

71. McGrath, *Iustitia Dei: The History of the Christian Doctrine of Justification;* Vol. 1, *From the Beginning to 1500* (Cambridge: Cambridge University Press, 1986), 1:30.

72. Wright, "Justification in Augustine," 55–56, 66.

73. Ibid., 71.

have endorsed faith alone, for his predestination theology emphasized that salvation is the Lord's work and faith is a gift from him.

The notion that we are justified by faith alone fits with Augustine's mature reading of Rom 7:14–25, for he believed that sin continues to bedevil Christians, and thus they fall remarkably short of God's standards. At the same time, Augustine emphasized Gal 5:6, which says that faith works through love. Augustine interpreted the verse differently from the Reformers, but the difference between them may not be as significant as some claim, for Augustine insisted that true faith expresses itself in works, supremely in love for God and others.[74] This is a notion that is shared by the Reformers as well. Augustine's theology of justification, while it differs in some ways from what we find in Luther and Calvin, stands on his theology of predestination and is influenced by his understanding of grace. Grace doesn't just make salvation possible; grace is effective and secures faith and love in the hearts of those God has chosen to be his people.

Regardless of where one believes Augustine's understanding of justification best fits, his place in the debate never grows old, for his influence on the Reformers and on Protestants today continues. At the same time, those who maintain that justification is a process and that it means "make righteous" also call upon Augustine to support their theology.

Thomas Oden's View

Thomas Oden, a well-known scholar of the early church, argues forcefully that theologians in the patristic era faithfully understood Paul and agreed with the Reformational teaching on faith and grace, though he doesn't claim that the teaching was "always rightly remembered or consistently appropriated," nor was it "always rightly integrated into preaching and pastoral care and moral instruction" or "grasped in a perfect way."[75] If we understand what Oden says in broad terms, he is almost certainly right.[76] At the same time we must beware of taking isolated sayings out of context and claiming that the fathers and the Reformers were on the same page. Individual statements must be interpreted in context, and typically the fathers weren't expounding justification in any detail.[77]

The earliest fathers repeated what they understood Paul to be saying

---

74. Cf. ibid., 66–69.
75. Oden, *Justification Reader*, 143.
76. But against this, see McGrath, *Iustitia Dei*, 1:180–87.
77. See here the wise comments of Lane, *Justification by Faith in Catholic-Protestant Dialogue*, 136.

about justification, affirming grace and faith and disavowing works as a basis for justification. McGrath says that in the patristic period "matters such as predestination, grace, and free will" are "somewhat confused, and would remain so until controversy forced a full discussion of the issue upon the church."[78] The word confusion seems apt from our perspective, but we must be reminded again that these early Christians weren't trying to synthesize the biblical teaching on justification and salvation.

Conclusion

If we are looking for a direct parallel between what the early church fathers wrote and the Reformation call to *sola fide*, we won't find it. The early church did not have the clarity on justification by faith alone that we find in the Reformers. By the same token, those who claim that the early fathers denied this truth go far beyond the evidence. Even a cursory tour of some of their writings indicates that they frequently upheld the truth that we are justified by faith rather than by works. In saying that works are necessary for final salvation as well, they were simply reproducing the message of the NT. Again, this is not to say that Protestants can claim the early fathers in support of the views articulated later, during the Reformation. Yet Roman Catholics can scarcely argue that the writings of the fathers are a ringing endorsement of the teaching of the Council of Trent either. In many respects, we find that a number of the fathers endorsed teachings that are similar to what we know today as the doctrine of justification by faith alone.

---

78. McGrath, *Iustitia Dei*, 1:19. McGrath probably underestimates the understanding of justification in the first 350 years of the church's life (see his discussion, 1:17–23).

CHAPTER 2

Martin Luther on Justification by Faith Alone

> "Wherefore it ought to be the first concern of every
> Christian to lay aside all confidence in works and grow
> in the knowledge, not of works, but of Christ Jesus, who
> suffered and rose for him." — *Martin Luther*

A s I mentioned in chapter 1, our examination of the historical roots of the doctrine of justification will be more of a tour than a comprehensive and thorough analysis of all that has been written or said on the subject. Instead, we are taking soundings and visiting a few important figures to gain some sense of the history of the church on this doctrine. In the next two chapters, we jump ahead several centuries from chapter 1 to the time of the Reformation to consider two of the brightest luminaries of that period, Martin Luther and John Calvin. In what follows, we want to learn what they taught about justification and, in particular, *sola fide*. This chapter will be devoted to what Luther has to say on the subject, and the next one will be on Calvin's thought.

Because our investigation is necessarily brief, I'll freely quote from both Luther and Calvin so that readers can see for themselves what they taught. These two Reformers, geniuses that they were, are much more interesting than all their commentators, including this one! And while many other theologians and pastors contributed to the Reformation, Luther and Calvin stand out as key representatives of the Reformation tradition, voices that continue to inform Protestant theology to this day.[1] Before we jump into Luther, let's take a look at the context for the Reformation.

---

1. I am not claiming that Calvin is *the* representative of the Reformed tradition. The Reformed tradition is wide and varied and it existed before Calvin. See J. V. Fesko, *Beyond Calvin: Union with Christ and Justification in Early Modern Reformed Theology, 1517-1700* (Reformed Historical Theology 20; Göttingen: Vandenhoeck & Ruprecht, 2012).

Context of the Reformation

Before we can understand discussions about justification during the Reformation, we should make a few observations about the medieval view of justification that was widely understood and accepted at the time. It is safe to say that Augustine's definition of justification had triumphed in the church. All understood justification to mean that believers are *made righteous*. Hence, justification for medieval thinkers didn't merely refer to a status by which one was declared to be in the right before God, but denoted the ongoing change and transformation in the lives of Christians. In that sense, the understanding of justification we find in Aquinas doesn't differ all that much from Augustine. The medieval consensus was clear: justification portrays the renewal of the human being *and* the process of that renewal.[2]

Alister McGrath helpfully charts out three ways the phrase "righteousness of God" was understood in the medieval period.[3] In the first view, God is righteous because he is faithful to his promises to save his people. In this understanding, God's righteousness is demonstrated in his faithfulness to the promises of salvation found in the OT. In the second view, the righteousness of God is also understood in an objective sense, denoting the righteousness God gives to sinners, so that it is a righteousness from God and granted to those who trust in Christ. McGrath maintains that these first two views are "complementary," and that a number of writers espoused both notions without seeing any contradiction. The third view McGrath mentions is that God is righteous in rewarding people in accord with their actions. Here God's righteousness manifests itself in rewarding human beings according to their merits.

One of the precursors to Luther, Gabriel Biel, understood righteousness in covenantal terms.[4] He emphasized that human beings must meet the conditions of the covenant to be in a right relationship with God. God is required, according to the terms of the covenant that he himself set, to grant grace to those who do their best.[5] One medieval theologian illustrates this concept with the example of opening the shutters to let the light in. In the same way, he says, people should remove those things that

---

2. McGrath, *Iustitia Dei*, 1:40–41, 50.
3. Ibid., 1:51–54.
4. For Biel, see ibid., 1:64–66, 76–78, 89.
5. See Timothy George, *Theology of the Reformers* (rev. ed.; Nashville: B & H Academic, 2013), 67; McGrath, *Iustitia Dei*, 1:83. Thomas Aquinas initially placed the emphasis on one doing one's best, but he later emphasized that one can't even prepare to receive grace apart from grace moving and arousing the human will (see McGrath, *Iustitia Dei*, 1:85–86).

obstruct the grace of God so that the light of his love can stream into their lives.[6] Another example is taken from sailing. A ship won't receive the wind in its sails if the sails aren't up. The wind here stands for God's grace and the sails for human preparation.[7] If human beings don't prepare for God's grace by putting their sails up, God's grace cannot empower them.

The covenant was understood to be a gracious gift of God. Nevertheless, if God didn't honor the terms of the covenant, he would fail to be just, for God must honor his promises and commitments. Biel believed that human beings had the capacity by virtue of their free will to meet the terms of the covenant, to take the first steps toward God.[8] Many scholars have maintained that Biel's understanding should be understood as semi-Pelagianism, since the capacity of human beings plays a role in justification.[9]

The Reformers, of course, understood matters differently and rejected Biel's synergism, for even though God acts graciously in offering the covenant, the first impetus for covenant inclusion lies with the human being, with the choices and decisions made by us. Luther and Calvin certainly thought such a notion was contrary to the grace of God, which explains why for them justification was closely tied to predestination. They vigorously rejected the notion that we take any first steps on our own. In any case, the notion that human beings needed to prepare themselves, to make themselves ready for justification, became increasingly popular in the medieval period.

McGrath argues that there were three main features in the Lutheran and Protestant doctrine of justification.[10] First, justification is forensic rather than transformative, denoting a change in status rather than a change in nature. Second, justification is clearly distinguished from sanctification. Justification refers to the declaration that one stands in the right before God, while sanctification denotes the ongoing renewal and transformation in one's life. Third, justification denotes alien righteousness, which means that Christ's righteousness is imputed to the believer. Believers aren't righteous because of a righteousness inherent to them.[11]

---

6. McGrath, *Iustitia Dei*, 1:84–85.

7. Ibid., 1:90.

8. Ibid., 1:78.

9. See Matthew Barrett, *Salvation by Grace: The Case for Effectual Calling and Regeneration* (Phillipsburg, NJ: Presbyterian & Reformed, 2013), 10–11.

10. Alister E. McGrath, *Iustitia Dei: A History of the Christian Doctrine of Justfication*, vol. 2, *From the 1500s to the Present Day* (Cambridge: Cambridge University Press, 1986), 2.

11. The forensic and imputed nature of righteousness was developed particularly by Melanchthon. See McGrath, *Iustitia Dei*, 2:25, though McGrath notes that Melanchthon isn't totally clear since he also makes statements about being made righteous.

More specifically, Luther rejected the idea that human beings can do anything to prepare for grace. They cannot do their best and as a result receive God's righteousness.[12] Luther categorically rejected the notion that one can prepare oneself for grace by doing good works, as Biel advocated.[13]

Luther insists that good works cannot be understood as the cause or ground of justification.[14] McGrath summarizes Luther's position, "works are a condition, but not a cause of salvation."[15] The word "condition" is acceptable if one understands works as the fruit or evidence of justification. This means that Luther stands apart from Augustine in rejecting the idea that human beings are made righteous in justification.[16] Although Luther didn't formulate imputation the same way as those who were in the Reformed tradition, his emphasis on a righteousness that is extrinsic to us (on the truth that all our righteousness is in Jesus Christ) prepared the way for Melanchthon's later teaching on imputed righteousness.[17]

Sin and the Law

At this juncture, it will be helpful for us to look at some of Luther's own words on justification and *sola fide*.[18] Philip Watson has argued that the fundamental issue in Luther's theology isn't philosophical or psychological but theological. What concerned Luther was one's relationship with God.[19] Luther's vision of God was the foundation for what he thought about everything else, and because of his view of God Luther believed justification was the doctrine by which the church stands or falls.[20] Luther insisted that "nothing in this article can be given up or compromised, even

---

12. Ibid., 2:6.

13. Martin Luther, "Preface to the Epistle of St. Paul to the Romans," in *Martin Luther: Selections from His Writings* (ed. John Dillenberger; Garden City, NY: Doubleday, 1961), 21.

14. McGrath, *Iustitia Dei*, 2:16.

15. Ibid., 2:27.

16. Ibid., 2:18.

17. Ibid., 2:14.

18. Trueman observes that Luther's understanding of justification differs from many modern evangelicals in his theology of baptism. See Carl Trueman, "*Simul peccator et justus*: Martin Luther and Justification," in *Justification in Perspective: Historical Developments and Contemporary Challenges* (ed. Bruce L. McCormack; Grand Rapids: Baker, 2006), 92–94. As a Baptist, I would argue Luther is inconsistent here, but, in any case, my focus is on where there is agreement between Lutherans and Baptists.

19. Philip S. Watson, *Let God Be God! An Interpretation of the Theology of Martin Luther* (London: Epworth, 1947), 23.

20. See McGrath, *Iustitia Dei*, 2:10. "Because if this article [of justification] stands, the church stands; if this article collapses, the church collapses" (*WA* 40/3.352.3). All citations from *WA* are from Martin Luther, *Luthers Werke: Kritische Gesamtausgabe [Schriften]* (65 vols.; Weimar: H. Böhlau, 1883–1993). I am particularly grateful to my PhD student, Aubrey Sequeira, who tracked down and verified the translations from Luther's Works.

if heaven and earth and things temporal should be destroyed."[21] Moreover, "the Article of justification is the Master and the prince, the lord, the ruler and judge, over all the kinds of doctrine, which preserves and governs the entire church doctrine and sets up our conscience in the sight of God."[22] Human beings cannot enjoy a relationship with the Holy One of Israel apart from the radical grace of God. In other words, we cannot understand what Luther meant when he insisted on *sola fide* if we don't grasp Luther's understanding of the one true God, the creator of all.

Luther knew that human beings stood condemned before a holy God because he had a profound theology of sin.[23] Timothy George captures Luther's thought on this: "Luther came to view sin as a seething rebellion."[24] Human beings as creatures owe God everything, and yet they treacherously turn against him. Carl Trueman explains Luther's view this way, "Thus it is not healing that the sinner needs; rather, it is death and resurrection, for only these radical steps can address the truly radical nature of sin itself as involving primarily a certain status before God."[25] Luther *felt* and experienced the awfulness of sin. "If anyone would feel the greatness of sin he would not be able to go on living another moment; so great is the power of sin."[26] As human beings we fail to grasp on our own what sin truly is. "Radical sin, deadly and truly mortal, is unknown to men in the whole wide world.... Not one of all men could think that it was a sin of the world not to believe in Christ Jesus the Crucified."[27]

This means that the failure to believe isn't a minor matter, nor can it be ascribed simply to ignorance. Sin is rooted in unbelief, in the failure to entrust oneself entirely to God.[28] Those who think they keep the law are guilty of idolatry; such a person "denies God and makes himself into God."[29] In what is perhaps his most famous book, *The Bondage of the Will*, Luther declared that human beings are captives to sin.[30] Freedom

21. WA 50, 199.

22. WA 39/I.205.

23. See the masterful exposition in Gordon Rupp, *The Righteousness of God: Luther Studies* (London: Hodder and Stoughton, 1953), 102–20.

24. George, *Theology of the Reformers*, 68.

25. Trueman, *"Simul peccator et justus:* Martin Luther and Justification," 85.

26. Quotation taken from George, *Theology of the Reformers*, 69.

27. Quotation taken from ibid., 69, n. 52.

28. Luther, "Preface to Romans," 22.

29. Martin Luther, *Lectures on Galatians 1535: Chapters 1–4* (vol. 26 of *Luther's Works*; ed. Jaroslav Pelikan; St. Louis: Concordia, 1964), 258. I especially focus on Luther's 1535 commentary on Galatians, for it represents his mature work.

30. Martin Luther, *De Servo Arbitrio*, in *Luther and Erasmus: Free Will and Salvation* (trans. and ed. Philip S. Watson in collaboration with B. Drewery; LCC; Philadelphia: Westminster, 1969), 185, 293–94.

for sinners means that our wills are bent to do what is evil, for we are evil trees, and hence the fruit of our lives is also wicked.[31] We need to become a new tree, and only the grace of God can make the tree new. Luther's strong doctrine of predestination wasn't a speculative matter for him. It was tied to his firm belief that justification could not be merited by works (Rom 11:5–6) and was rooted in his conviction that salvation was entirely God's work.

Luther didn't restrict himself to one "use" of the law, yet he especially argued that God gave the law to expose human sin. The law reveals the rebellion, idolatry, and unbelief of the human heart. Partial obedience to the law does not justify before God, for it is evident from Gal 3:10 and other texts that perfect obedience is required,[32] and hence it is impossible to keep the law (Rom 8:7–8).[33]

God gave the law, then, to put us to death, to kill us, so that we would see the enormity of our sin.[34] One of Luther's favorite illustrations was that God uses the law as a hammer.[35] Human beings are convinced of their righteousness, and God needs a mighty tool to crush our self-righteous presumption. "Therefore this presumption of righteousness is a huge and horrible monster. To break and crush it, God needs a large and powerful hammer, that is, the Law, which is the hammer of death, the thunder of hell, and the lightning of divine wrath. To what purpose? To attack the presumption of righteousness, which is a rebellious, stubborn, and stiff-necked beast."[36] God shatters our self-confidence and self-righteousness, so that we will put our faith in Jesus Christ. Luther goes on to say that "hunger is the best cook. As the dry earth thirsts for rain, so the Law makes the troubled heart thirst for Christ. To such hearts Christ tastes sweetest, to them He is joy, comfort, and life. Only then are Christ and His work understood correctly."[37]

---

31. Luther, *Galatians 1–4*, 126.

32. Ibid., 253, 260, 274 (on Gal 3:12). Timothy Wengert points out that Luther believed perfect obedience was required for justification, and the law, according to Luther, refers to the entire law and can't be restricted to the ceremonial law. See Timothy Wengert, "Martin Luther on Galatians 3:6–14: Justification by Curses and Blessings," in *Galatians and Christian Theology: Justification, the Gospel, and Ethics in Paul's Letter* (ed. Mark W. Elliott, Scott J. Hafemann, N. T. Wright, and John Frederick; Grand Rapids: Baker, 2014), 59, n. 115; 76, n. 194, 196.

33. Luther, *Galatians 1–4*, 254.

34. Ibid., 335, 345.

35. Ibid., 312, 314, 336.

36. Ibid., 310.

37. In the discussion below we see that all three elements appear under each of the topics considered.

Imputation

Timothy George has identified three elements in Luther's theology, all closely connected:[38] (1) imputation; (2) faith-alone justifies; and (3) believers are justified and at the same time sinners.[39] We begin with imputation. George says that Luther emphasized that righteousness is imputed to us instead of imparted.[40] In other words, the righteousness of a believer is extrinsic rather than intrinsic; it is declared instead of being inherent.

Luther's understanding of righteousness is disputed. Bernhard Lohse, for instance, argues that Luther didn't clearly define righteousness, that on some occasions he defined it as being declared righteous, but in other places he saw it as a process by which one is made righteous.[41] Trueman brings some clarity to the debate, pointing out that the *early Luther* understood justification in terms of a process and growing in righteousness (1515–1520), but the *mature Luther* came to the conviction that justification had to do with one's status and relation before God.[42] Hence, the notion that the mature Luther and Melanchthon were at odds over justification is historically improbable.[43] Indeed, as Trueman suggests, conversations between Luther and Melanchthon may have solidified Luther's own view on the matter.

We can confidently say, then, that Luther believed righteousness is fundamentally a gift and extrinsic. Luther often emphasized that our righteousness is passive; that is, we don't do anything to prepare for it or to receive it.[44] "But this righteousness is heavenly and passive. We do not have it of ourselves; we receive it from heaven."[45] The righteousness that belongs to believers is an alien righteousness, one that isn't intrinsic to human beings.[46] "Through faith in Christ, therefore, Christ's righteousness becomes our righteousness and all that he has becomes ours."[47]

---

38. In the discussion below we see that all three elements appear under each of the topics considered.

39. George, *Theology of the Reformers*, 70.

40. Ibid., 70–71. What George says here stands in some tension with McGrath's claim that Luther didn't hold a strong doctrine of imputation, but McGrath is probably thinking of the technical language of imputation developed in Reformed theology later.

41. Bernhard Lohse, *Martin Luther's Theology: Its Historical and Systematic Development* (trans. and ed. Roy A. Harrisville; Minneapolis: Fortress, 1999), 260.

42. Trueman, "*Simul peccator et justus:* Martin Luther and Justification," 72–88.

43. Ibid., 88–92.

44. For a discussion of the righteousness of God in Luther, see Rupp, *The Righteousness of God*, 121–37.

45. Luther, *Galatians 1–4*, 8.

46. Martin Luther, "Two Kinds of Righteousness," in *Martin Luther: Selections from His Writings* (edited with an introduction by John Dillenberger; Garden City: Doubleday, 1961), 86. See also here Fesko, *Beyond Calvin*, 132.

47. Martin Luther, "Two Kinds of Righteousness," 87.

Luther goes on to say, "He who trusts in Christ exists in Christ; he is one with Christ, having the same righteousness as he."[48]

The extrinsic nature of righteousness is evident, for Christ is the bridegroom and church is the bride, and as the bride it possesses all that belongs to the bridegroom.[49] "Therefore this is a marvelous definition of Christian righteousness: it is a divine imputation for reckoning as righteousness or to righteousness, for the sake of our faith in Christ or for the sake of Christ."[50] As Timo Laato says about Luther, "For the Reformer, Christ alone is the basis of justification."[51] The righteousness of believers does not lie in themselves. They are righteous because they belong to Jesus Christ; they are righteous because they are married to Christ.

Faith Alone

Luther also emphasized that faith alone justifies.[52] He famously adds the word "alone" ("allein") to Rom 3:28. Such a translation isn't an imposition on the text, but represents the meaning of the verses in context.[53] The famous Roman Catholic scholar Joseph Fitzmyer agrees.[54] Luther emphasizes repeatedly that faith alone justifies—faith directed to God's Word, faith focused on what God has done for us in Jesus Christ crucified and risen. Luther rejects the notion that we take the first step toward God by doing our best, since such a view smuggles in works and fails to recognize that faith is God's gift to us. Works cannot and do not justify, and the Scriptures often posit a disjunction between faith and works. A person "is justified by faith alone and not any works."[55] "We are pronounced righteous solely by faith in Christ, not by the works of the Law or by love."[56] And, "Wherefore it ought to be the first concern of every Christian to lay aside all confidence in works and grow in the knowledge, not of works, but of Christ Jesus, who suffered and rose for him."[57]

---

48. Ibid., 88.
49. Ibid., 87. Cf. here Mark A. Seifrid, "Paul, Luther, and Justification in Gal 2:15–21," *WTJ* 65 (2003): 223–24.
50. Luther, *Galatians 1–4*, 233.
51. Timo Laato, "Justification: The Stumbling Block of the Finnish Luther School," *CTQ* 72 (2008): 337.
52. George, *Theology of the Reformers*, 71–72.
53. See Thomas R. Schreiner, *Romans* (BECNT; Grand Rapids: Baker, 1998), 204–5.
54. Joseph A. Fitzmyer, *Romans* (AB; New York: Doubleday, 1993), 360–62.
55. Martin Luther, "The Freedom of a Christian," in *Three Treatises* (trans. W. A. Lambert; rev. Harold J. Grimm; Philadelphia: Fortress, 1970), 280.
56. Luther, *Galatians 1–4*, 137.
57. Luther, "The Freedom of a Christian," 281.

It is vital to see that justification, for Luther, is ultimately and finally *not* grounded on faith. Rather, faith is the means by which one lays hold of Christ, who is our righteousness. Faith alone justifies "because faith brings us the Spirit gained by the merits of Christ."[58] Faith saves because it "takes hold of Christ and believes that my sin and death are damned and abolished in the sin and death of Christ."[59] Faith saves, then, because it unites believers to Christ.

Faith looks away from oneself and trusts in what Christ has done. The story of Dr. Krause helps to illustrate what Luther teaches.[60] Dr. Krause committed suicide because he thought he denied Christ and was convinced Christ was accusing him at the Father's right hand because of his defection. Luther countered that such despair was a lie of the devil. The notion that Christ is an accuser of believers is "an alien Christ, about which Scripture knows nothing at all."[61] Scripture "depicts Christ, not as a judge or tempter or an accuser but as the Reconciler, the Mediator, the Comforter, the Savior, and the Throne of grace."[62]

Faith looks particularly to Christ crucified for the forgiveness of sins so that "His righteousness is yours; your sin is His."[63] Faith means that we "learn ... in every temptation to transfer sin, death, the curse, and all the evils that oppress us from ourselves to Christ, and, on the other hand, to transfer righteousness, life, and blessing from Him to us."[64] The substitutionary work of Christ is emphasized. "He has and bears all the sins of all men in His body—not in the sense that He has committed them but in the sense that He took these sins committed by us, upon His own body, in order to make satisfaction for them with His own blood."[65]

Luther puts this in a striking and unforgettable way in commenting on Gal 3:13. God "sent His Son into the world, heaped all the sins of all men upon Him, and said to Him: 'Be Peter the denier; Paul the persecutor, blasphemer and assaulter; David the adulterer; the sinner who ate the apple in Paradise; the thief on the cross. In short, be the person of all men, the one who has committed the sins of all men."[66] Justification is by faith alone, because it looks to Christ alone for forgiveness of sins and salvation.

---

58. Luther, "Preface to Romans," 22.
59. Luther, *Galatians 1–4*, 160.
60. Ibid., 195.
61. Ibid.
62. Ibid.
63. Ibid., 233.
64. Ibid., 292.
65. Ibid., 277.
66. Ibid., 280.

Faith itself doesn't save, but faith saves because we receive Christ by faith, because we possess and grasp Christ by faith.[67]

Since faith looks to God and to Christ, it honors God. It gives glory to him for saving us, so that wisdom, love, and righteousness are ascribed to him.[68] "There is no other honor equal to the estimate of truthfulness with which we honor him whom we trust."[69] Hence, "the very highest worship of God is this that we ascribe to him truthfulness, righteousness, and whatever else should be ascribed to one who is trusted."[70] He goes on to say, "What greater rebellion against God, what greater wickedness, what greater contempt of God is there than not believing his promise?"[71] Hence, Luther rejected the Roman Catholic notion that one couldn't have assurance of salvation.[72] Believers enjoy assurance because they don't save themselves, because they look only to Christ for salvation, and so their faith gives them assurance because faith grasps and possesses who Christ is for us.

For Luther, *sola fide* is an essential entailment of the gospel because it ascribes salvation to Christ alone (*solus Christus*) and glory to God alone (*soli Deo gloria*). Faith is God's gift in us.[73]

Simul Iustus et Peccator

The third element of Luther's thought is his famous motto that believers are *simul iustus et peccator* ("justified and at the same time sinners"). Luther declares, "We are in truth and totally sinners, with regard to ourselves and our first birth. Contrariwise, in so far as Christ has been given for us, we are holy and just totally. Hence from different aspects we are said to be just and sinners at one and the same time."[74] Faith doesn't transport us to paradise immediately because we still struggle with sin. "Thus a Christian man is righteous and a sinner at the same time, holy and profane, an enemy of God and a child of God."[75] Nevertheless, we also enjoy assurance because our righteousness isn't our own. We take hold of Christ who is our righteousness. Righteousness is outside us in Christ and is grasped in faith.[76] Luther says, "But because faith is weak, it is not perfected without

---

67. Lohse, *Martin Luther's Theology*, 260–63.
68. Luther, *Galatians 1–4*, 66, 226–27.
69. Luther, "The Freedom of a Christian," 284.
70. Ibid., 285.
71. Ibid.
72. Luther, *Galatians 1–4*, 377–78.
73. Luther, "Preface to Romans," 23–24.
74. Quotation taken from George, *Theology of the Reformers*, 72.
75. Luther, *Galatians 1–4*, 232.
76. Ibid., 229–35.

the imputation of God. Hence faith begins righteousness, but imputation perfects it until the day of Christ."[77] And, "Sins remain in us, and God hates them very much. Because of them it is necessary for us to have the imputation of righteousness, which comes to us on account of Christ, who is given to us and grasped by our faith."[78]

The paradoxical reality of Christian existence keeps us humble. Luther says that the Christian "really and truly feels that there is sin in him and that on this account he is worthy of wrath, the judgment of God, and eternal death. Thus he is humbled in this life."[79]

Luther captured, perhaps better than any theologian, the weakness that still bedevils our lives. He says, "The words 'freedom from the wrath of God, from the Law, sin, death, etc.,' are easy to say, but to feel the greatness of the freedom and to apply its results to oneself in a struggle, in the agony of conscience, and in practice—this is more difficult than anyone can say."[80] Living by faith is not easy in this fallen world.

> From this it is evident how difficult a thing faith is, it is not learned and grasped as easily and quickly as those sated and scornful spirits imagine who immediately exhaust everything contained in the Scriptures. The weakness and struggle of the flesh with the spirit in the saints is ample testimony how weak their faith still is. For a perfect faith would soon bring a perfect contempt and scorn for this present life.[81]

Our boldness and confidence would transform everything we face in life. But presently we are in the midst of a battle between the flesh and the Spirit.

Luther pours scorn on fanatics who seem to think that they live so powerfully in the Spirit. They have a dim grasp of their own sin. By way of contrast Luther says, "But I and others like me hardly know the basic elements of this art [living by faith], and yet we are studious pupils in the school where this art is being taught. It is indeed being taught, but so long as the flesh and sin remain, it cannot be learned thoroughly."[82] The division that rages within a believer fits with Luther's last known written words where he focuses on human need and God's grace, "We are beggars. That is true."[83]

---

77. Ibid., 230.

78. Ibid., 235.

79. Ibid.

80. Martin Luther, *Lectures on Galatians, 1535: Chapters 5–6* (vol. 27 of *Luther's Works*; ed. Jaroslav Pelikan; St. Louis: Concordia, 1964), 5.

81. Luther, *Galatians 1–4*, 393.

82. Ibid., 342.

83. Martin Luther, *Table Talk* (vol. 54 of *Luther's Works*; ed. and trans. Theodore G. Tappert; Philadelphia: Fortress, 1967), 476.

Role of Good Works

Luther didn't rule out the importance or necessity of good works. Lohse says that in Luther's thought good works are not a cause of salvation but they are still necessary, even if Luther didn't strongly emphasize this truth. Luther believed good works are evidence of a genuine faith.[84] Luther, responding to the situation of his day, was primarily worried that Roman Catholics had exalted love over faith and thereby subverted the biblical order.[85] Furthermore, he believed that if we concentrate on our works, the focus easily shifts from Christ and his sacrifice to our love. Much of the discussion on the role of works centered on Gal 5:6. The question was whether faith is formed by love or whether love is the result or expression of faith. Luther clearly believed the latter, insisting that works flow from faith and lead to love. He argued that we should reject the notion that love is the basis of our justification.[86] Instead, the order must be reversed. Faith expresses itself and is active through love.[87] "Behold, from faith thus flow love and joy in the Lord."[88] Commenting on Gal 5:6, Luther says, "works are done on the basis of faith through love, not that a man is justified through love."[89]

Luther often appeals to Jesus' illustration of good and rotten trees (Matt 7:17–19). "As the trees are, so are the fruits they bear."[90] Again, "good works do not make a good man, but a good man does good works; evil works do not make a wicked man, but a wicked man does evil works."[91] Luther does not discount the importance of good works; he certainly believed they were vital: "It is true that faith alone justifies, without works; but I am speaking about genuine faith, which after it has justified, will not go to sleep but is active through love."[92] All genuine obedience flows from faith.[93] Thus the obedience that pleases God stems from trusting God, which, Luther claims, Hebrews 11 makes clear. Works are a fruit of faith for Luther but cannot be understood as the ground or cause of justification.[94]

---

84. Lohse, *Martin Luther's Theology*, 264–65; cf. also Alan C. Clifford, *Atonement and Justification: English Evangelical Theology 1640-1790: An Evaluation* (Oxford: Clarendon, 1990), 175.

85. Luther, *Galatians 1–4*, 269–70; idem, *Galatians 5–6*, 28–30.

86. See George, *Theology of the Reformers*, 73–74.

87. Luther, "The Freedom of a Christian," 302.

88. Ibid., 304.

89. Luther, *Galatians 5–6*, 28.

90. Luther, "The Freedom of a Christian," 297.

91. Ibid.

92. Luther, *Galatians 5–6*, 30.

93. Luther, *Galatians 1–4*, 262–66.

94. So Timothy J. Wengert, *Defending Faith: Lutheran Responses to Andreas Osiander's Doctrine of Justification 1551-1559* (Studies in the Late Middle Ages, Humanism and the Reformation 65; Tübingen: Mohr Siebeck, 2012), 300.

The Finnish Interpretation of Luther

The notion that justification is by faith alone is one of the signature themes of the Reformation. In a book of this length, it is hardly necessary to demonstrate in detail that the Reformers argued such a case. The response of the Council of Trent alone indicates that Roman Catholics understood the Reformers in such a way.

In Lutheran scholarship, however, a recent recasting of Luther's thought has been articulated. The so-called Finnish school claims that Luther has been misunderstood. Probably the most prominent advocate of this view is Tuomo Mannermaa.[95] Mannermaa emphasizes that believers truly participate in Christ, and thus they are granted the attributes of his divine presence. When believers are united with Christ, they are truly joined with him, and there are ontological dimensions to this union.[96] Hence, they participate in the divine nature. This view fits with Luther's teaching that believers become a new tree. The Finnish view suggests that justification in Luther cannot be restricted to the categories of imputation or alien righteousness. Justification also includes our participation in the divine nature, in what is called in Greek orthodoxy *theosis*. Thus, imputation is more than merely a legal declaration, it has ontological ramifications as well.[97] Christians share ontologically, says Mannermaa, in what Christ is; that is, they really are free from sin and death. Christians truly have Christ living in them (Gal 2:20) since they are united with Christ. This notion of deification, they argue, is a constituent part of Luther's theology. Human beings are divinized through their union with Christ.

It follows, then, that justification and sanctification are really two different ways of discussing the same reality. Paul Louis Metzger says, "Luther maintains that *real* transformation occurs in justification."[98] This means that justification and sanctification should *not* be sharply distinguished from one another as they commonly are in Lutheran theology. Such a view

---

95. For Manneremaa's view as it is sketched in here, see his *Christ Present in Faith: Luther's View of Justification* (ed. and intro. by K. Stjerna; Minneapolis: Fortress, 2005). Other advocates of the Finnish view include Carl E. Bratten and Robert W. Jenson, eds., *Union with Christ: The New Finnish Interpretation of Luther* (Grand Rapids: Eerdmans, 1998), and Paul Louis Metzger, "Luther and the Finnish School. Mystical Union with Christ: An Alternative to Blood Transfusions and Legal Fictions," *WTJ* 65 (2003): 201–13.

96. See Robert W. Jenson, "Response to Mark Seifrid, Paul Metzger, and Carl Trueman on Finnish Luther Research," *WTJ* 65 (2003): 247–48. There are differences between Metzger and Jenson (see 249–50), but that is not my concern here.

97. See ibid., 248–49.

98. Metzger, "Luther and the Finnish School," 204 (italics his).

of sanctification does not threaten the grace of the gospel, they argue, for sanctification is the work of Christ in believers, and hence it has a supernatural quality instead of being seen as the contribution of the human being.

The question we need to consider is whether Luther's notion of imputation or *simul iustus peccator* contradicts Mannermaa's reading of Luther. Mannermaa notes that Luther believed that the imputation of sin is necessary since believers are still imperfect and struggle with sin. Metzger says that imputation doesn't do justice to the whole of Luther's understanding of justification, for "Christ is truly present in faith."[99] Metzger appeals particularly to Luther's notion that believers are married to Christ, which must designate who we are, for those who are married are not just given a certificate![100] Justification, Metzger avers,

> occurs not by way of a legal act so much as through the sovereign indwelling love of the Spirit of life, who now creates and quickens a desire for Christ within us.... Such personal union with Christ by faith through the Spirit is what justifies, giving rise to the declaration of Christ's righteousness being ours, not by nature, nor by a legal act as such, but again, by the Spirit.[101]

Mannermaa insists that for Luther justification cannot be restricted to a forensic category. Righteousness is not only God's favor but also a gift. The gift denotes Christ's real and transforming presence, for in faith believers truly enjoy Christ's real presence within them.

The concern raised by Mannermaa is that a forensic view lends itself to a legal fiction, where believers are declared to be righteous, even though they aren't changed at all. Actually, Mannermaa veers off here, for God's verdict, even though it isn't transformative ethically, is effective.[102] Mannermaa also misunderstands the union between Christ and the believer in Luther's thought, failing to see that the believer retains his distinctiveness and does not become one in essence with Christ.[103] Union with Christ should not be interpreted ontologically and realistically as Mannermaa does.[104]

---

99. Ibid., 207.

100. Ibid., 205–8.

101. Ibid., 208. Metzger argues that the Spirit is the missing element in forensic interpretations of justification (ibid., 209–11).

102. Cf. Robert Kolb, *Martin Luther: Confessor of the Faith* (Oxford: Oxford University Press, 2009), 128. For a careful and full assessment of the new Finnish view, see William W. Schumacher, *Who Do I Say That You Are? Anthropology and the Theology of Theosis in the Finnish School of Tuomo Mannermaa* (Eugene, OR: Wipf & Stock, 2010).

103. Kolb, *Martin Luther: Confessor of the Faith*, 128–29; Seifrid, "Paul, Luther, and Justification," 227.

104. Rightly, Carl R. Trueman, "Is the Finnish Line a New Beginning? A Critical Assessment of the Reading of Luther Offered by the Helsinki Circle," *WTJ* 65 (2003): 235. Wengert notes

A significant problem with the Finnish view is Luther's own teaching on imputation.[105] Yes, Christ is present in believers, but the language Luther actually used is imputation instead of transformation. Jenson, as noted above, thinks imputation itself is transformative, but we should note that Luther endorsed Melanchthon's articulation of imputation penned in 1531. Since Luther supported Melanchthon's notion that righteousness is imputed and extrinsic to us, the notion that Luther believed that justification was renovative and transformative is unlikely. Michael Allen agrees that both justification and participation are important to Luther, but he rightly observes that it doesn't follow from this that the former has the same meaning as the latter: the forensic and the formative are not confused or identified, though the former is the foundation for the latter.[106] Along the same lines, Timo Laato has argued convincingly that Mannermaa has misunderstood grace (favor) and gift in Luther. Laato shows that for Luther favor precedes gift, which mean that the forensic precedes the transformative.[107] In other words, alien righteousness, in contrast to Mannermaa, is fundamental and foundational for one's relationship to God.

Carl Trueman raises significant, and I think devastating, critiques of the Finnish view. He notes that the context and time of Luther's writings must also be considered.[108] Often those who support the Finnish view cite the early Luther, the pre-Reformation Luther, instead of documenting the views of the mature Luther. Furthermore, there are instances where statements of Luther are taken out of context and wrongly read as if they supported the Finnish view. The notion that Luther was at odds with subsequent Luther tradition, though possible, is unlikely.[109]

Furthermore, the Finnish view has not accounted for Luther's

---

that Luther agreed with Melanchthon that justification was forensic. Hence, "The central point for Luther was *not* that justification was an ontological joining of Luther to Christ, but precisely the opposite: In place of a quality or virtue in the soul, Luther pronounced an absolution and union with Christ to himself.... Thus, despite obvious differences in style and expression, Luther and Melanchthon both placed justification by faith in the Word and the comfort it afforded the sinner, not in the sinner's renewal or supposed participation in God's essential righteousness but in God's declared promise" (*Defending Faith: Lutheran Responses to Andreas Osiander's Doctrine of Justification 1551-1559*, 69).

105. Trueman, "Is the Finnish Line a New Beginning?" 239–41; Wengert, *Defending Faith: Lutheran Responses to Andreas Osiander's Doctrine of Justification 1551-1559*, 378–79.

106. R. Michael Allen, *Justification and the Gospel: Understanding the Context and Controversies* (Grand Rapids: Baker, 2013), 47–51.

107. Laato, "Justification: The Stumbling Block of the Finnish Luther School," 327–46.

108. Trueman, "Is the Finnish Line a New Beginning?" 236–37; see also Schumacher, *Who Do I Say That You Are?*, 130–39.

109. Trueman, "Is the Finnish Line a New Beginning?," 243.

distinction between active and passive righteousness.[110] In reading Luther's 1535 commentary on Galatians, as was noted above, we see a persistent emphasis on the continuing presence of sin in the believer.[111] Such a notion sits awkwardly with the emphasis on deification and the conception that justification also brings renovation. Indeed, it seems that Luther distinguished clearly between justification and sanctification, for the former demands perfection, which is still lacking in those who are united to Christ.[112]

Another problem surfaces with the Finnish view. If Luther believed that justification was sanative and transforming instead of being imputed and forensic, how is it that Lutherans rejected Osiander so dramatically?[113] It is possible, of course, that the mainstream Lutheran tradition misunderstood Luther, but as Timothy Wengert observes, such a scenario is unlikely.[114] If Luther espoused a transformative view of justification, it seems likely that many more Lutherans would have endorsed Osiander.[115]

Conclusion

Martin Luther's understanding of justification is rooted in his anthropology and his doctrine of God, in his understanding of human sin and God's holiness. God's radical grace was necessary for human beings to be right before God because human obedience could never qualify. Luther viewed human sin as so pernicious because of his conception of God's

---

110. Ibid., 238–39. When Luther speaks of active and passive righteousness, this should not be confused with the Reformed notion of imputation (the active and passive obedience of Christ), for Luther wasn't addressing this issue in speaking of passive righteousness. By passive righteousness Luther meant that believers don't do anything to be righteous in God's sight; they receive God's righteousness by faith in Jesus Christ, not by virtue of anything they do.

111. Javier Garcia raises another issue with the 1535 commentary on Galatians. Mannermaa's starting point for unpacking Luther is the incarnation, but the preface of the commentary shows that Luther's own starting point was the distinction between law and gospel. See Javier A. Garcia, "'Not an Idle Quality or an Empty Husk in the Heart': A Critique of Tuomo Mannermaa on Luther and Galatians," in *Galatians and Christian Theology: Justification, the Gospel, and Ethics in Paul's Letter* (ed. Mark W. Elliott, Scott J. Hafemann, N. T. Wright, and John Frederick; Grand Rapids: Baker, 2014), 136–37.

112. Trueman, "Is the Finnish Line a New Beginning?," 241.

113. Wengert, *Defending Faith: Lutheran Responses to Andreas Osiander's Doctrine of Justification 1551-1559*, 4. See also Garcia, "A Critique of Tuomo Mannermaa on Luther and Galatians," 140–41.

114. "How can one argue that Luther was such a brilliant teacher if nearly all of his closest students completely misunderstood his teaching on justification by faith and if the only person to understand his position never sat in his classroom and was universally vilified by the very students who did" (Wengert, *Defending Faith: Lutheran Responses to Andreas Osiander's Doctrine of Justification 1551-1559*, 3).

115. See ibid., esp. 242–316.

holiness. The only righteousness that could save, then, was passive instead of active righteousness. Believers needed an imputed righteousness, a righteousness that is given to them instead of earned by them. Such righteousness, as Luther loved to teach, was by faith alone. Faith receives what God gives, and those who put their faith in Jesus Christ as the crucified and risen one are right with God. Believers are, so to speak, married to Christ, and all that Christ is belongs to them.

Luther did not deny the importance or necessity of good works, but he saw such works as the fruit or consequence of faith. They were never understood as qualifying human beings to stand in God's presence. The notion that Luther's view of justification is akin to the Orthodox conception of *theosis* is unconvincing. Such a view does not account for Luther's agreement with Melanchthon and his teaching on imputation. Finally, it falls short because it fails to distinguish between the early and mature Luther.

CHAPTER 3

John Calvin on Justification by Faith Alone

> "Now we shall possess a right definition of faith if we call it a firm and certain knowledge of God's benevolence toward us, founded upon the truth of the freely given promise in Christ, both revealed to our minds and sealed upon our hearts through the Holy Spirit."
>
> —*John Calvin*

Justification played a significant role in John Calvin's theology.[1] Calvin wrote that justification is "the main hinge upon which religion turns,"[2] and he believed that a saving relationship with God cannot exist apart from justification. In this chapter, we will investigate Calvin's teaching on justification under five headings: (1) why we need justification; (2) justification by faith alone; (3) justification and assurance; (4) justification by imputation; and (5) justification and sanctification (i.e., the role good works play in justification). We will spend much of our time looking at what Calvin himself has written, and since his *Institutes* represent his theology and developed thought, that work will be the primary source for our discussion.

Why We Need Justification

We begin with the necessity of justification. Why did Calvin believe justification was so crucial and important? His answer is that apart from justification human beings cannot be right with God, for God requires perfect obedience.[3] Partial obedience will not do, and if we think our

---

1. For a summary of Calvin's teaching on justification, see Lane, *Justification by Faith in Catholic-Protestant Dialogue*, 17–43.
2. John Calvin, *Institutes of the Christian Religion* (ed. John T. McNeill; trans. and indexed by Ford Lewis Battles; LCC 20; Philadelphia: Westminster, 1960), 3.11.1.
3. Ibid., 3.2.1, 38; 3.17.7.

works are sufficient, we have an inadequate view of both sin and God's justice. When we rightly understand the depth of our sin, says Calvin, our conscience testifies against us and reveals to us that God is our enemy on account of our transgressions.[4] Sin is pervasive in human beings, for it is located in desires and can't be confined to the will.[5] Hence, it is obvious that righteousness cannot be obtained by works since all fall short of what God requires.[6] Works of law in Paul can't be restricted to the ceremonial law but include the entire law,[7] revealing again the radical need of human beings as they stand before God. Since human beings are sinners, no one can boast before God on the basis of works.[8]

Boasting in one's works is also ruled out because of God's majesty and holiness. Calvin says that human beings vainly imagine they can be right before God "because they do not think about God's justice."[9] In a striking passage, Calvin asks readers to consider themselves as they truly are before God.

> Let us envisage for ourselves that Judge, not as our minds naturally imagine him, but as he is depicted for us in Scripture: by whose brightness the stars are darkened [Job 3:9], by whose strength the mountains are melted; by whose wrath the earth is shaken [cf. Job 9:5–6]; who catches the wise in their craftiness [Job 5:13]; beside whose purity all things are defiled [cf. Job 25:5]; whose righteousness not even the angels can bear [cf. Job 4:18].... Let us behold him, I say, sitting in judgment to examine the deeds of men; Who will stand confident before his throne? "Who ... can dwell with the devouring fire?" asked the prophet. "Who ... can dwell with the everlasting burnings?"[10]

We see the radical depth of our sin by seeing a vision of God in his holiness, and when we see God, we will despair of righteousness by works. We will realize that righteousness can never be obtained by the law but will only be granted through the gospel.[11] An understanding of our sin is fundamental, for "we will never have enough confidence in him unless we become deeply distrustful of ourselves."[12]

Luther and Calvin hold similar views of sin and the law. In Calvin,

---

4. Ibid., 3.2.20.
5. Ibid., 3.3.10–12.
6. Ibid., 3.11.3.
7. Ibid., 3.11.19.
8. Ibid., 3.11.13.
9. Ibid., 3.12.1.
10. Ibid.
11. Ibid., 3.11.17.
12. Ibid., 3.12.8.

works of law refer to the entire law and cannot be restricted to the ceremonial law. The law exposes our sin and drives us to Christ, for the law reveals the depth and power of sin in the lives of human beings.

Justification by Faith Alone

Calvin, like Luther, stresses that justification is by *faith alone*.[13] A right relationship to God can't be gained by works since all people sin; thus the only pathway to salvation is faith. Calvin is careful to say, however, that faith shouldn't be construed as a work, as if faith itself justifies us, for if such were the case, then faith would be a good work that makes us right with God. Instead, faith is the instrument or vessel that joins us to Christ, and ultimately believers are justified by Christ as the crucified and risen one. Faith itself, strictly speaking, doesn't justify. Rather, faith justifies as an instrument, receiving Christ for righteousness and life.[14] Indeed, faith is not something that originates with human beings. Yes, human beings believe the gospel and are saved, and so in that sense faith is exercised by human beings. At the same time, however, faith ultimately comes from the Holy Spirit and is a gift of God.[15] Faith alone accords with the God-centered character of the gospel, for faith gives all glory to God for our salvation.[16]

Faith, according to Calvin is living, active, and vital; merely agreeing that certain things happened in gospel history should not be confused with genuine faith.[17] True faith sees "Christ's splendor ... beamed upon us."[18] Those who put their trust in God see God and Jesus Christ for who they truly are; their eyes are opened to the beauty and loveliness of Jesus Christ. Those who think that Calvin was cold and devoid of emotions should think again, for his description of genuine faith almost certainly reflects his own experience.

> But how can the mind be aroused to taste the divine goodness without at the same time being wholly kindled to love God in return? For truly, that abundant sweetness which God has stored up for those who fear him cannot be known without at the same time powerfully moving us. And once anyone has been moved by it, it utterly ravishes him and draws him to itself.[19]

---

13. Ibid., 3.3.1; 3.11.19.
14. Ibid., 3.11.7. See also François Wendel, *Calvin: Origins and Development of His Religious Thought* (trans. Philip Mairet; Durham: Labyrinth, 1963), 262–63.
15. *Institutes*, 3.1.4; 3.2.33–35.
16. Ibid., 3.13.1–2.
17. Ibid., 3.2.1.
18. Ibid.
19. Ibid., 3.2.41.

True faith for Calvin has a powerful effect on our lives. We sense the sweetness of God's love and are overwhelmed with it. Indeed, we are so ravished by his love that our hearts are drawn to put our trust in God.

We have already seen that faith is a gift of God, but we can also say that faith derives from the word of God, the gospel.[20] As Paul says, "So faith comes from what is heard" (Rom 10:17). Faith, then, puts its trust in God's Word and his promises.[21] Faith doesn't come, says Calvin, from just any source. It must be derived from God's Word and the gospel of Jesus Christ.

Calvin's definition of faith is famous and rightly so. "Now we shall possess a right definition of faith if we call it a firm and certain knowledge of God's benevolence toward us, founded upon the truth of the freely given promise in Christ, both revealed to our minds and sealed upon our hearts through the Holy Spirit."[22] Those who believe are convinced that God loves them, and this love, which is revealed in the promises of the Word, is authenticated by the Holy Spirit. Calvin puts it this way in another place: "He alone is truly a believer who, convinced by a firm conviction that God is a kindly and well-disposed Father toward him, promises himself all things on the basis of his generosity; who, relying upon the promises of divine benevolence toward him, lays hold on an undoubted expectation of salvation."[23] Faith knows the love of God in Jesus Christ through the Holy Spirit and trusts God's promise to save.

Justification and Assurance

Calvin taught that believers can have a sure and certain knowledge, an assurance that they are justified by faith in Christ. Calvin's emphasis on assurance in faith raises questions about the role of doubt, for on first glance his definition seems to say that believers never suffer from doubt.[24] Calvin, however, affirms that believers struggle with doubts; what characterizes genuine faith is not that it never doubts but that it perseveres to the end.[25] Believers experience ups and downs in their lives, but the final reality of their lives is faith. The divided experience of believers is captured well by Calvin:

20. Ibid., 3.2.6.
21. Ibid., 3.2.21.
22. Ibid., 3.2.7.
23. Ibid., 3.2.16.
24. For a helpful discussion on assurance and faith in Calvin, see Joel R. Beeke, "Appropriating Salvation: The Spirit, Faith and Assurance, Repentance: (3.1–3, 6–10)," in *Theological Guide to Calvin's Institutes: Essays and Analysis* (ed. David W. Hall and Peter A Lillback; Phillipsburg, NJ: Presbyterian & Reformed, 2008), 276–95.
25. *Institutes*, 3.2.17.

Therefore the godly heart feels in itself a division because it is partly imbued with sweetness from its recognition of the divine goodness, partly grieves in bitterness from the awareness of its calamity; partly rests upon the promises of the gospel, partly trembles at the evidence of its own iniquity; partly rejoices at the expectation of life, partly shudders at death. This variation arises from imperfection of faith, since in the course of the present life it never goes so well with us that we are wholly cured of the disease of unbelief and entirely filled and possessed by faith.[26]

Another way of putting it is that even a small amount of faith brings comfort, even in the midst of trials and difficulties. Calvin says, "When even the least drop of faith is instilled in our minds, we begin to contemplate God's face, peaceful and calm and gracious toward us. We see him afar off, but so clearly as to know we are not at all deceived."[27]

The life of faith is not simple and easy; rather, it is a fight. Calvin compares such a life to a person in prison who truly sees the rays of the sun, even though there is darkness on every side.[28] Calvin understood the rough and tumble of the Christian life, saying that "faith is tossed about by various doubts, so that the minds of the godly are rarely at peace — at least they do not always enjoy a peaceful state. But whatever siege engines may shake them, they either rise up out the very gulf of temptations, or stand fast upon their watch."[29] The life of faith is difficult, but we see again that true faith endures and rises victorious in the struggle. Faith is never snuffed out entirely from the godly, but "lurk[s] as it were beneath the ashes."[30] Sometimes it appears that faith is dead, but we know that faith is real because it ultimately triumphs.

Both Calvin and Luther emphasized that righteousness is by faith alone. They also both emphasized the assurance of faith, but neither of them had a simplistic conception of faith. They recognized the anguish and doubts that beset believers. Still, genuine faith persists and lasts, making it through every storm. Faith may be battered and even quenched for a time but at the end of the day it arises victorious. Both Calvin and Luther also emphasized that faith itself doesn't save. Faith justifies because it connects believers to Jesus Christ and to his death and resurrection on their behalf. Faith, then, is rooted in the word of God, in the good news of the gospel, for believers put their faith in the glad tidings of what God has done for them in Christ.

---

26. Ibid., 3.2.18.
27. Ibid., 3.2.19.
28. Ibid.
29. Ibid., 3.2.37.
30. Ibid., 3.2.21.

Justification as Imputation

God's righteousness is granted to human beings as a gift of God, as a fruit of his grace.[31] The phrase "righteousness of God" signifies that God "is its author and bestows it upon us."[32] Righteousness can't come from ourselves since even our best works are still marred by sin.[33] Our works can't bring right standing with God since he demands perfection, and we all fall short in many ways. Those who are in the right before God, then, are forgiven of their sins; their sins are no longer counted against them or imputed to them.[34] This is another way of saying that justification is forensic. Forgiveness of sins and standing in the right before God is a forensic notion.[35]

It follows, then, that justification, according to Calvin, doesn't mean that we are made righteous, but that we are counted as righteous; believers are not transformed in justification but forgiven.[36] Justification is extrinsic instead of intrinsic,[37] so that those who are justified have a new status before God.[38] Our justification, then, is perfect from the beginning.[39] Believers don't become more justified as they progress in holiness, for justification doesn't denote inner renewal, but the declaration from God that one is acquitted and not guilty before him.

We saw earlier that Calvin teaches that our faith, even after our conversion, is still imperfect and flawed.[40] He appeals to 1 Cor 13:12, where Paul says our faith is incomplete and partial in this life.[41] In other words, sin continues to bedevil believers. The continuing presence of sin indicates that righteousness has to be forensic, for no one can claim to be right before God while they are still stained with sin.[42] Similarly, faith can't count for our righteousness since it isn't perfect or constant,[43] and hence we need righteousness to be imputed to us to rest assured that we are right

---

31. Ibid., 3.11.18; 3.18.5.
32. Ibid., 3.11.9.
33. Ibid. See also Wendel, *Calvin*, 260–61.
34. *Institutes*, 3.11.22.
35. Ibid., 3.11.4.
36. Ibid., 3.11.6.
37. So Wendel, *Calvin*, 258. See Richard B. Gaffin Jr., "Justification and Union with Christ (3.11–18)," in *A Theological Guide to Calvin's Institutes: Essays and Analysis* (eds. David W. Hall and Peter A. Lillback; Phillipsburg, PA: Presbyterian & Reformed, 2008), 262–64.
38. See Paul Helm, *Calvin: A Guide for the Perplexed* (New York: T&T Clark, 2008), 75.
39. Wendel, *Calvin*, 257.
40. *Institutes*, 3.2.4.
41. Ibid., 3.2.20.
42. Ibid., 3.11.21.
43. So Wendel, *Calvin*, 262.

with God.[44] Trusting in our works troubles our conscience since we all fail, and thus believers must rely on Christ to enjoy peace with God.[45] Calvin teaches that we won't have peace and rest unless we "are entirely righteous before him."[46] And this righteousness is ours by imputation.

We can see, then, why imputation is so important in Calvin's theology, for assurance rests on the truth that Christ's righteousness is imputed to believers.[47] Believers don't locate righteousness in themselves; rather, they are righteous because Christ's righteousness is reckoned to them.[48] Calvin says, "He is said to be justified in God's sight who is both reckoned righteous in God's judgment and has been accepted on account of his righteousness."[49] Or even more clearly, "Therefore, we explain justification simply as the acceptance with which God receives us into his favor as righteous men. And we say that it consists in the remission of sin and the imputation of Christ's righteousness."[50] A person "is not righteous in himself but because the righteousness of Christ is communicated to him by imputation."[51]

In Calvin's interpretation of Rom 5:19, which speaks of believers being made righteous on account of Christ's obedience, he says, "What else is this but to lodge our righteousness in Christ's obedience, because the obedience of Christ is reckoned to us as if it were our own."[52] According to Calvin, Christ's righteousness is imputed to us because of our union with Christ, because we become members of his body when we believe.[53] Hence, believers are counted righteous as those who belong to Jesus Christ, as those who are engrafted into him.[54] The crucial role that union with Christ plays in imputation is often expressed in Calvin.[55] "You see that righteousness is not in us but in Christ, that we possess it only because we are partakers in Christ."[56]

---

44. *Institutes*, 3.13.10.
45. Ibid., 3.13.3.
46. Ibid., 3.11.11.
47. For a contrary view, see Clifford, *Atonement and Justification*, 171–72.
48. John C. Olin, ed., *A Reformation Debate: John Calvin and Jacopo Sadoleto* (Grand Rapids: Baker, 1966), 67.
49. *Institutes*, 3.11.2.
50. Ibid.
51. Ibid., 3.11.23.
52. Ibid.
53. See Wendel, *Calvin*, 256–58; Helm, *Calvin*, 76; McGrath, *Iustitia Dei*, 2:37–38.
54. *Institutes*, 3.11.10.
55. See Gaffin, "Justification and Union with Christ," 252–54, 258–69. Craig B. Carpenter, "A Question of Union with Christ? Calvin and Trent on Justification," *WTJ* 64 (2002) 363–86.
56. *Institutes*, 3.11.23.

Calvin and Luther don't use the same wording and expressions in describing imputation, but they both emphasize that our consciences have peace with God because we enjoy Christ's righteousness. Both use the language of imputation, and both stress union with Christ. Luther particularly stresses that believers are married to Christ so that Christ is theirs. This same notion is evident in Calvin's emphasis on imputation and union with Christ. Both Luther and Calvin, then, teach that Christ is our righteousness.

Justification and Sanctification

The claim that *sola fide* nullifies the importance of good works is rejected by Calvin. Good works flow from faith and are a fruit of faith.[57] Calvin remarks that "faith alone first engenders love in us."[58] Faith is the root that produces every good thing in the life of those who belong to Jesus Christ. Good works are not rejected as inconsequential. Instead, they are vital, "for we dream neither of faith devoid of good works nor of justification that stands without them."[59] Good works are "not the foundation by which believers stand firm before God that is described but the means whereby our most merciful Father introduces them into his fellowship, and protects and strengthens them."[60] When it comes to Jas 2:24–26, Calvin argues that James refers to proving our righteousness, not the imputation of righteousness.[61]

According to Calvin, sanctification or regeneration (the latter term in Calvin refers to what we normally call sanctification) can't be separated from justification. All those who belong to Christ are also transformed.[62] Those who are united to Christ are both justified and sanctified in him.[63] But even though sanctification and justification are inseparable, they must

---

57. Ibid., 3.13.19.
58. Ibid., 3.2.41.
59. Ibid., 3.16.1.
60. Ibid., 3.27.6.
61. Ibid., 3.17.12.
62. Olin, *A Reformation Debate,* 68–69.
63. See Karla Wübbenhorst, "Calvin's Doctrine of Justification: Variations on a Lutheran Theme," in *Justification in Perspective: Historical Developments and Contemporary Challenges* (ed. Bruce L. McCormack; Grand Rapids: Baker, 2006), 99–118. Wübbenhorst says that Calvin emphasizes that in Christ believers are both justified and sanctified. By formulating matters in this way, he avoids antinomianism, while at the same time maintaining the foundational role of justification. See also on this matter Gaffin, "Justification and Union," 255–56. Still, justification is the foundation for sanctification in the Reformed tradition, as J. V. Fesko rightly contends (*Beyond Calvin: Union with Christ and Justification in Early Modern Reformed Theology* [Göttingen: Vandenhoeck und Ruprecht, 2012]).

be distinguished. For instance, the sun both illumines with its light and warms with its heat, and yet heat and light are not the same thing. It is best to hear the notion in Calvin's own words, "It is therefore faith alone which justifies, and yet the faith which justifies is not alone: just as the heat alone of the sun which warms the earth, and yet in the sun it is not alone, because it is constantly conjoined with light."[64]

Calvin emphasizes that believers are both justified and sanctified by union with Christ, and hence union with Christ becomes critical for understanding his view of both justification and sanctification. Gaffin says that the ultimate "source" of sanctification for Calvin is not justification per se, but Christ and his Spirit, to whom believers are united by faith.[65] At the same time, we must recognize that justification is foundational for sanctification in Calvin. Calvin declares,

> Why, then, are we justified by faith? Because by faith, we grasp Christ's righteousness, by which alone we are reconciled to God. Yet you could not grasp this without at the same time grasping sanctification also. For he "is given unto us for righteousness, wisdom, sanctification, and redemption" [I Cor. 1:30]. Therefore Christ justifies no one whom he does not at the same time sanctify.[66]

The emphasis on union is even clearer when Calvin says, "Although we may distinguish them [justification and sanctification], Christ contains both of them inseparably in himself."[67] The close relationship between justification and sanctification and their roots in union with Christ is a regular theme in Calvin. He remarks that God "bestows both of them at the same time, the one never without the other. Thus it is clear how true it is that we are justified not without works yet not through works, since in our sharing in Christ, which justifies us, sanctification is just as much included as righteousness."[68]

Calvin was clearer than Luther on the importance of good works in those who are justified. Yet, as we saw above, Luther also contended that good works were an expression and fruit of faith. Neither Calvin nor Luther thought that good works were inconsequential or unnecessary. True faith expresses itself in works, yet our works can never be the *basis* of our relationship with God since we continue to sin. Works are not the foundation

---

64. The citation is taken from Lane, *Justification by Faith in Catholic-Protestant Dialogue*, 181.
65. Gaffin, "Justification and Union," 256–57.
66. *Institutes*, 3.16.1.
67. Ibid.
68. Ibid.

of our relationship with God but they are the fruit of it. The foundation of our right relationship with God is justification by faith alone.

Conclusion

The fundamental agreement on justification by faith alone between Calvin and Luther is striking. The holiness of God and the depth of human sin ensure that human works are insufficient to be right with God. Calvin emphasizes the assurance of faith, but also acknowledges that faith is imperfect in this life. Calvin doesn't teach that faith *is* our righteousness. Our righteousness lies in the imputed righteousness of Christ, and through faith we are united with Christ, who is both our righteousness and sanctification. Good works (or sanctification) are not the foundation of our right standing with God. They are the evidence that we belong to God, and thus justification and sanctification are not identical, even though they are both ours through union with Christ.

CHAPTER 4

Sola Fide and the Council of Trent

> "If any one saith, that by faith alone the impious is justified ... let him be anathema."   —*Council of Trent*

The Reformation provoked a number of reactions from Roman Catholics politically, socially, and theologically. Before the Council of Trent (1545–1563) took place, in the early 1540s some prominent Roman Catholics and Protestants attempted to find a rapprochement on justification and other doctrines in a number of colloquies, the most significant being the Regensburg colloquy (1541). Surprisingly, there was substantial agreement in Article 5 on justification.[1] In the end, the colloquy discussions broke down, but the disagreement centered on the authority of the church and the Eucharist, not on justification.[2]

Remarkably, Calvin was quite positive about the article on justification, noting that the Catholics had given much ground and that he was in substantial agreement with what was written.[3] Perhaps Calvin's openness was due to his youth and his relationship to Martin Bucer, who was inclined toward unity.[4] As time passed, Calvin lost interest in uniting with Rome.[5] Luther, however, was far more negative about the Regensburg colloquy, complaining that the document was a patchwork of Catholic and Protestant views. He worried that it would be interpreted in a way that subverted what the Scriptures taught about justification.[6] The contents of

---

1. The text of Article 5 can be conveniently found in Lane, *Justification by Faith in Catholic-Protestant Dialogue*, 233–37.
2. So Lane, *Justification by Faith in Catholic-Protestant Dialogue*, 52.
3. For Calvin's thoughts, see ibid., 56.
4. Cf. Bruce Gordon, *Calvin* (New Haven, CT: Yale University Press, 2009), 99–102.
5. Herman J. Selderhuis, *John Calvin: A Pilgrim's Life* (trans. Albert Gootjes; Downers Grove, IL: InterVarsity Press, 2009), 102–3.
6. Again, see Lane, *Justification by Faith in Catholic-Protestant Dialogue*, 53–54.

the colloquy are quite astonishing, definitely leaning in a Protestant direction. Lane rightly says "that it is ambitious of a Protestant interpretation, though patient of a Catholic one."[7]

The Council of Trent

A reconciliation between Roman Catholics and Protestants was not to be. A few years after the Regensburg colloquy, the Council of Trent (1545–1563) formulated its own view of justification in response to Protestant and especially Lutheran teaching on justification.[8] What interests us here in our look at *sola fide* is the *Decree on Justification* (1547). We must recognize that this decree was formulated in a specific historical context, about which more will be said shortly, but let's first take a quick look at some of the key propositions in the decree.

The Council of Trent (6.9) directly refuted *sola fide*—the idea that we can be justified by faith alone. Indeed, in its reflection on James 2 the Council says that faith cooperates with good works and increases our justification, and that this proves that justification is not by faith alone (6.10). Such words also demonstrate that justification is a process that may wax or wane in this life. Good works play a role in justification, so that the grace of justification increases in those who belong to God, as they perform works that are pleasing to God (6.10). Those who believe they are justified by faith alone flatter themselves, for perseverance is necessary (6.11), and no one can be sure he or she is among the predestined (6.12).

Eternal life is granted to those who continue in good works until the end, for God's justice is infused in us through Christ's merit (6.16). Canon IX contains these thunderous words, "If any one saith, that by faith alone the impious is justified; in such wise as to mean, that nothing else is required to co-operate in order to the obtaining the grace of Justification, and that it is not in any way necessary, that he be prepared and disposed by the movement of his own will; let him be anathema." On the one hand, these words reflect a misunderstanding of the Protestant view, as if the latter claimed that good works were unnecessary. On the other hand, the language of preparation reflects the theology of Gabriel Biel and a view of grace that differs sharply from the Reformers, who taught there is nothing we can do to prepare ourselves to receive God's grace. The

7.   Ibid., 59.
8.   For a careful discussion of Trent and Catholic deliberations on justification during this period, see McGrath, *Iustitia Dei*, 2:54–97; Lane, *Justification by Faith in Catholic-Protestant Dialogue*, 45–85.

sacramental theology of Roman Catholicism is what distinguishes it from the Reformers. For instance, canons 4, 8 (Section 6) pronounce an anathema on those who claim that we can be justified by faith alone *without* the sacraments.[9]

Roman Catholic theology emphasizes the free will of human beings, so that human beings cooperate in their justification (6.1).[10] Justification, in this view, isn't merely forensic, nor is it limited to forgiveness of sins, for those who are justified are also made new within, so that justification includes the notion of renovation or what evangelicals have typically identified as sanctification (6.7). Still, justification is recognized to be a gift of grace that is freely given to human beings, for works or faith preceding justification do not merit justification (6.8). The notion that one can be justified autonomously apart from God's grace is categorically rejected.[11]

The Council was clear in saying that human beings cannot obtain God's grace through the exercise of their free will alone. Nevertheless, they do say that free will cooperates with divine grace and obtains justification and merit before God by virtue of the works that are done (6.32). Good works are not merely "the fruits and signs of Justification" but are also understood to be "a cause of the increase thereof" (6.24), which means that good works are part of the basis for justification. Hence, the notion that we are justified by faith alone or by the imputed righteousness of Christ alone is rejected (Canon 9, 11, 12).

Conclusion

At Trent, justification is understood to be a process and is defined in terms of inherent righteousness. Justification by faith alone is categorically rejected, and justification is based in part on human works. Hence, the notion that righteousness is imputed to us is also repudiated, along with the notion that one can have assurance of final salvation.

The interesting question for us, however, is what Trent means for us today. It has often been pointed out that the anathemas of Trent reflect a misunderstanding of the Reformers, and hence don't apply to the issues of today. The Catholic Church changes through time, and what matters to believers is the official Roman Catholic position in our day.[12] For instance,

---

9.   Cf. also canon 7 and canon 11 (much later in the document).
10.   Canons 4 and 5 (Section 6) teach that free will, assisted by God's grace, is not lost through Adam's sin and is still able to respond to divine overtures.
11.   Section 6, Canons 1 and 2.
12.   So Lane, *Justification by Faith in Catholic-Protestant Dialogue*, 85.

Pope John Paul II spoke positively about Luther in 1980.[13] We should also recognize that the beliefs of individual Catholics vary, for some like Peter Kreeft and Thomas Howard claim that they agree with the Protestant understanding of justification, while others like Scott Hahn sharply disagree.[14] The Roman Catholic Church isn't where it was in the sixteenth century, and thus one might hope that it will embrace a Protestant view of justification.

Still, it is difficult to see how that will happen, for the anathemas of Trent, even if they misunderstand the Reformers' view in part, also strike at vital and central elements of the Reformation view of justification. It is difficult to imagine the Roman Church rescinding what Trent says, especially in light of the fact that Rome views its councils as part of infallible tradition, and therefore just as authoritative as Scripture. Furthermore, as we will see in due course, the Catholic Church today is not embracing a Protestant view. In fundamental ways the recent Catholic Catechism endorses the perspective of Trent. Thus, it is difficult to imagine a significant shift relative to justification, because it would involve not only a repudiation of formulations at Trent and the Catholic Catechism, but also a change in Rome's sacramental theology, and such a change seems improbable.

---

13. Ibid., 94.

14. For references, see ibid., 95. See also the vigorous Roman Catholic rejection of the view of the Reformers in Robert A. Sungenis, *"Not by Faith Alone": The Biblical Evidence for the Catholic Doctrine of Justification* (Santa Barbara, CA: Queenship, 1997).

CHAPTER 5

Glimpses into Further Reformed Discussions on *Sola Fide:* The Contribution of John Owen, Richard Baxter, and Francis Turretin

"We are justified by faith alone, but not by faith that is alone."

—John Owen

A fter the Reformation one of the most fascinating and complete expositions on justification by faith alone hails from John Owen, whose writings on the topic of imputation are a helpful contribution to our understanding of what the Reformers and those who followed them meant by *sola fide*. At the same time, we will also consider the perspective of Richard Baxter, for he differed quite dramatically from Owen and even debated him in his writings. By examining Owen and Baxter we see how the understanding of justification by faith alone continued to be shaped and reappropriated within the broader Protestant and Reformed tradition. In addition to these voices, we will also take a quick look at Francis Turretin, who represents Protestant orthodoxy and a mature Protestant view of justification.

John Owen: His Charity and Pastoral Spirit

One of the classic post-Reformation books on imputation was written by John Owen (1616–1683).[1] Owen wrote this work in 1677, and it represents a mature Protestant position, well-summarizing the Reformed consensus

---

1. See *The Doctrine of Justification by Faith through the Imputation of the Righteousness of Christ; Explained, Confirmed, and Vindicated*, in *The Works of John Owen*, (vol. 5; ed. William H. Goold; Carlisle, PA: Banner of Truth, 1965), 2–400.

after more than a hundred years of debate with Roman Catholicism and various other opponents, such as the Socinians.[2] It is not my intention here to summarize the work fully or to delineate Owen's specific contribution over against his detractors.[3] Instead, we'll focus on the main lines of his argument, written amidst accusations, by Richard Baxter among others, that *sola fide* and the doctrine of imputation encouraged an antinomian lifestyle of sinful behavior.

Despite Owen's contention for imputation in this impressive and detailed work, he wrote out of a catholic and charitable spirit, as is evidenced in a remarkable passage in the book.

> To believe the *doctrine* of it [imputation], or not to believe it, as thus or thus explained, is one *thing*; and to enjoy the *thing*, or not to enjoy it, is another. I no way doubt but that many men do receive more grace from God than they understand or will own, and have a greater efficacy of it in them than they will believe. Men may be really saved by that grace which doctrinally they do deny; and they may be justified by the *imputation of that righteousness*, which, in opinion, they deny to be imputed: for the faith of it is included in that *general assent* which they give unto the truth of the gospel, and such an *adherence unto Christ* may ensue thereon, as that their mistake of the way whereby they are saved by him shall not defraud them of a real interest therein. And for my part, I must say, that notwithstanding all the disputes that I see and read about justification ... I do not believe but that the authors of them ... do really trust unto the mediation of Christ for the pardon of their sins and their acceptance with God, and not their own works or obedience; nor will I believe the contrary unless they expressly declare it.[4]

Owen affirms here that some may be justified by faith alone and the imputed righteousness of Christ, even though they deny such doctrines. The heart may be better than the head, so that one may actually be trusting Christ alone for salvation without fully realizing that one is leaning on Jesus' righteousness for right standing with God.

---

2. For an essay that sums up well the political and theological context in which Owen wrote, see Carl R. Trueman, "John Owen on Justification," in John Owen, *The Doctrine of Justification by Faith through the Imputation of the Righteousness of Christ; Explained, Confirmed, and Vindicated* (Grand Rapids: Reformation Heritage, 2006), iii–xxii. See also his more comprehensive work on Owen: Carl R. Trueman, *The Claims of Truth: John Owen's Trinitarian Theology* (Carlisle, UK: Paternoster, 1998). Trueman shows that Owen's thought can't be dismissed simply by labeling it Aristotelian (34–44, 233–40, *passim*).

3. For a more complete summary of Owen's book on justification, see the chapter titled "Justification by Faith Alone," in Matthew Barrett and Michael A. G. Haykin, *Owen on the Christian Life: Living for the Glory of God in Christ* (Wheaton, IL: Crossway, 2015).

4. Owen, *Justification by Faith*, 164.

On the flip side, Owen says that some who promote and defend imputation may actually be unbelievers.[5] His point is that simply contending for
imputation doesn't necessarily prove that one belongs to God. At the same
time, he readily agrees that many who affirm imputation live holy lives, and
there is no basis for saying that the doctrine itself encourages people to live
lawlessly. Nor is there any indication that those who repudiate imputation
live holier lives. The same charge of antinomianism was also leveled against
Paul (Rom 3:31; 6:1, 15), and hence it is unsurprising that a similar charge
is raised against those who defend the imputation of Christ's righteousness.
Such accusations don't support the notion that imputation is contrary to
apostolic teaching.

What leaps out at the reader in these writings is the pastoral character
of Owen's understanding. He remarks that it is one thing to hear theologians dispute about justification, but quite another to hear someone's
prayers. When we pray, Owen says, we never plead our own righteousness,
but rely on the mercy of God.[6] When we truly apprehend God's holiness
and majesty, we recognize that our obedience and righteousness fall dramatically short of what God requires.[7] "Those who know the terror of the
Lord, who have been really convinced and made sensible of the guilt and
their apostasy from God, and of their actual sins in that state, and what a
fearful thing it is to fall into the hands of the living God" don't trust in
themselves.[8]

Justification by Faith instead of Works

According to Owen, justification by faith alone fits with the scriptural
teaching that we are justified by faith instead of works.[9] If salvation is by
grace and not by works, then works can't be, even in part, the foundation
of our righteousness.[10] Even our evangelical post-conversion righteousness
(Titus 3:5) isn't sufficient for us to stand in the right before God.[11] For
instance, says Owen, the present tense in Phil 3:8 demonstrates that Paul
didn't place any trust in his works after his conversion, as if those works

---

5. Ibid., 376–78.
6. Ibid., 18–19, cf. also p. 9.
7. Ibid., 13–14. See also p. 20.
8. Ibid., 42.
9. Ibid., 24, 27.
10. Ibid., 361, cf. also 365–67.
11. Ibid., 369. Owen argues that the word "filth" in Phil 3:8 doesn't mean that Paul's works
were necessarily "dung" but that he estimated or counted them to be such (371).

were the basis of his righteousness.[12] Indeed, the letter to the Galatians was written to believers who were tempted to rely on their own works in their relationship with God, showing that works in any sense are excluded as a basis of justification.[13] Owen says that those who

> are acquainted with God and themselves in any spiritual manner, who take a view of the time that is past, and approaching eternity, into which they must enter by the judgment-seat of God, however they have thought, talked, and disputed about their own works and obedience, looking on Christ and his righteousness only to make up some small defects in themselves, will come at last unto a universal renunciation of what they have been and are, and betake themselves unto Christ alone for righteousness or salvation.[14]

Owen emphasizes that salvation is by faith alone.[15] Still, it is not just any faith that saves, for justifying faith puts its trust in what God has revealed in his Word and should not be confused with mental assent to doctrines.[16] After all, the devils themselves give assent to divine truth.[17] Owen considers our experience as Christians, remarking that believers don't rest on what they have done, but look entirely to God for pardon and justification.[18] More specifically, those who are saved put their trust in the mercy of God offered in Jesus Christ and the promises of the gospel.[19] Justifying faith is placed especially in the work Jesus accomplished on the cross, where he functioned as our mediator before God.[20] Hence, saving faith is directed personally toward the Lord Jesus Christ.[21] There is a "temporary faith" that doesn't truly rest in Christ, and such faith must be distinguished from faith that flows from the heart where one rests on the salvation given by Jesus Christ for the forgiveness of sin.[22] Faith, then, accords with God's work in salvation, for in faith all glory is given to God for the salvation accomplished in Jesus Christ.[23]

---

12. Ibid., 368.
13. Ibid., 370.
14. Ibid., 33.
15. Ibid., 73.
16. Ibid., 80–81.
17. Ibid., 82.
18. Ibid., 83.
19. Ibid., 84–87.
20. Ibid., 89–90.
21. Ibid., 90–91.
22. Ibid., 95–96, 97–101.
23. Ibid., 97.

Faith and Obedience

Owen next considers the relationship between faith and obedience. Faith is a gift God gives to his own and all obedience flows from faith, so that faith is the root of one's relationship to God.[24] Owen defends *sola fide* and thus stands against Rome, but, like Luther and Calvin before him, he also thinks genuine faith is never an isolated reality: "we are justified by faith alone, but not by faith that is alone."[25] Faith rests and receives Christ alone for right standing before God,[26] and obedience is a fruit of faith.[27] We must carefully attend to the relationship between faith and final perseverance since the latter is a condition for final salvation. Admittedly, the word "condition" is tricky and ambiguous and must be defined carefully.[28] What must be answered, then, is exactly what someone means by their use of the word "condition." Owen insists that perseverance isn't required for initial justification, and perseverance is obtained in the same way as our initial justification—by faith alone.[29]

James 2:14–26 has often been raised in opposition to the view of imputation espoused by Protestants.[30] Owen maintains that one must consider the context in which the letter was written. James responds to a wrong understanding of justification, but he doesn't correct or explain Paul's meaning, as if he is contesting Pauline teaching.[31] Furthermore, Paul and James mean different things by faith.[32] James rejects a dead faith, a faith that the devils have, but affirms the power of a living faith that is dynamic and active. James and Paul are also using the word "justify" differently, for in James it means that faith is manifested or proved or evidenced, so that justification is before people instead of before God.[33] James doesn't contradict the notion that justification is by faith alone, nor does he stand against the truth that Christ's righteousness is imputed to believers.

The faith that justifies should be understood as the instrument or means of salvation.[34] Faith doesn't constitute our righteousness, as if faith *is our righteousness,* for faith justifies because it apprehends and receives Christ

---

24. Ibid., 103–4.
25. Ibid., 104.
26. Ibid., 290–94.
27. Ibid., 122.
28. Ibid., 105.
29. Ibid., 105–6.
30. Ibid., 384–400.
31. Ibid., 388–89.
32. Ibid., 390–92.
33. Ibid., 392–94.
34. Ibid., 109–11.

both for righteousness and for pardon of sins.[35] Faith can be understood as a condition of justification as long as it is not construed as constituting our righteousness, for it is an instrument by which we are united with Christ who is our righteousness.[36] Believers are justified, then, because they are united with Christ; he is their righteousness.[37] Faith saves because of its object, because we put our trust in Jesus' blood.[38] Justifying faith puts its faith in Jesus Christ as the great high priest who gave his life as atonement for sin.[39] Faith can't be imputed for righteousness, for faith itself is imperfect, and what is imperfect can't be counted as if it were perfect.[40]

Justification as Forensic

Owen then considers the meaning of the word justification, arguing in detail that the term is forensic, denoting right standing before God as judge.[41] The term, therefore, doesn't denote *inherent* righteousness but *imputed* righteousness. Justification doesn't rest on a righteousness that is in us, as if we are counted righteous before God because of the transformation that has taken place in us. Owen vigorously contests the notion that there is a second or later justification that is established on the basis of works or merit.[42] At the final judgment the justification we already enjoy by faith is publicly announced and declared to the world.[43] Owen returns to human experience, noting that believers don't plead their righteousness, but the mercy of Christ and his sacrifice. They don't rest on their own obedience or righteousness.[44] God demands complete obedience, and the Scriptures plainly indicate that all works are excluded as the ground of justification, and hence they can't be reintroduced by the back door as a ground for right standing with God.[45] The obedience of believers, or their holiness or sanctification, isn't the ground of their justification.[46]

---

35. Ibid., 111–12.
36. Ibid., 112–16.
37. See Fesko, *Beyond Calvin*, 290–91.
38. Owen, *Justification by Faith*, 317–19.
39. Ibid., 116–20.
40. Ibid., 319–20; cf. Fesko, *Beyond Calvin*, 292–93.
41. Owen, *Justification by Faith*, 123–37.
42. Ibid., 137–52.
43. Fesko, *Beyond Calvin*, 294.
44. Owen, *Justification by Faith*, 148.
45. Ibid., 278–90.
46. Ibid., 152–62. It should be pointed out here that the typical Reformed view distinguishes between justification and sanctification, so that justification is the basis for sanctification. Believers are justified and sanctified because they are united with Christ, but such a truth doesn't rule out the truth that justification is the basis for sanctification. See here the important study of Fesko, *Beyond Calvin*.

Imputation of Righteousness

Owen then turns to a long discussion on imputation. We can have something imputed or counted or reckoned to us that truly belongs to us (say a debt or a good deed), or, conversely something can be imputed that doesn't belong to us by nature.[47] The imputation of Christ's righteousness belongs obviously to the latter category, so that in this case we have an imputation by grace.[48] The righteousness of Christ is granted to believers because they are mystically united to Christ as their covenant surety when he took upon himself the guilt we deserved.[49] In Owen's view, as Trueman remarks, "the union of natures in the Incarnation is what qualifies Christ as capable of acting as mediator, and this is because that union is determined by the voluntary covenant of redemption, the doctrinal context for understanding the incarnate Mediator."[50] Trueman goes on to exposit Owen's view of Christ's work.

> His whole life, having its causal ground in the covenant of redemption, is that of the sponsor of the covenant of grace, and thus in its entirety it has a significance which embraces all of the objects of the covenant of grace. The theology of federal headship, rooted in the covenant of redemption between the Father and Son, thus repeatedly connects to the debate on justification and allows for conceptual precision in clarifying the status and role of Christ as mediator.[51]

Owen's conception of imputation must be understood within a covenantal context.[52] Owen argues for imputation in a number of texts, and I will note a few of them here. In Rom 4:6–8 David's forgiveness isn't equated with righteousness, as if forgiveness and righteousness are the same thing.[53] Instead, we see that believers are both forgiven of their sins *and* granted the righteousness of Christ, so that sins are erased and a positive righteousness is given to believers. That believers have received the righteousness of Christ is argued especially from Rom 5:12–21.[54] Just as the sin of Adam was imputed to all people, so also the obedience of Christ has been imputed to believers. Adam and Christ are understood to be covenant heads. Along the same lines, Owen sees imputation in Rom

---

47. Owen, *Justification by Faith*, 162–75.
48. See his long discussion on imputation, ibid., 205–94.
49. Ibid., 175–205.
50. Trueman, "John Owen on Justification," ix.
51. Ibid., x.
52. See again ibid., xix–xx.
53. Owen, *Justification by Faith*, 320–21.
54. Ibid., 321–35.

9:30–10:4 since those who had no righteousness of their own (cf. Phil 3:9) are now counted righteous because the righteousness of Christ is given to them.[55]

Owen also adduces 1 Cor 1:30, which states that Christ is our righteousness.[56] Socinus objected that this exegesis of the passage is wrong, for then we would have to say that Christ's wisdom and redemption and sanctification are imputed to us as well.[57] But Owen counters that such an objection fails, for there isn't any reason to think that Christ is our righteousness *in the same way* that he is our wisdom, sanctification, and redemption. Thus, there are solid reasons to think that Christ's righteousness was imputed to us in contrast to wisdom, sanctification, and redemption.[58]

Finally, 2 Cor 5:21 testifies to the imputation of God's righteousness in Jesus Christ.[59] Jesus was made sin in that our sins were imputed to him. As in Lev 1:4 (cf. Lev 16:21), our sins were transferred to Christ and counted against him, even though he was sinless. Conversely, believers are counted or imputed as righteous as those who are united with Christ. Owen summarizes his view, "The righteousness of Christ (in his obedience and suffering for us) imputed unto believers, as they are united unto him by his Spirit, is that righteousness whereon they are justified before God, on the account whereof their sins are pardoned, and a right is granted them unto the heavenly inheritance."[60]

Believers need the imputed righteousness of Christ for justification, for their sins testify that they can't be righteous before God on the basis of their works.[61] Inherent righteousness is required of believers, but not for justification. It is the result of justification instead of the basis for it. Inherent righteousness can't justify since God requires perfection, for God can't declare those as righteous who fail to do all that he requires.[62] Otherwise, God would declare to be righteous those who aren't righteous,

---

55. Ibid., 338–44.

56. Ibid., 344–47.

57. We shall see in due course that N. T. Wright raises the same objection today. We have another reminder that most debates aren't new. When we read history, we see that most of the issues we raise have been examined previously.

58. Owen, *Justification by Faith*, 346–47.

59. Ibid., 349–54.

60. Ibid., 208. Most of this citation is in italics, which I removed. Owen answers many objections to this teaching (208–23, 251–75).

61. Ibid., 223–41.

62. Ibid., 233–41. The necessity of perfect obedience to the law is argued as well in the next chapter (241–50).

and hence we need the perfect righteousness of Christ to stand truly in the right before God. As Owen says, "The conscience of a convinced sinner, who presents himself in the presence of God, finds all practically reduced unto this one point, — namely, whether he will trust unto his own personal inherent righteousness, or, in a full renunciation of it, betake unto the grace of God and the righteousness of Christ alone."[63] Believers are counted as righteous because they are united to Christ as their covenant head.[64]

Conclusion on John Owen

John Owen represents a mature and carefully formulated theology of justification by faith alone. The fundamental tenets of his thought are already expressed by Luther and Calvin, but Owen writes in a new context where objections to *sola fide* and imputation have been disseminated. Owen locates his understanding of justification in a covenantal context and answers his critics in an in-depth analysis, and thus he advances and deepens the Reformed understanding of *sola fide*.

A Brief Word on Richard Baxter[65]

While we won't be considering the writings of Richard Baxter (1615–1691) to the same extent that we have looked at Owen, a short discussion of his view provides an illuminating contrast.[66] Though Baxter held to a form of imputation, it was distinctive, for he rejected the notion of double imputation promoted by Owen and other Protestants, worrying that it would lead to antinomianism. In saying that Baxter rejected double imputation, we mean that he accepted single imputation (the forgiveness of sins in Christ), but rejected the second dimension of imputation (i.e., that the righteousness of Christ is credited or imputed to believers). In this respect, Baxter to some degree anticipates the theology of John Wesley, though at the end of the day Wesley seems to have believed in double imputation.

Contrary to Owen, Baxter believed that faith *is* our righteousness, rejecting the notion that faith is counted as righteousness because it

---

63. Ibid., 230.

64. Ibid., 275–77.

65. Baxter believed Owen held to eternal justification, but he misunderstood Owen on this matter. See Trueman, "John Owen on Justification," xvii–xxi.

66. For Baxter, see especially Hans Boersma, *A Hot Pepper Corn: Richard Baxter's Doctrine of Justification in Its Seventeenth-Century Context of Controversy* (Zoetermeer: Uitgeverij Boekencentrum, 1993), esp. 257–330; Tim Cooper, *John Owen, Richard Baxter and the Formation of Nonconformity* (Burleigh, VT: Ashgate, 2011), esp. 75–80; Fesko, *Beyond Calvin*, 300–17.

unites believers with Jesus Christ.[67] According to Baxter, Christ's sacrifice fulfilled what was required for *legal righteousness*, and thus believers are justified by faith alone initially. Still, he finds a secondary role for what he calls *evangelical righteousness*. Our *evangelical righteousness* is imperfect, but God graciously accepts it in the lives of believers. Baxter's conception is often called *neonomian*, which means that a "new law" is required for Christians. Baxter's view is also tied to his understanding of the atonement and the covenant,[68] for he doesn't believe that the penalty for sin was strictly paid for on the cross. He held to a variant of Hugo Grotius's view on the atonement.[69] Grotius believed that Christ atoned for the sin of human beings, but in contrast to the satisfaction theory, the exact payment for sins was not visited on Jesus at his death.[70]

Baxter believed, then, in two justifications, one at the inception of the Christian life and one on the last day. The second justification is dependent on perseverance, and thus works are a condition of justification. Others also believed that works and perseverance were necessary for justification, but Baxter sees these works as being a ground — or at the very least a proximate ground. Such a view separated him from those who were confessionally Reformed. At the same time, Baxter also believed that justification was continuous in the life of believers, that it was a process. Even though he wasn't Roman Catholic and inveighed against Catholicism, his notion that justification as a process is similar to the view of Rome. We should not be surprised to learn, then, that for Baxter obedience was a necessary condition for secondary justification.

A Glimpse at Francis Turretin's Perspective

I opened this book with a quote from Francis Turretin (1623–1687) that revealed the pastoral heart behind his view of justification by faith alone. Turretin's understanding of justification must be construed in terms of his covenant theology and his understanding of the covenantal pact between the Father and the Son.[71] The notion that Turretin was innovative

---

67. See here J. I. Packer, *Quest for Godliness: The Puritan Vision of the Christian Life* (Wheaton, IL: Crossway, 1990), 158. Packer rightly observes that this makes faith "a work of some strength and merit" (159).

68. Cf. Fesko, *Beyond Calvin*, 304–5, 307–8.

69. See here Packer, *Quest for Godliness*, 159.

70. For Baxter's appropriation of Grotius's view, see Trueman, *John Owen's Trinitarian Theology*, 210–25, 244.

71. For a helpful exposition of Turretin's theology of union with Christ and justification, see Fesko, *Beyond Calvin*, 318–39.

in his theology of the covenant should be rejected.[72] He stands as a classic example of Reformed orthodoxy,[73] in line with the Reformers as well as John Owen. Because of this, we do not need to linger long on his views. Still, the controversies that roiled during the 1500s and 1600s spurred Turretin and others to define justification carefully. Turretin is particularly helpful in clarifying the nature of justifying faith:

> The question is not whether solitary faith (i.e., separated from the other virtues) justifies (which we grant could not easily be the case, since it is not even true and living faith); but whether it "alone"(*sola*) concurs to the act of justification (which we assert).... The coexistence of love in him who is justified is not denied; but its coefficiency or cooperation in justification is denied.... The question is not whether the faith "which justifies" (*quae justificat*) works by love (for otherwise it would not be living but dead); rather the question is whether faith "by which it justifies" (*qua justificat*) or in the act itself of justification, is to be considered under such a relation (*schesei*) (which we deny).[74]

Turretin goes on to state:

> It is one thing for love and works to be required in the person who is justified (which we grant); another [to be required] in the act itself or causality of justification (which we deny). If works are required as concomitants of faith, they are not on that account determined to be causes of justification with faith or to do the very thing which faith does in this matter."[75]

Turretin's technical statement accords with the theology of both Luther and Calvin. Justification is by faith alone, but it isn't a faith that is alone, for true faith produces good works. Still, good works are not the ground or cause of salvation; they are the fruit of one's faith. The perfect righteousness of Christ is imputed to believers, so that their righteousness is not inherent but is theirs because they are united to Jesus Christ.[76] At the final judgment God will declare publicly what was already the case in the lives of believers, i.e., that they are righteous by faith, and their works will verify (but will not be the foundation of) that declaration.[77]

Turretin's discussion on justification and faith alone is important, for it

---

72. Ibid., 322.

73. Though some of the Reformed embraced eternal justification, Turretin clearly rejected it (see Fesko, *Beyond Calvin*, 336–39).

74. Turretin, *Institutes of Elenctic Theology*, 2:677.

75. Ibid., 2:680.

76. Fesko, *Beyond Calvin*, 329, 331.

77. See ibid., 333, 336.

represents a mature Reformed statement in light of the controversies and discussions that had taken place since the Reformation. We see in Turretin the pastoral concern that animated those who insisted that justification was by faith alone. At the same time, we also see the precision and care with which he formulates the doctrine. Turretin took into account objections and misunderstandings of *sola fide* and articulated it clearly for the Reformed of his day.

Conclusion

John Owen's formulation of justification represents a mature articulation of the doctrine, one which was minted in debates with Roman Catholics, Socinians, and people like Richard Baxter. Owen particularly emphasized the covenantal context for understanding the justifying work of Christ, and his fundamental convictions are the same as Calvin's. Human sin means that salvation cannot come from works. Justification is by faith alone and should be understood forensically, and this faith is in the one who sent his divine Son to ransom us from sin. Faith is not our righteousness but is an instrument that unites us to Jesus Christ. The righteousness of believers isn't inherent but imputed and belongs to believers through union with Jesus Christ as their covenant representative. Owen differed dramatically from Baxter, who feared antinomianism and rejected the notion that Christ's righteousness is imputed or credited to believers. Baxter believed that the evangelical righteousness of believers functioned as a secondary ground for justification. Such notions were also persuasive to Baxter because in his view, the atonement of Christ was not a strict repayment for sins, and thus the atonement was understood in a modified Grotian sense.

Finally, with Turretin we find a consolidation and representation of mainstream Reformed thinking. The righteousness of Christ is imputed to believers, and it is faith *as an instrument* that unites believers to Jesus Christ. The faith that saves leads to works, but works themselves aren't the ground of justification. Rather, they function as evidence of the salvation that is ours.

CHAPTER 6

The Status of *Sola Fide* in the Thought of Jonathan Edwards and John Wesley

"Now God takes delight in the saints for both these: both for Christ's righteousness imputed and for Christ's holiness communicated, though 'tis the former only that avails anything to justification."   —*Jonathan Edwards*

"That we are justified by faith, is spoken to take away clearly all merit of our works, and wholly to ascribe the *merit and deserving* of our justification to Christ only."
                                                            —*John Wesley*

Jonathan Edwards (1703–1758) was a profound and creative thinker, and his creativity and depth manifest themselves in his discussion of justification.[1] Like others we have looked at, Edwards affirmed justification by faith alone, but scholars debate whether his view departed from Reformed understandings and wandered to some extent into Roman Catholic territory. In this section, I will argue that such a reading of Edwards is mistaken, and that when he is rightly interpreted, Edwards's view of justification fits within the Protestant conception of the doctrine. I will also examine briefly the views of John Wesley (1703–1791). While Wesley didn't write systematically, which makes nailing down his views difficult, his perspective on faith alone, imputation, and good works is remarkably similar in many ways to Edwards, even though they held different views of the sovereignty of God in salvation.

---

1. I am especially thankful to Gary Steward for steering me to the sources here and for the help given in an unpublished paper (Dec. 7, 2011) titled "Jonathan Edwards's Innovative Additions to the Reformed Doctrine of Justification by Faith." Even though Steward and I read Edwards differently on some points, I have learned much from his careful reading and his discussion with me on these matters.

Edwards on Faith and Works

Though we cannot delve deeply into a full and comprehensive understanding of Edwards's theology,[2] we will consider his teaching on the matter of justification, which captures well the complexity of what we mean by *sola fide*. On the one hand, Edwards emphasizes that our righteousness is in Christ alone and by faith alone.[3] Edwards rejected the neonomian ("new law") notion that repentance and obedience are the condition for salvation.[4] At this point, however, things get tricky, for Edwards also says that faith is "that in us by which we are justified."[5] Edwards doesn't use the language of faith as an instrument of justification, but says that faith qualifies us to be right with God.[6] He even speaks of faith as "one chief part of the inherent holiness of a Christian."[7] This language of "inherent holiness" makes it sound as if faith *is* our righteousness, especially since Edwards doesn't describe faith as an instrument of justification. We can certainly see why some think Edwards wanders from the Reformed view, for in this regard his formulations sound a bit like Baxter.

Edwards also attempts to account for Scripture's emphasis on the importance of good works for final salvation, especially in the epistle of James, where good works are said to be necessary for justification. Here Edwards speaks of the reward believers receive because of their good works.[8] The reward is clearly eternal life, though good works are rewarded in a "secondary and derivative sense."[9] Works express our faith, and so we can say that a person "is not justified by faith only, but also by works."[10]

Because of this, Hunsinger argues that Edwards tilts against three

---

2. Supporting the notion that Edwards inadvertently strayed from the Reformation are George Hunsinger, "Dispositional Soteriology: Jonathan Edwards on Justification by Faith Alone," *WTJ* 66 (2004): 107–20; Gerald McDermott, "Jonathan Edwards on Justification by Faith—More Protestant or Catholic?" *ProEccl* 17 (2008): 92–111; Thomas A. Schäfer, "Jonathan Edwards and Justification by Faith," *CH* 20 (1951): 55–67. For a vigorous refutation of Schäfer's views, see Jeffrey C. Waddington, "Jonathan Edwards's 'Ambiguous and Somewhat Precarious' Doctrine of Justification?" *WTJ* 66 (2004): 357–72.

3. "Quaestio," in *The Works of Jonathan Edwards*; Vol. 14, *Sermons and Discourses, 1723-1729* (ed. K. P. Minkema; New Haven, CT: Yale University Press, 1997), 62. See also "Justification by Faith Alone," in *The Works of Jonathan Edwards*; Vol. 19, *Sermons and Discourses, 1734-1738* (ed. M. X. Lesser; New Haven, CT: Yale University Press, 2001), 149. For the entire treatise, see 147–242.

4. Edwards, "Quaestio," 63.

5. Edwards, "Justification by Faith," 153, 222.

6. Ibid., 153–54.

7. Ibid., 154.

8. Ibid., 199, 213–15.

9. Ibid., 215.

10. Ibid., 236.

essential teachings of the Reformation.[11] First, Edwards sees a place for inherent righteousness and not *only* imputed righteousness for justification. Second, Edwards, in contrast to Luther, saw a place for active righteousness and not merely passive righteousness. Third, Edwards, in contrast to Calvin, didn't really understand the personal nature of our union with Christ; he understood it in legal terms instead of as a personal communion.

Hunsinger says that faith "as a subjective act and disposition was ... interpreted by Edwards as a secondary derivative reason why the believer was pleasing to God and rewarded by God."[12] Thus, Hunsinger believes that for Edwards faith is a ground of justification, even though Edwards speaks of faith as a gift of God.[13] Since Edwards uses the word "qualification" for faith, faith is not merely a condition in Edwards's thought, but "a positive qualification," which "functions as a secondary and ex post facto ground."[14] Acceptance at the final judgment isn't based only on the alien righteousness of Christ, but in a secondary sense also rests on inherent righteousness.[15]

Edwards as Faithful to the Reformers

Contrary to this argument, I would suggest that Edwards does not depart from the Reformational understanding in his view of justification, even if his terminology isn't always the same and his explanations are occasionally confusing.[16] Edwards declaims,

---

11. Hunsinger, "Dispositional Soteriology," 111–12. In support of the notion that Edwards's understanding of justification doesn't fit a mere forensic model and hence is closer to Thomas Aquinas and Catholicism, see McDermott, "Jonathan Edwards on Justification by Faith," 92–111; Michael J. McClymond and Gerald P. McDermott, *The Theology of Jonathan Edwards* (Oxford: Oxford University Press, 2012), 400.

12. Hunsinger, "Dispositional Soteriology," 113.

13. Ibid., 113–14.

14. Ibid., 114.

15. Ibid., 115. Cf. "'Controversies' Notebook: Justification," in *The Works of Jonathan Edwards*; Vol. 21, *Writings on the Trinity, Grace, and Faith* (ed. S. H. Lee; New Haven, CT: Yale University Press, 2003), 367.

16. In support of the notion that Edwards did not depart from the Reformation, see Samuel T. Logan Jr., "The Doctrine of Justification in the Theology of Jonathan Edwards," *WTJ* 46 (1984): 26–52; John H. Gerstner, *The Rational Biblical Theology of Jonathan Edwards* (Powhatan, VA, and Orlando, FL: Berea Publications and Ligonier Ministries, 1993), 3:208–12; John J. Bombaro, "Jonathan Edwards's Vision of Salvation," *WTJ* 65 (2003): 45–67, esp. 61–67; Waddington, "Edwards's Ambiguous and Precarious Doctrine of Justification," 357–72; Josh Moody, "Edwards and Justification Today," in *Jonathan Edwards and Justification* (ed. J. Moody; Wheaton: Crossway, 2012), 17–43; Kyle Strobel, "By Word and Spirit: Jonathan Edwards on Redemption, Justification, and Regeneration," in *Jonathan Edwards and Justification*, 45–69; Douglas A. Sweeney, "Justification by Faith Alone? A Fuller Picture of Edwards's Doctrine," in *Jonathan Edwards and Justification*, 129–54.

> There is a two-fold righteousness that the saints have; an imputed righteousness, and 'tis this only that avails anything to justification; and an inherent righteousness, that is, that holiness and grace which is in the hearts and lives of the saints. This is Christ's righteousness as well as imputed righteousness; imputed righteousness is Christ's righteousness accepted for them, inherent holiness is Christ's righteousness communicated to them.... Now God takes delight in the saints for both these: both for Christ's righteousness imputed and for Christ's holiness communicated, though 'tis the former only that avails anything to justification.[17]

I would suggest that Edwards's understanding of inherent righteousness must be interpreted in light of this clear statement. Here Edwards says that justification depends on and is grounded in imputed righteousness, not inherent righteousness. In fact, he specifically rejects the idea that inherent righteousness justifies us.

Sometimes Edwards's language is confusing, but when all is said and done, he doesn't offer us a Roman Catholic view of justification. For instance, Edwards refers to "infused grace," but in doing so he isn't endorsing the Catholic notion of justification. Edwards uses the word "infusion" to describe what is typically identified as regeneration.[18] When Edwards says that works are "necessary to salvation"[19] and that they "are the expression of the life of faith,"[20] he is trying to be faithful to James among other biblical writers.[21] So, he speaks of works as "proper evidence."[22]

Hunsinger says that for Edwards works "are necessary to the efficacy of faith."[23] That is close, of course, to what James teaches, and we must ask what Edwards actually means when he says faith isn't efficacious without works. We could easily import a meaning to the term "efficacious" that doesn't accord with Edwards's intention. If works are construed as the basis for justification, we have a clear contradiction of Reformed teaching,

---

17. "None Are Saved by Their Own Righteousness," in *The Works of Jonathan Edwards*; Vol. 14, *Sermons and Discourses, 1723–1729* (ed. Kenneth P. Minkema; New Haven, CT: Yale University Press, 1997), 340–41. I owe this citation to Sweeney, "Justification by Faith Alone?," 135–36.

18. See Moody, "Edwards and Justification Today," 20–24. Similarly, there are occasions where Edwards uses the term "sanctification," but the referent is to regeneration (27–28).

19. Edwards, "Justification by Faith," 234.

20. Ibid., 236.

21. Cf. Logan, "Justification in the Theology of Jonathan Edwards," 43–45. McDermott ("Jonathan Edwards on Justification by Faith," 103) also points out the emphasis in Edwards on works as an expression of faith.

22. Edwards, "Justification by Faith," 233; cf. 235.

23. Hunsinger, "Dispositional Soteriology," 117.

but if the notion is that they are efficacious as fruit, as evidence of new life, then the term fits the Reformation understanding of *sola fide*.

Hunsinger says Edwards moves against the Reformed view, for "works not only declare but also complete or contribute to the efficacy of faith."[24] It is possible, however, that Hunsinger misunderstands Edwards on this point. Edwards compares faith and works to "strings in consort, if one is struck, others sound with it; or like links in a chain, if one is drawn, others follow."[25] But again, this illustration probably means that works are the fruit of faith. Hunsinger says Edwards discounts the notion that faith alone is sufficient,[26] but it is far more probable that Edwards teaches that faith and works are inseparable, and that true faith always results in works and in that sense works are necessary.[27]

Faith and Obedience

Gary Steward raises another question about Edwards's understanding of justification. He maintains that Edwards goes astray in his definition of faith, for faith in Edwards's thought embraces love and obedience, and thus the distinction between these two is confused.[28] Indeed, Edwards seems to come close to the Roman Catholic view that faith is formed by love.

> Faith is a duty required in the first table of the law, and in the first commandment; and there it will follow that it is comprehended in the great commandment, "Thou shall love God with all thy heart, and with all thy soul, and with all thy mind" [Matt. 22:37]. And so it will follow that love is the most essential thing in a true faith.... Love is the very life and soul of a true faith ... it is love that is this active working spirit which is in true faith. That is its very soul without which it is dead.[29]

Steward may be on target here. Edwards could be read to say something similar to the Roman Catholic view that faith is formed by love. Yet Edwards insists elsewhere that justification is by faith alone. The quote

---

24. Ibid., 118.

25. *The Works of Jonathan Edwards*; Vol. 20, *The "Miscellanies" 833–1152* (ed. A. P. Pauw; New Haven, CT: Yale University Press, 2002), 393.

26. Hunsinger, "Dispositional Soteriology," 119.

27. See *The Works of Jonathan Edwards*, "None Are Saved by Their Own Righteousness," 14:333, and "Justification by Faith," 19:152. Again, I owe these references to Sweeney, "Justification by Faith Alone?," 143–45. Edwards makes it clear that perseverance is evidential in his discussion.

28. Steward, "Innovative Additions," 9–12; see Edwards, "Quaestio," 60–61; "Justification by Faith," 160.

29. "Charity and Its Fruits," in *The Works of Jonathan Edwards*: Vol, 8, *Ethical Writings* (ed. P. Ramsey; New Haven, CT: Yale University Press, 1989), 140.

above is taken from "Charity and Its Fruits," and in his writing here Edwards may not be as precise given the emphasis of the text (he exposits the nature of love) and the occasional nature of the writing. When he speaks of faith as being dead without love, we have a clear allusion to Jas 2:14, 26. Love is the soul ("spirit" in James) and faith is the "body."[30] I suggest that Edwards maintains love as the necessary fruit or evidence of faith. Edwards also alludes to Gal 5:6, where Paul says that faith expresses itself in love. His allusions to Gal 5:6 and Jas 2:26 suggest that he isn't saying that faith is formed by love, but that faith necessarily expresses itself in love. Steward may be right in his interpretation, for Edwards writes imprecisely, and yet given his polemics against Roman Catholic teaching elsewhere, his affirmation that justification is by faith alone, and his insistence on imputation, I believe it is better to interpret him as saying that love is the fruit of faith.

Steward points to several other comments Edwards makes that raise questions about whether he fits with the traditional Reformed view of justification. Edwards says,

> When it is asserted that a sinner is justified by this faith alone, we mean, of course, that God receives the sinner into his grace and friendship for this reason alone, that his entire soul receives Christ in such a way that righteousness and eternal life are offered in an absolutely gratuitous fashion and are provided only because of his reception of Christ. We are not even asking whether or not we are justified by this evangelical obedience, but whether we are justified by this evangelical obedience because of its intrinsic goodness, or *merely because it is only by evangelical obedience that Christ is received. For every part of evangelical obedience is an implicit reception of Christ and an act of justifying faith.*[31]

The last sentence may indicate that Edwards has smuggled obedience into justification, so that justification ends up, unintentionally to be sure, being a combination of faith and works. Once again, it seems unlikely that Edwards intends to say that obedience functions as part of the basis for our justification. In the same citation he reaffirms faith alone and the gracious character of justification, so I would suggest that Edwards intends to say here that faith and obedience are inseparable—that, in accord with James, all faith *results* in works. It would have helped clarify the matter if Edwards had said that faith and works were inseparable but distinguishable, or if

---

30. Cf. here Moody, "Edwards and Justification Today," 33–34.
31. Edwards, "Quaestio," 61. Italics mine.

he had said that works aren't in any sense a basis of faith. And in fact he does say this elsewhere and affirms this in the quote above regarding imputation. Also, he says here that justification isn't due to "evangelical obedience," by which he means that our obedience after salvation cannot justify us, presumably because believers continue to be stained by sin. Salvation is in Christ alone.

Other citations, however, continue to raise questions about Edwards's adherence to justification by faith alone:

> Faith unites to Christ, and so gives a congruity to justification, not merely as remaining a dormant principle in the heart, but as being, and appearing in its active expressions. The obedience of a Christian, so far as it is truly evangelical, and performed with the spirit of the Son sent forth into the heart, has all relation to Christ the Mediator, and is but an expression of the soul's believing union to Christ: all evangelical works are works of that faith that worketh by love; and every such act of obedience, wherein it is inward, and the act of the soul, is only a new effective act of reception of Christ.... So that as was before said of faith, so may it be said of a child-like, believing obedience, it has no concern in justification by any virtue, or excellency in it; but only as there is a reception of Christ in it.[32]

Edwards could be interpreted variously here. One could read this as if justification is a process sustained by every act of obedience. Again, Edwards takes seriously the demand for good works in the scriptural testimony. It seems doubtful that he thinks justification is a process, even if what he wrote could be more precise. We note again an allusion to Gal 5:6, and hence he affirms that obedience is an expression and fruit of genuine faith. So, when he says that obedience is "a new effective act of reception of Christ," he isn't suggesting that such obedience gives a basis for justification. What he is doing is describing the nature of the faith that saves. Genuine saving faith isn't merely notional but has an affective dimension to it, where Christ is embraced and loved. Such faith expresses itself necessarily in obedience, in works that are pleasing to God. Edwards emphasizes that such faith is faith in Christ. He is not suggesting, then, that obedience is the ground of justification. He is simply saying that faith and obedience are inseparable.

Such an interpretation fits with Edwards's reading of James on justification, "if we take works as acts or expressions of faith, they are not

---

32. Edwards, "Justification by Faith," 207.

excluded; so a man is not justified by faith only, but also by works; i.e. he is not justified only by faith as a principle in the heart, or in its first and more immanent acts, but also by the effective acts of it in life, which are the expressions of the life of faith."[33] Edwards reflects on James, even in saying that justification is not only by faith but also by works (see Jas 2:24). But he doesn't see works as the basis or ground of justification, for he speaks of "the expressions of the life of faith." So, the "effective acts" of obedience aren't effective in the sense that they merit justification.

Some believe Edwards compromises *sola fide* in asserting the necessity of works. For Edwards says,

> The Scripture doctrine of justification by faith alone ... does in no wise diminish, either the necessity, or benefit of a sincere evangelical universal obedience: in that man's salvation is not only indissolubly connected with it, and damnation with the want of it, in those that have opportunity for it, but that it depends upon it in many respects ... even in accepting of us as entitled to life in our justification, God has respect to this, as that on which the fitness of such an act of justification depends: so that our salvation does truly depend upon it, as if we were justified for the moral excellency of it.[34]

Saying that salvation depends on works looks suspicious to us at first glance. Still, there are many texts in Scripture, as I will show later in this book, that demonstrate that good works *are* necessary for salvation. Simply saying this is not a problem in itself, for we must discern and understand precisely *in what sense* good works are required. I suggest that Edwards is not compromising *sola fide* here, for he asserts that good works are a necessary fruit of justification, that they must be there for a person to be declared righteous on the last day. This fits with Logan's interpretation of Edwards, who contends that Edwards sees works as a condition but not as a cause of justification.[35]

Faith and Perseverance

Yet another question arises in our reading of Edwards on justification and his understanding of *sola fide*. Does Edwards depart from the Reformed view in his understanding of the role perseverance plays in faith? According to Edwards,

---

33. Ibid., 236.
34. Ibid.
35. Logan, "Justification in the Theology of Jonathan Edwards," 39.

Justification is by the first act of faith, in some respects, in a peculiar manner, because a sinner is actually and finally justified as soon as he has performed one act of faith; and faith in its first act does, virtually at least, depend upon God for perseverance, and entitles to this among other benefits. But yet the perseverance of faith is not excluded in this affair; it is not only certainly connected with justification, but it is not to be excluded from that on which the justification of a sinner has dependence, or that by which he is justified.[36]

Whether what Edwards says about the first act of faith is biblically warranted is not my concern here. Certainly what he writes on this matter is quite speculative, showing Edwards's philosophical inclinations. We would be hard pressed, though, to say that Edwards compromises *sola fide*, for perseverance flows from and is virtually contained in the first act of faith. When Edwards says that justification depends on perseverance, he is not grounding justification on perseverance; he is insisting that genuine faith *necessarily manifests* itself as a persevering faith, as a faith that abides.

In fact, Edwards continues on this theme:

Although the sinner is actually, and finally justified on the first act of faith, yet the perseverance of faith, even then, comes into consideration, as one thing on which the fitness of acceptance to life depends. God in the act of justification ... has respect to perseverance, as being virtually contained in that first act of faith.... God has respect to the believer's continuance in faith ... as though it already were, because by divine establishment it shall follow.[37]

I interpret this text in a similar way. The necessity of perseverance is evident in Scripture, which explains why Edwards isn't content to say that faith without perseverance saves or justifies. Edwards knows the Bible too well to say that "faith alone" means that perseverance is somehow optional. *But he does not ground justification in perseverance, for perseverance flows from the first act of faith.* It is to be seen as an expression of faith and is even contained in the first act of faith. Perseverance "follows" faith. Edwards certainly could have been clearer in defining the relationship between faith and perseverance, but he does not merge them together as if they play the same role in justification. When we carefully observe his language, perseverance seems to be the result of faith.

---

36. Edwards, "Justification by Faith," 201–2.
37. Ibid., 203.

Steward worries that Edwards compromises the Reformation, for he says that perseverance is no longer just a fruit of faith, but is necessary in order to be justified.[38] But the language of necessity isn't precise enough to solve the problem before us. Nor does it follow that Edwards is somewhat Catholic in merging justification with sanctification. What we must get at is what Edwards means here. He isn't as clear as we would like him to be, but I would suggest that Edwards sees perseverance as a necessary fruit. The same could be said about sanctification. Those who show no transformation in their lives reveal that they were never justified. Edwards isn't grounding justification on perseverance or on progressive sanctification. He is saying that genuine faith necessarily results in perseverance, just as when you pluck on a guitar string it necessarily issues a sound.[39]

Conclusion

According to Hunsinger, Edwards can be understood to be in harmony with the Reformation if one reads him with "a soft focus," but that "a crisper focus" calls into question whether his teaching accords with faith alone.[40] We can certainly understand why Hunsinger says this, for Edwards's writings on justification lack clarity, and hence he is interpreted in different ways. I have suggested, however, that Edwards fits with the Reformed tradition in teaching justification by faith alone. Perhaps I have taken "a soft focus" view in arguing that his questionable statements should be read in light of places where he affirms justification by faith alone. Still, such a view is defensible, for Edwards knew the Bible and the Reformers well, and he specifically and emphatically endorses the formula that justification is by faith alone.

Moreover, Edwards clearly says that justification is due to imputed instead of inherent righteousness. Even in the contested passages we have seen that Edwards sees perseverance or obedience to be *an expression* of faith. I conclude that Edwards believed that works and obedience were necessary for justification. However, he did not see them as a necessary ground, but as a necessary fruit of faith.

---

38. Steward, "Innovative Additions," 20. McDermott argues that Edwards merges together sanctification and justification since justification is dependent on sanctification ("Jonathan Edwards on Justification by Faith," 98–99).

39. Edwards, "Justification by Faith," 203–6.

40. Hunsinger, "Dispositional Soteriology," 119.

A Brief Look at John Wesley

As I mentioned earlier, because John Wesley didn't write systematic treatises, the occasional and situational nature of his writing can make it difficult
to pin down his views. According to Charles Brockwell, Wesley's view on
justification and imputed righteousness were in line with the Reformers.[41]
Scott Kisker, by contrast, argues more convincingly that Wesley's conception
of justification was not consistent with the Reformers. Sometimes, it seems
that Wesley understands justification forensically, but on other occasions he
explains it in terms of deliverance from the power of sin.[42]

So what was Wesley's view of *sola fide*?[43] Alan Clifford argues that
Wesley rejected *sola fide* because he feared it led to antinomianism.[44] Yet
Clifford doesn't read Wesley broadly enough in making such an assertion.
In fact, Wesley embraced *sola fide*, for he criticizes those who teach that
good works are required for justification[45] and claims that he believed in
justification by faith alone.[46] On the one hand, in Sermon V ("Justification
by Faith," 1746), he explicitly asserts that salvation is by faith alone, claiming that "faith is the *only* condition of justification."[47] Twenty years later,
in 1766, he said, "I believe justification by faith alone as much as I believe
there is a God."[48]

On the other hand, Wesley seems to reject the imputation of Christ's
righteousness, saying that we can't be considered righteous on the basis of

---

41. Charles W. Brockwell Jr., "John Wesley's Doctrine of Justification," *Wesleyan Theological Journal* 18 (1983): 18–32.

42. See Scott Kisker, "Justified but Unregenerate? The Relationship of Assurance to Justification and Regeneration in the Thought of John Wesley," *Wesleyan Theological Journal* 28 (1993): 44–58. See Ted M. Dorman, who shows that Wesley didn't restrict himself to a forensic understanding of justification ("Forgiveness of *Past* Sins: John Wesley on Justification: A Case Study Approach," *ProEccl* 10 2001. : 286). Wesley rejects the notion that justification is complete when we believe, remarking about justification, "There may be as many degrees in the favour as in the image of God." See "Preface to a Treatise on Justification," in *The Works of John Wesley* (3rd ed.; vol. 10; Grand Rapids: Baker, 1978), 320.

43. My thanks to my PhD student and research assistant Aubrey Sequeira, whose research particularly helped me to understand Wesley's view.

44. Clifford, *Atonement and Justification*, 59, 65, n. 58, 176 (where he says Wesley was ambivalent).

45. Ibid., 59.

46. See Sermon I, "Salvation by Faith" (1738), in *Wesley's Standard Sermons* (ed. Edward H. Sugden; London: Epworth, 1951), 1:37–52, where he affirms *sola fide* but doesn't mention imputed righteousness. See also William Ragsdale Cannon, *The Theology of John Wesley: With Special Reference to the Doctrine of Justification* (Lanham, MD: University Press of America, 1974), 81–82; Dorman, "John Wesley on Justification," 278–79. Cf. Oden, *Justification Reader*, 41.

47. *Sermons*, 1:127.

48. "Some Remarks on 'A Defense of the Preface to the Edinburgh Edition of Aspasio Vindicated,'" in *The Works of John Wesley* (3rd ed.; Grand Rapids: Baker, 1978), 10:349.

Christ's righteousness.[49] Wesley appears to hold at this juncture what is sometimes called single imputation: a justification that pardons and forgives sins but does not also involve the imputation of Christ's righteousness. In any case, Wesley believes justification is by faith alone.[50] "That we are justified by faith, is spoken to take away clearly all merit of our works, and wholly to ascribe the *merit and deserving* of our justification to Christ only."[51]

So we can say that while Wesley affirmed *sola fide*, he questioned the imputation of Christ's righteousness. We see this in his 1762 response to James Hervey[52] when he says, "'The righteousness of Christ' is an expression which I do not find in the Bible."[53] Wesley was particularly concerned that those who defended imputed righteousness opened the door to antinomianism. In his *Treatise on Justification* (1764–65) Wesley again responds to Hervey, questioning Christ's imputed righteousness while emphasizing that it leads to antinomianism.[54]

Still, we should be cautious and acknowledge that Wesley's view was complicated, for at the end of 1765 in a sermon on Jer 23:6 he affirms strongly the active obedience of Christ![55] He says, "to all believers the righteousness of Christ is imputed."[56] Here Wesley accepts gladly the idea, "For the sake of Thy active and passive righteousness, I am forgiven and accepted of God."[57] Our inherent righteousness is not the "ground" but the "fruit" of "our acceptance with God."[58] And, "The righteousness of Christ is the whole and sole foundation of all our hope."[59] Wesley maintains, "I always did, and do still continually affirm, that the righteousness of Christ is imputed to every believer."[60] Still, he worries about some using the phrase to justify antinomianism.[61]

49. *Sermons*, 1:120. For the trajectory of Wesley's view, see E. H. Sugden in the introduction to Sermon XLIX in *Sermons*, 2:421–23.

50. Ibid., 1:124–30.

51. Ibid., 2:431.

52. See John Wesley, "Thoughts on the Imputed Righteousness of Christ" (1762), in *The Works of John Wesley*, 10:312–15.

53. Ibid., 10:312. He goes on to say, "'the imputing the righteousness of Christ'" is a phrase "I dare not insist upon, neither require any one to use, because I cannot find it in the Bible" (ibid., 10:314–15). He says about the imputation of Christ's righteousness elsewhere, "It is not scriptural; it is not necessary" (ibid., 10:318).

54. Ibid., 10:322–31.

55. *Sermons*, "The Lord Our Righteousness," 2:420–41.

56. Ibid., 2:428.

57. Ibid., 2:433.

58. Ibid., 2:434–35.

59. Ibid., 2:434.

60. Ibid., 2:435.

61. Ibid., 2:438.

In 1773 Wesley hesitates. Again, he fears using the phrase imputed righteousness of Christ "in the Antinomian sense."[62] He says that the phrase itself isn't important since it isn't in Scripture.[63] And he says he won't speak of the imputation of Christ's righteousness in the future.[64] Yet Wesley's last written sermon, "On the Wedding Garment," returns to the matter.[65] He still questions the phrase, saying it isn't a biblical expression, but at the same time he strongly affirms that believers are saved only through the merits of Jesus Christ.[66] Wesley even uses the phrase "righteousness of Christ." He writes,

> The righteousness of Christ is, doubtless, necessary for any soul that enters into glory. But so is personal holiness, too, for every child of man. But it is highly needful to be observed that they are necessary in different respects. The former is necessary to *entitle* us to heaven; the latter, to *qualify* us for it. Without the righteousness of Christ, we could have no *claim* to glory; without holiness we could have no *fitness* for it.[67]

Wesley's back and forth stance on the imputation of Christ's righteousness has filtered down to the scholarly evaluations of his work. Clifford says he rejected the notion that Christ is our righteousness, so that imputation is limited to forgiveness of sins.[68] Similarly, Frederick Dale Bruner maintains that Wesley rejected imputed righteousness.[69] Dorman charts the trajectory of Wesley's view, arguing from Wesley's 1738 sermon "Justification by Faith," from his 1744 minutes, and from his 1756 letter to James Hervey that Wesley rejected the imputation of Christ's righteousness.[70] However, by 1765 in his sermon "The Lord Our Righteousness," and in 1790 in his sermon on "The Wedding Garment," Wesley subscribes to a form of imputation.[71] Dorman argues, however, that Wesley departed from the Reformed view in his articulation, for he believed that our sins were forgiven by imputation, but Christ's righteousness wasn't credited to us.[72] At

---

62. "Mr. Hill's Farrago Double-Distilled" in *The Works of John Wesley*, 10:428.
63. Ibid.
64. Ibid., 2:430.
65. "On the Wedding Garment," in *The Works of John Wesley* (ed. Albert Outler; Nashville: Abingdon, 1987), 4:140–48.
66. Ibid., 4:142–43.
67. Ibid., 4:144. Italics his.
68. Clifford, *Atonement and Justification*, 65, n. 59, 188–91.
69. Frederick Dale Bruner, *A Theology of the Holy Spirit* (Grand Rapids: Eerdmans, 1970), 332, n. 37.
70. Dorman, "John Wesley on Justification," 279–80, 283–86.
71. Ibid., 289–92.
72. Ibid., 293.

the same time, Wesley thinks good works are necessary for final justification, which Clifford sees as a development away from his early views.[73]

Again, because Wesley didn't write systematic treatises, tracing out his view is difficult. I would suggest that Thomas Oden captures Wesley's view most accurately, so that Wesley, when rightly understood, believes in the imputation of Christ's righteousness.[74] When Wesley speaks against imputation, he has in mind the abuses of the teaching. He doesn't insist on the phrase since it isn't scriptural and worries about those who would demand that every Christian embrace the formula since many believers are trusting in Christ alone for their salvation but don't understand imputation. Nevertheless, Wesley affirms that believers find their righteousness in Jesus Christ and that his righteousness is the basis for their heavenly hope. He says he has always believed and taught imputation in this sense.

It seems that Wesley isn't always consistent, and he is also confusing, for in some instances he appears to merge justification and sanctification. Still, I suggest that we should take Wesley's own words to best understand his belief in imputation. When he speaks negatively about imputation, he rejects the notion that someone must use the phrase or understand the phrase to be orthodox. What especially worried Wesley, then, is the notion that imputation would cancel out the necessity of holiness, for as Heb 12:14 says, "without [holiness] no one will see the Lord." In conclusion, Wesley tried to maintain the balance of the Scriptures. He affirmed that salvation is by faith alone and that our righteousness is grounded in Jesus Christ. Still, good works are necessary as a fruit for our salvation, and if they aren't present, we have no hope for eternal life.

Conclusion

I have argued in this chapter that Edwards, despite his use of confusing language in some instances, stands in fundamental continuity with Luther, Calvin, Owen, and Turretin. Edwards crafts things in his distinctive way, but he didn't believe inherent righteousness qualified believers for justification. Believers rely on the imputed righteousness of Christ to be right with God. Edwards insisted on the necessity of good works, but such a claim did not compromise justification by faith alone, for such works were never conceived by Edwards as the basis for one's relationship with God. They were the fruit or evidence of one's standing before him.

---

73. Clifford, *Atonement and Justification*, 60.

74. Thomas C. Oden, *John Wesley's Scriptural Christianity: A Plain Exposition of His Teaching on Christian Doctrine* (Grand Rapids: Zondervan, 1994), 206–11.

It is also difficult to discern John Wesley's views on justification. Though he clearly taught justification by faith alone, he didn't speak with one voice on imputation. Yet rightly interpreted, he and Edwards shared the same concern, even though they came from different theological backgrounds. Wesley affirmed that our righteousness was in Jesus Christ, but he likewise insisted on the necessity of good works and worried about the threat of antinomianism when people insisted on imputation.

PART 2

A Biblical and Theological Tour of *Sola Fide*

CHAPTER 7

Human Sin

"Now we know that whatever the law says speaks to those who are subject to the law, so that every mouth may be shut and the whole world may become subject to God's judgment. For no one will be justified in His sight by the works of the law, because the knowledge of sin comes through the law."   —Romans 3:19–20

Our tour of history relative to the doctrine of justification by faith alone has been selective, yet it provides a context for our biblical interpretation. We must always remember that we are not the first ones to interpret the Scriptures. We would be foolish to plunge into the meaning of the biblical texts without considering the work of those who have gone before us. The careful work of our predecessors has shaped us whether we are aware of it or not. Still, as Protestants we believe in *sola scriptura*. We must, in the end, turn to what the Scriptures say and cannot simply rely on tradition or interpretations from the past. Hence, the second part of this book investigates the biblical witness regarding justification by faith alone. Once again, we are conducting a tour, since we cannot provide a detailed examination of every text in question.

Broadly speaking, we will examine four themes as we study the Scriptures:

- First, why is it that justification is by faith alone? Here the role of human sin in particular will be explored.
- Second, we will explore the role of faith and its nature since it is claimed that righteousness is *sola fide*.
- Third, as we have seen in our historical survey, the meaning of righteousness has been examined and debated for hundreds of years, and so the meaning of this term must be investigated. Several chapters will be required to work out this matter.

- Fourth, we must account for the texts that say good works are necessary for salvation and justification. How do texts that demand good works fit with *sola fide*?

Our study will focus particularly on Paul, for the debates have centered on his writings, though I will also try to indicate here and there that Jesus taught the same truth. Along the way I will interact with the New Perspective on Paul which has made such a splash in the last generation. An excursus on the recent view of Doug Campbell will also be included.

Works of Law Don't Justify

When we say justification is by faith alone, the works or good deeds of human beings are excluded as a ground for right standing before God. Justification must be by faith alone because it can't be obtained or secured by works. But why is it the case that righteousness cannot be gained by works? What reasons does the Bible give for such an assessment of human beings? We should not be surprised to learn that different answers have been given to this question, and because the debate centers on the Pauline epistles, we will focus on Paul in attending to this question.

Paul teaches that no one can be justified or receive the Spirit by the works of the law (*erga nomou*, Rom 3:20, 28; Gal 2:16; 3:2, 5, 10). The meaning of "works of the law" in Paul has been fiercely contested. Historically, during the time of the Reformation, Roman Catholics argued that the term referred to the ceremonial law. On this reading Paul doesn't deny that justification stems from works. According to Roman Catholics, Paul agrees with James (Jas 2:14–26) that justification is based on obedience to the moral law. What Paul rules out is justification on the basis of the ceremonial law. In other words, one doesn't have to be circumcised and to keep the other commands that distinguished Jews from Gentiles. Earlier, in our historical tour, we saw that Calvin and Luther vigorously disagreed with those who limited works of law to the ceremonial law, contending that the phrase refers to the entire law.

New Perspective on Works of Law

A similar interpretation has been proposed today by those who espouse what is commonly called the New Perspective on Paul.[1] The context today, of course, is different, for proponents of the New Perspective have

---

1. For an excellent survey recent work on justification in Paul, see David E. Aune, "Recent Readings of Paul Relating to Justification by Faith," in *Rereading Paul Together: Protestant and Catholic Perspectives on Justification* (Grand Rapids: Baker, 2006), 188–245.

typically been Protestant and are not advancing a Roman Catholic agenda. Nevertheless, there is a fascinating convergence with the Roman Catholic view on works of law.[2] Both James Dunn and N. T. Wright have maintained that works of law focus on the laws that separate Jews from Gentiles.[3]

Hence, when Paul excludes works of law from justification, he thinks particularly of matters like circumcision, Sabbath, and food laws. The laws that segregate Jews from Gentiles come to the forefront and are the particular object of Paul's irritation. On the New Perspective reading Paul doesn't criticize legalism, for the notion that Judaism was legalistic doesn't accord with the sources. Nor is Paul's fundamental complaint that human beings can't or don't obey the law. Instead, what concerns him is the nationalistic and jingoistic spirit of his Jewish opponents. The issue is nationalism, not legalism; exclusivism, not works-righteousness; ethno-centricism, not human inability to obey. The works of law were boundary markers or badges of Jewish identity. What concerned Paul and what Paul rejects is the notion that one had to become Jewish to be a Christian.

Evaluation of New Perspective on Works of Law

Advocates of the New Perspective have unearthed an important truth in the notion that Paul rejects the ceremonial law or the boundary markers.[4] There was an ethnic and cultural dimension to the Torah, and some Jews were convinced that as the chosen people of Yahweh, they were pleasing to God by virtue of their ethnicity. They believed that Gentiles had to join the Jewish people to belong to God. Paul, by contrast, declares that Jews and Gentiles are now one people of God in Jesus Christ (Eph 2:11–3:13). He argued that Gentiles didn't need to adopt the OT law or circumcision to be members of the church, for both Jews and Gentiles are united to God and to one another through the cross of Jesus Christ. Paul was concerned about Jewish ethnocentricism and nationalism, and he clearly rejected it.

---

2. For a wide-ranging discussion and evaluation of the New Perspective from a systematic theologian, see Gerald Bray, "Justification: The Reformers and Recent New Testament Scholarship," *Churchman* 109 (1995): 102–26.

3. James D. G. Dunn, "The New Perspective on Paul," *BJRL* 65 (1983): 95–122; idem, "Works of the Law and the Curse of the Law (Galatians 3.10–14)," *NTS* 31 (1985): 523–42; idem, "Yet Once More—'The Works of the Law': A Response," *JSNT* 46 (1992): 99–117; idem, "The Justice of God: A Renewed Perspective on Justification by Faith," *JTS* 43 (2003):13–14. N. T. Wright, *Paul and the Faithfulness of God* (2 vols., Christian Origins and the Question of God; Minneapolis: Fortress, 2013), 184–87.

4. For a balanced assessment of the New Perspective, see Michael F. Bird, *The Saving Righteousness of God: Studies on Paul, Justification, and the New Perspective* (Paternoster Biblical Monographs; Eugene, OR: Wipf and Stock, 2007), 88–154. This is not to say I agree with all of Bird's conclusions.

Despite these strengths in the New Perspective view, their understanding of works of law isn't persuasive.[5] The term doesn't limit its focus on the boundary markers but instead refers to the entire law. In other words, Paul's fundamental criticism wasn't that the badges of the law were imposed on the Gentiles, as if they were compelled to become Jews. Instead "works of law" refers to the entire law, which includes, of course, the boundary markers. Further, the reason why justification or receiving the Spirit doesn't come by works of law is not ascribed to exclusivism. Nor does the phrase denote legalism. "Works of law" refers to all the deeds or actions mandated in the Sinai covenant, in what is often called the Mosaic law.[6] It is almost certainly the case (more on this below) that some Jews were legalistic, but the real issue under discussion is what the phrase "works of law" means. The most common sense definition should be assigned to the phrase—it denotes everything mandated in the law.

Works of Law in Romans

The reading proposed here is verified when we read the context of Romans 3 and Galatians 2 and 3. Paul indicts both Jews and Gentiles (Rom 1:18–3:20), and in his ringing conclusion he declares, "Now we know that whatever the law says speaks to those who are subject to the law, so that every mouth may be shut and the whole world may become subject to God's judgment. For no one will be justified in His sight by the works of the law, because the knowledge of sin comes through the law" (3:19–20). What fault does Paul find with the Jews in 1:18–3:20? He doesn't breathe a word here about excluding the Gentiles. Yes, he mentions the Jewish reliance on circumcision, but he doesn't go on to intimate that the Jews used this as a club to oust Gentiles (2:25–27). Rather, he criticizes the Jews because they are transgressors of the law (2:25, 27).

And so it goes elsewhere in this section. Paul doesn't deny that the Jews have great privileges as the chosen people (Rom 2:17–20; 3:1–2), nor does he dispute their role as teachers and instructors of Gentiles. What

---

5.   It should be noted that Dunn has moderated his position, so that he is now friendlier to the old perspective, without withdrawing his claim that the New Perspective is fundamentally correct. See James D. G. Dunn, *The New Perspective on Paul* (rev. ed.; Grand Rapids: Eerdmans, 2008), 1–97.

6.   See, e.g., Stephen Westerholm, *Israel's Law and the Church's Faith: Paul and His Recent Interpreters* (Grand Rapids: Eerdmans, 1988), 106–21; Thomas R. Schreiner, "'Works of Law' in Paul," *NovT* 33 (1991): 217–44; idem, *DPL*, 975–79; Joseph A. Fitzmyer, "Paul's Jewish Background and the Deeds of the Law," in *According to Paul: Studies in the Theology of the Apostle* (New York: Paulist, 1993), 18–35.

he complains about is their disobedience to the Torah (2:21–24). And the sins he puts under the searchlight are *moral infractions of the law*: stealing, adultery, and robbing temples. Paul could have easily said that he was troubled by Jewish nationalism and ethnocentricism, but instead he complains about their failure to keep the law—their disobedience. All of this suggests that works of law refer to the entire law, and that the fundamental problem is human disobedience.

Such a reading fits well with the logic of Rom 3:20. Justification doesn't come by works of law, since the knowledge of sin is disclosed through the law. Paul does not say that the law fails to justify because the Jews excluded the Gentiles. Instead, the law uncovered their sin, demonstrating that they failed to keep what God enjoined. Such a reading fits most naturally with the preceding verses (3:9–18), where Paul declares that "no one" is "righteous, not even one" (3:10). "All have turned away.... There is no one who does what is good, not even one" (3:12). All human beings have become polluted in their speech (3:13–14) and their actions (3:15–17). The problem is not the boundary markers but a failure to do what God demands.

The interpretation offered here is supported further by Rom 3:23, "for all have sinned and fall short of the glory of God." This verse is important because Paul reaches back in the midst of a new section and a new theme (3:21–26) to capture the substance of what he argued for in 1:18–3:20, and he declares that all are sinners—all are transgressors. No one keeps the prescriptions of the law.

What we have just seen in Rom 1:18–3:23 illuminates the meaning of works of law in 3:28. Boasting is excluded (3:28), "For we conclude that a person is justified by faith apart from the works of the law." The "for" (*gar*) in v. 28 demonstrates that Paul explains v. 27 in v. 28. If boasting is excluded because no one is justified by works of law and if works of law refer to the whole law (as argued above), then boasting is ruled out because no one does the works mandated in the law. Human beings cannot boast since they fail to keep the stipulations and commands given by God.

New Perspectivists point to the immediately following verses, for there we find that both Jews and Gentiles are justified by faith since God is one (3:29–30). In response, we can say: yes, Paul is concerned about the equality of Jews and Gentiles in the people of God. The New Perspective has that right. Still, such an observation doesn't lead to the conclusion that works of law focus on boundary markers or badges. Paul teaches in 3:29–30 that works of law don't justify either Jews or Gentiles. Both are saved by faith alone and not because they have practiced the works of the law. Given the previous argument (1:18–3:20 and 3:23), the reason works of law don't justify is because all people (both Jews and Gentiles) fail to keep what the law commands.[7]

Works of Law in Galatians

The same question arises in Galatians where the term "works of law" is found six times (Gal 2:16 [3x]; 3:2, 5, 10). One might think that works of law focus on boundary markers since the matter comes up in a debate over foods. Peter and other Jews have by their actions implied that the Gentile Christians must also observe the food laws (2:11–14). Paul strikes back at this by insisting that works of law don't justify. Right standing with God doesn't come through works of law but by faith in Jesus Christ (2:16). The importance of what Paul says is underscored, for the notion that works of law don't justify is stated three times in the verse.

In Paul's letter to the Galatians the term "works of law" is introduced in the context of a discussion about food regulations, and in the letter as a whole it is clear that the opponents advocated circumcision for entrance into the people of God (Gal. 2:3–5; 5:2–6, 11–12; 6:12–13). So works of law in Galatians are certainly tied up with the boundary markers, but there are several pieces of evidence in the letter that call into question the notion that *the focus* is on boundary markers. One of the most important verses in this regard is Gal 3:10. "For all who rely on the works of the law are under a curse, because it is written: *Everyone who does not continue doing everything written in the book of the law is cursed*." The verse is intensely controversial, and I have examined it in further detail elsewhere.[8] What we must see here is that the phrase "works of law" (*erga nomou*) is defined further by "everything written in the book of the law." Paul draws on Deut

---

7.   I am not attempting here to engage in a full scale investigation of Paul's theology of law. I believe his arguments are salvation historical and anthropological. See Thomas R. Schreiner, *The Law and Its Fulfillment: A Pauline Theology of Law* (Grand Rapids: Baker, 1993); idem, *Forty Questions about Christians and Biblical Law* (Grand Rapids: Kregel, 2010). For salient criticisms of the notion that Paul's theology of justification can be restricted to apocalyptic or eschatology, see Bruce McCormack, "Can We Still Speak of 'Justification by Faith'? An In-House Debate with Apocalyptic Readings of Paul," in *Galatians and Christian Theology: Justification, the Gospel, and Ethics in Paul's Letter* (ed. Mark W. Elliott, Scott J. Hafemann, N. T. Wright, and John Frederick; Grand Rapids: Baker, 2014), 159–84.

8.   Thomas R. Schreiner, *Galatians* (ZECNT; Grand Rapids: Zondervan, 2010), 203–7. See the discussion there for further literature. For a very different reading, one that sees the statements in Gal 3:10–14 as situationally constrained, see Timothy H. Gombis, "Arguing with Scripture in Galatia: Galatians 3:10–14 as a Series of Ad Hoc Arguments," in *Galatians and Christian Theology: Justification, the Gospel, and Ethics in Paul's Letter* (ed. Mark W. Elliott, Scott J. Hafemann, N. T. Wright, and John Frederick; Grand Rapids: Baker, 2014), 82–90.

27:26 ("cursed is the one who does not continue in all the words of this law to do them") and Deut 28:50 ("if you are not careful to obey all the words of this law, which are written in this scroll").[9]

Works of law, then, are defined as *everything* written in the law, and the curse is unleashed on those who fail to keep everything commanded. The fundamental reason for the curse, then, is not the imposition of the law on the Gentiles (though that is clearly wrong), but disobedience—the failure to keep what the law says. Such an interpretation fits with the contrast between justification by works of law and justification through faith in Jesus Christ.[10] Justification doesn't come from works of law but through faith. Indeed, it is by faith alone instead of by faith and works.

Demand for Perfect Obedience

Two other verses in Galatians point us in the same direction. Galatians 5:3 says, "Again I testify to every man who gets himself circumcised that he is obligated to keep the entire law." We should notice right off the emphasis on "the entire law [*holon ton nomon*]."[11] There isn't a focus on only a portion of the law here or on the boundary markers. The readers are reminded that they are required to observe the whole law if they submit to circumcision. Moreover, we see from the next verse (5:4) that they were tempted to obtain justification through keeping the law ("You who are trying to be justified by the law"). The Galatian readers could have responded to the warning here by saying that if justification required keeping the entire law, then that's what they would do!

Such a response would have signaled that they misunderstood Paul's intention, for he isn't merely saying that taking on the law is a heavy burden. His criticism goes deeper than this. He reverts to what he said in Gal 3:10. The requirement of keeping the law to be justified places the readers in an impossible situation, for no one can carry out all that the law requires. Such a reading of 5:3 is confirmed by 6:13, where Paul says about the opponents, "For even the circumcised don't keep the law themselves." Paul has a consistent message in both Romans and Galatians. Justification doesn't come via the law (cf. Gal 3:12) since no one keeps all that the law demands. Justification is by faith alone, for right standing with God can't be obtained by works since all fall short of divine requirements.

---

9. This represents my translation of the LXX.
10. The meaning of faith in Jesus Christ is contested, and the matter is discussed in chapter 13.
11. For further discussion of this verse, see Schreiner, *Galatians*, 313–14.

We have other indications that Paul thinks of the law generally in Galatians. Paul says he died to the law (Gal 2:19), which certainly can't be limited to boundary markers. The law played a role ("through the law I have died to the law") in putting him to death. Paul also declares that righteousness does not come via the law (2:21). The law reveals transgressions (3:19) and is described in terms of a covenant given to Moses with all the statutes contained therein (3:17). The Galatians come under criticism for desiring to be under the law (4:21; cf. 5:18), which demonstrates that the matter isn't limited to boundary markers. The Galatians are inclined to devote themselves to the entire law, and Paul's fundamental objection is that the law can't bring salvation or justify on account of human disobedience.

Works Don't Justify

Paul doesn't simply say that works of law don't justify. He speaks more generally as well, insisting that "works" (*erga*) don't justify either. Notice, for instance, that though Paul speaks of works of law not justifying in Rom 3:20 and 28, when he comes to Romans 4 Paul no longer refers to works of law. The subject is works in general, so that the issue is whether Abraham "was justified by works" (4:2). It makes perfect sense that Paul drops the phrase "works of law," for Abraham wasn't under the Mosaic law. Paul carefully distinguishes the era of Abraham from the era of the law, for the law was inaugurated 430 years after the covenant with Abraham (Gal 3:15–18; cf. Rom 5:12–14, 20). Abraham didn't perform the works of law, for he wasn't under the law. Hence, Paul asks whether Abraham was justified by works in general (Rom 4:2). Yes, the boundary marker issue of circumcision surfaces in 4:9–12, but it isn't broached in 4:1–8.[12]

Paul places justification by faith and justification by works in opposition (Rom. 4:2–3), insisting that Abraham was justified by believing instead of doing. It is obvious that Paul thinks of works in general instead of boundary markers from the illustration introduced in 4:4. Here he considers the wages that are paid to someone who works for an employer. Employees don't think their wages are a gift since they worked hard to receive pay. The illustration demonstrates conclusively that Paul fixes his attention on whether our works can obtain salvation.

Paul rejects works as a way of salvation, because human beings are ungodly (Rom 4:5). Paul doesn't imply or suggest that boasting is wrong

---

12. For a further defense of the interpretation proposed here, see Schreiner, *Romans*, 212–21.

even if works are carried out (4:2, 4). If someone actually does the works, then boasting is entirely legitimate. If we do the works, we get the praise! But Abraham wasn't justified before God (see 4:2!) because he was ungodly (4:5). God justifies the ungodly, and Abraham was ungodly because he worshiped false gods along with his ancestors before God called him (Josh 24:2). Paul doesn't limit himself to or even focus on boundary markers in Rom 4:1–8. Works don't justify because of human disobedience, and thus justification comes from faith alone. Faith is "counted" as "righteousness" for those who "[believe] in him who justifies the ungodly" (4:5, ESV).

Paul then turns to the life of David to confirm the claim that "righteousness" is "apart from works" (Rom 4:6). It is striking that Paul again speaks of "works" (*erga*) in general instead of "works of law." Clearly, the issue isn't boundary markers, for Psalm 32 is cited in Rom 4:7–8, where David celebrates the forgiveness of his "lawless acts" and "sins." David and Paul were almost certainly thinking of his adultery with Bathsheba and his murder of Uriah the Hittite. Righteousness doesn't come by works since David was a sinner who desperately needed forgiveness for his transgressions. By implication, the blessing of forgiveness and justification is granted by faith alone.

Another illuminating text on works and faith is Rom 9:30–10:21. My purpose isn't to provide a full exegesis of this text but to feature some highlights that underscore that righteousness is granted by faith instead of works. New perspectivists claim that this text supports their understanding of Paul, so that "their own righteousness" (10:3) refers to the nationalistic or ethnic righteousness of Israel over against the Gentiles. As I said earlier, I don't doubt that the inclusion of Gentiles apart from the boundary markers was an important issue for Paul (cf. 4:9–12). But the boundary markers issues must be read against the broader backdrop of Paul's thought, where he rejects righteousness by works fundamentally.

This utter polarity between faith and works is evident in Romans 9:30–10:21.[13] Once again Paul uses the word "works" (*erga*) instead of works of law, and he speaks of "the one who does these things" (10:5), where "these things" refers to the works mandated in the Mosaic law. Nothing is said in this context about boundary markers like circumcision, Sabbath, or purity laws. Nor is anything said about excluding Gentiles. Instead, Paul says that Israel didn't obtain righteousness because they pursued it by works instead of faith (9:31–32). The fundamental opposition between righteousness by faith and righteousness by works again surfaces.

---

13. See further ibid., 533–58.

Israel stumbled because they relied on works, though God called them to put their faith in Jesus Christ (Rom 9:33). The chapter division isn't the best here, for the same subject matter continues into chapter 10. Israel's attempt "to establish their own righteousness" (10:3) is parallel with the desire to obtain righteousness by works in 9:32. Hence, the desire to establish their own righteousness doesn't pertain to exclusivism but represents a righteousness by works over against a righteousness by faith. Israel submits to God's righteousness by believing (10:3–4). The righteousness of the law is based on doing (10:5) in contrast to the righteousness of faith, which relies on what God has done in Jesus Christ (10:6–8). Why doesn't righteousness by law succeed? Paul, quoting Lev 18:5 says, "the one who does these things will live by them" (Rom 10:5). Given the previous discussion of these matters in Romans (1:18–3:20; 3:23), Paul likely implies that works don't bring righteousness because of human failure, because human beings are unable to do what the law commands.

Once again, we see the contrast between doing and believing. It is "the righteousness that comes from faith" that saves (Rom 10:6), where one confesses that Jesus is Lord and believes that God raised him from the dead (10:9–10). Salvation is available to all, both Jews and Gentiles, by faith (10:11–13). Those who hear the message about Jesus Christ and put their faith in the good news will be saved (10:14–17). To sum up: Paul teaches clearly in 9:30–10:21 that one is righteous by faith alone—faith alone justifies. Works are excluded altogether because of human disobedience, and they play no role in obtaining righteousness.

Philippians 3:2–9

Philippians 3:2–9 is an important text for our purposes as well.[14] Once again, we will not attend to every element of the text but comment briefly on matters that pertain to the subject at hand. Paul warns the believers about adversaries in this passage, and they are almost certainly Jewish since they advocate circumcision (3:2). Boundary markers, then, play an important role, for circumcision was the initiation rite into Judaism and divided Jews from Gentiles. The ethnic character of the opponents can be surmised from Paul's defense of himself in 3:5, "circumcised the eighth day; of the nation of Israel, of the tribe of Benjamin, a Hebrew born of Hebrews; regarding the law, a Pharisee." Paul presents his own Jewish

---

14. Cf. here Robert H. Gundry, "Grace, Works, and Staying Saved in Paul," *Bib* 66 (1985): 1–38, esp. 13–14.

credentials, and they are impeccable. Indeed, they exceed the qualifications of his opponents. He was circumcised on the day specified in the law (Lev 12:3) and was from the nation of Israel. Many Jews in Paul's day would no longer know their tribal background, but Paul knew he was from the tribe of Benjamin, the tribe from which Israel's first king (Saul) came. When Paul says he was a Hebrew of Hebrews, he probably means that he spoke Aramaic (or Hebrew). He was a speaker of the native language in the land. Finally, his devotion to the law was represented in his joining the sect of the Pharisees, who were known for their devotion to the law.

New perspectivists (who aren't all the same, of course) often comment on how Philippians 3 fits with their paradigm. And they are certainly right, at least to some extent. We see the ethnic and nationalist flavor of the Jewish opponents here. Still, this passage is interesting in another way, for nationalism is aligned with works-righteousness as well. We don't have an either-or between nationalism and activism, between ritual and works-righteousness. Instead, these are included together. Such a state of affairs is hardly surprising. If one ethnic group thinks it is superior to another, it typically believes that it is morally superior as well. Indeed, alleged moral superiority is often one of the chief reasons for believing that they are better than another people group.

We see the same phenomenon in the Philippians text, where the ethnic and moral superiority of the Jews are linked together. Paul's decision to become a Pharisee reflected his moral choice (Phil 3:5), his decision to join what he elsewhere calls the strictest sect in Judaism (Acts 26:5). Pharisaism can't be reduced to an ethnic matter, for most Jews weren't part of the Pharisaic sect. This reading is borne out by Phil 3:6. Paul mentions his persecution of the church. Obviously, we are given a preconversion perspective of Paul's activities here. Before Paul was converted on the Damascus Road, he was convinced that his zeal in persecuting the church commended him before God (cf. Gal. 1:13–14). He almost certainly believed that he was following the example of those who showed zeal for God in the past: Phinehas in slaying the Israelite man having sex with a Midianite woman (Num 25:6–15), Elijah's zeal in killing the prophets of Baal (1 Kgs 18; 19:10, 14), and Mattathias in resisting the pagan reforms of Antiochus Epiphanes (1 Macc. 2). After Paul's conversion, he recognized that his zealous persecution of the church was "filth" (*skybala*, Phil 3:8); but before he was saved, he was convinced that it was morally praiseworthy. Hence, Paul's persecution was a testimony to his virtue, attesting that works-righteousness was part of his problem.

That Paul also centered his identity on what he accomplished and attained is evident by his claim that he was "blameless" with respect to "the righteousness that is in the law" (Phil 3:6). Blamelessness doesn't mean that Paul thought he was sinless. The notion that anyone could live without sin was foreign to Jewish thought (1 Kgs 8:46; Ps 130:3; Prov 20:9; Eccl 7:20). What Paul means is that his righteousness was extraordinary and that he offered sacrifice when he sinned. It is crucial to recall what was said about the previous line in Phil 3:6, and remember that here we have Paul's preconversion view of himself. As a Christian looking back on his past life, he had a different view of his life under the Mosaic law. He now recognized that such a life was loss (Phil 3:7), and he realizes retrospectively (Rom 7:14–25) that sin was present in ways that he failed to understand before his conversion. The main point established in this section still stands, however. Paul, prior to his conversion, was proud not only of his Jewish heritage; he was also proud of his actions, of what he did, of his devotion to the Torah.

What Paul says in Philippians should be interpreted to fit with what he says in Romans and Galatians. Law-righteousness doesn't justify since human beings sin. Human beings may think they are righteous enough to obtain right standing with God, but they are dramatically wrong. Those who are "found" in God don't have "a righteousness of [their] own from the law" (Phil 3:9). This righteousness can't be restricted to boundary marker issues, given Paul's emphasis on his own choices and moral virtue in 3:5–6. Furthermore, we saw that the similar phrase in Rom 10:3 ("their own righteousness") is parallel to pursuing the law "by works" (9:31–32). Romans 10 shares another common feature with Philippians 3, for in both "zeal" for God is noted (Rom 10:2; Phil 3:6).

Paul's own righteousness based on the law, then, includes the notion that he believed he could gain right standing with God because of his obedience to Torah. But Paul discovered, presumably on the Damascus Road (though his insight deepened as time passed), that his own righteousness was "loss" and "filth" (Phil 3:7–8). His only hope was "the righteousness from God based on faith" (Phil 3:9). Since obedience to the law does not obtain righteousness, this is a way of saying that justification is by faith alone. Human obedience and actions can't bring one into a right relationship with God.

Later Pauline Reflections

The unity of Jews and Gentiles in the church is one of the central themes of Ephesians (Eph 2:11–3:13). Paul celebrates their oneness and solidarity in Christ Jesus. At the same time, when he reflects on salvation, he speaks, if I can put it this way, in "old perspective" terms. We read in Eph 2:8–10, "For you are saved by grace through faith, and this is not from yourselves; it is God's gift—not from works, so that no one can boast. For we are His creation, created in Christ Jesus for good works, which God prepared ahead of time so that we should walk in them." We might expect from the emphasis on the unity of Jews and Gentiles that Paul would refer to "works of law" or concentrate on the boundary markers in discussing salvation.[15] Instead, he speaks of "works" (*erga*) in general and says nothing about the identity markers or badges of Israel. The term "works" refers to everything and anything human beings might do to obtain salvation. Such a definition is evident, for if people do the required works, they can boast about what they have done. It seems "works" are also defined in the phrase "this is not from yourselves," so that works represent what is from ourselves; works represent what we do and contribute.

Works are contrasted as well with grace and faith. Grace features what God does, what God accomplishes, God's gift to human beings. The miraculous activity of God is evident because human beings are a new creation in Christ Jesus (Eph 2:10). And faith, in contrast to works, receives what God has done in giving new life to human beings (see Eph 2:1–7). No one can boast about faith, for faith itself is a gift of God.

Why does Paul say that salvation isn't gained by works? The implicit answer is: human disobedience. After all, we are told that we can boast if the works are performed, and that makes perfect sense. If human beings do what is required, they receive the reward and praise for carrying out what was mandated. But Paul has already said that human beings are dead in trespasses and sins and are children of wrath by nature (Eph 2:1–4). Their only hope is the grace of God, which is his new creation work (2:10) by which they are granted life when dead (2:4–6). Boasting isn't ruled out by definition. It is excluded because of human sin and failure.

We should point out another interesting parallel here between the use of the "works" here in Ephesians and "works of law" in Rom 3:28. In both contexts boasting is ruled out (3:27–28; Eph 2:8–9). This lends further

---

15. For the notion that later Pauline reflections support the old perspective view of works, see I. H. Marshall, "Salvation, Grace, and Works in the Later Writings in the Pauline Corpus," *NTS* 42 (1996): 339–58.

credence to the notion that "works of law" refers to all the works of the law. People would be tempted to boast because they were proud of all they did to observe the law. Let me put it another way. When Paul steps back and looks back in Ephesians at the issue of justification in Romans and Galatians, he excludes boasting in works. He drops the reference to the law. Such an omission indicates that the fundamental issue in Paul's mind wasn't boundary markers (as important as they were) but works in general. People are inclined to boast in what they have contributed, to brag about their moral virtue.

What Paul writes in Eph 2:8–10 indicates that salvation is by faith alone and by grace alone.[16] God raises the human being from the dead and grants faith. As God spoke the old creation into existence (Gen 1:1–2:3), so members of the church are the product of his new creation work. Their salvation is not on the basis of works but is granted through faith. Salvation is God's gift and his work. Ephesians 2:1–10 is a remarkable text, for we see in this one text *sola fide, sola gratia, solus Christus,* and *soli Deo Gloria* (Eph 2:7).

Paul also considers the role of works in two of his latest letters: Titus and 2 Timothy. In Titus 3:5–7 salvation is ascribed to God's mercy, to the renewing and regenerating work of his Spirit. Justification, Paul affirms, is by God's grace. The saving work of God stands in opposition to human "works." Human beings are not saved "by works of righteousness that we had done" (*ex ergōn tōn en dikaiosynē ha epoiēsamen hēmeis*). We don't find any mention of boundary markers here. Indeed, works are further described as the righteous things carried out by human beings, confirming that the moral virtue of human beings is the subject matter.

Works, though, do not bring salvation or justification. Justification is by grace *instead* of by works. Paul doesn't say here that justification is by faith alone, but what he writes fits with that notion, for justification is by grace and works are excluded. Why are works ruled out? Paul doesn't argue that works are legalistic. Instead, his comments in Titus 3:3 provide the reason. Before the advent of grace, "we too were once foolish, disobedient, deceived, enslaved by various passions and pleasures, living in malice and envy, hateful, detesting one another." Works don't justify, not because they are legalistic, but because of human sin and disobedience. Salvation

---

16. For further discussion of these verses, see Peter O' Brien, *The Letter to the Ephesians* (Pillar; Grand Rapids: Eerdmans, 1999), 174–78; Frank Thielman, *Ephesians* (BECNT; Grand Rapids: Baker, 2010), 143–44; Clint E. Arnold, *Ephesians* (ZECNT; Grand Rapids: Zondervan, 2010), 138–40.

has to be by grace because human works fall far short of the standard God requires. When we say salvation is by faith alone, we are saying that salvation is entirely God's work.

Paul's last letter, 2 Timothy, confirms what we have seen thus far. We read in 2 Tim 1:9, "He has saved us and called us with a holy calling, not according to our works, but according to His own purpose and grace, which was given to us in Christ Jesus before time began." Here works are contrasted with God's calling, grace, and purpose. God purposed and intended to pour his grace out on believers before history began. They were not chosen or granted grace because of their works but in spite of their works.

Conclusion

The notion that salvation is by faith alone is supported by the truth that righteousness isn't by works. In this chapter we examined the term "works of law," and we saw it doesn't refer fundamentally to boundary markers that divide Jews from Gentiles. Instead, the term focuses on the entire law, and Paul stresses that righteousness doesn't come by works of law since all people fail to perform what the law requires. Confirmation for this conclusion is derived from Paul's use of "works," for Paul makes the same point relative to works as he does when he speaks of works of law; that is, no one is justified by works, for all sin and fall short of the glory of God (Rom 3:23). If justification can't be obtained by works or works of law, how can it be achieved? The answer is: faith alone, and we turn to that subject in the next chapter.

CHAPTER 8

Faith Alone

> "I believe You are the Messiah, the Son of God, who
> comes into the world." —*Martha, in John 11:27*

> "Believe on the Lord Jesus, and you will be saved—
> you and your household." —*Act 16:31*

I n the previous chapter we examined what Paul means by the phrase "works of law" and saw that the word focuses on the entire law, and that Paul stresses that righteousness doesn't come by works of law since all people fail to perform what the law requires. This is due to human sin and disobedience. How, then, can a person be justified? The repeated answer we find in Scripture is *by faith*. If faith plays such a decisive role in one's relationship with God, we should expect it to be a prominent feature of the NT documents. In this chapter, we will investigate the role of faith in the Synoptic Gospels, John's gospel, Acts, and Paul. Once again we will be touring, for an entire book could be written about faith in each piece of literature we consult.

The Synoptic Gospels

The Synoptic Gospels don't discuss the relationship between faith and works in the same way as Paul's epistles or the letter of James does (which will be examined in a later chapter), presumably because the matter wasn't the subject of debate. Furthermore, the fundamental purpose of the Gospels was to present the life, ministry, death, and resurrection of Jesus Christ. Hence, we don't find the same emphasis on faith that we find elsewhere in the NT. Still, there are indications that faith plays a central role in one's relationship with God. I will discuss a few examples to illustrate the point.

Jesus commends the faith of the centurion, saying his faith is greater than any he had seen in Israel (Matt 8:10, 13; Luke 7:9). We should not read too much into this story since it is primarily a record of the healing of a servant. But we do learn that the centurion had a radically different view of himself than the Jewish leaders. They encouraged Jesus to heal his servant because of his concern for the Jewish people and his work in building a synagogue. Hence, they pronounced him "worthy" (*axios*) to receive the request for healing (Luke 7:4). The centurion, however, didn't share their perspective, for he confessed to Jesus that he was "unworthy": "I am not worthy [*ou hikanos*] to have you come under my roof" (7:6; cf. Matt 8:8), and "I don't consider myself worthy [*oude emauton ēxiōsa*] to come to you" (Luke 7:7). Jesus healed the centurion's slave because of the man's faith, not because of his noble efforts on behalf of the Jews or his worthiness.

Moreover, even though the story has to do with the healing of his slave, Jesus ties his faith to salvation, for he declares that many Gentiles "will come from east and west, and recline at the table with Abraham, Isaac, and Jacob in the kingdom of heaven" (Matt 8:11), whereas many Jews "will be thrown into the outer darkness. In that place there will be weeping and gnashing of teeth" (8:12). There seems to be an indication here that salvation is by faith, not by works, for the centurion received an answer to his request because of his faith, not because of his worthiness.

A connection between faith and forgiveness is forged in the story of the healing of the paralytic. Though the faith mentioned is that of his friends instead of his own faith (Matt 9:2; Mark 2:5; Luke 5:20), it is likely that the paralytic also exercised faith. The healings of Jesus often function at two levels, representing the wholeness of Jesus' work. Those who were healed physically were also spiritually healed. The woman with the hemorrhage for twelve years was healed when she touched Jesus' garment. Almost all English versions render Jesus' words to her as, "your faith has made you well." But literally Jesus declared to her, "your faith has saved [*sesōken*] you" (Matt 9:22; Mark 5:34; Luke 8:48).[1] Both her physical and spiritual healing were due to her faith. It is striking as well that in the story of Jairus's daughter, which frames the account of the woman healed of her hemorrhage, Jesus says to Jairus when his hope of his daughter's life continuing is beginning to fade: "Don't be afraid. Only believe" (Mark 5:36; cf. Luke 8:50), suggesting that faith is fundamentally what is required for human beings.

---

1. The wording is exactly the same in all three accounts.

Luke's use of the phrase "your faith has saved [*sesōken*] you" is particularly interesting. He uses it on three occasions, and each one of them is significant (Luke 7:50; 17:19; 18:42). The first instance occurs in the story of Jesus' meal with Simon the Pharisee (7:36–50). A disreputable woman enters and begins to weep, and her tears fall onto Jesus' feet. As she wipes off his feet with her hair, Simon is astonished that Jesus allowed such a woman to touch him, and concludes that Jesus isn't a prophet. Jesus, however, demonstrates his prophetic status by reading Simon's mind. He explains that the woman has loved much because she has been forgiven much (7:42–43, 47). The story features the forgiveness of sins: "her many sins have been forgiven" (7:47), and Jesus declares to her, "Your sins are forgiven." The story concludes with Jesus' ringing affirmation. "Your faith has saved you. Go in peace" (7:50). This story accords with the notion that justification is by faith alone, for the forgiveness Jesus offers here is not secured by obedience—the woman was a notorious sinner. Instead, she was forgiven because of her faith, her trust that Jesus would forgive her.

In Luke 17:10–19 we read that Jesus healed ten lepers. One leper, a Samaritan, returned and gave glory to God by thanking Jesus for what he had done. None of the other lepers returned and gave thanks. Jesus singled out the one who returned and gave thanks, and his concluding words, "your faith has saved you," are limited to this man. It seems fair to conclude that only the Samaritan was "saved" in this encounter, for he was both physically and spiritually healed.[2] The other nine were healed physically, but the words of salvation are limited to the one who returned and gave thanks. He differs from the other nine in truly exercising faith, and thus the wholeness of salvation is restricted to him.

The final story we should consider is the healing of the blind man in Luke 18:35–43 (cf. Matt 9:28–29; Mark 10:52). When the blind man heard Jesus was passing by, he pleaded with him as the Son of David to have mercy on him. People tried to convince him to be quiet, but he shouted all the more, "Son of David, have mercy on me" (Luke 18:39). The blind man requested that Jesus open his eyes, and Jesus granted his request. The opening of the eyes isn't limited to his physical sight, for he recognized

---

2. In a careful study Yeung says both physical and spiritual healing are intended here. Maureen W. Yeung, *Faith in Jesus and Paul: A Comparison with Special Reference to 'Faith That Can Move Mountains' and "Your Faith Has Healed/Saved You"* (WUNT 2/147; Tübingen: Mohr Siebeck, 2002), 53–195. See also Ben Witherington III, "Salvation and Health in Christian Antiquity: The Soteriology of Luke-Acts in Its First Century Setting," in *Witness to the Gospel: The Theology of Acts* (ed. I. H. Marshall and David Peterson; Grand Rapids: Eerdmans, 1998), 145–66.

that Jesus was the Son of David, the Messiah of Israel. Thus, when Jesus declared, "Your faith has saved you," his words aren't restricted to physical healing. This is borne out by the conclusion of the story, for the blind man followed Jesus to Jerusalem, to the place where he would suffer as the Son of David on the cross. The blind man didn't just believe in Jesus for healing and forgiveness, he followed him in discipleship. Luke emphasizes in these three narratives that salvation is by faith, that those who trust in Jesus are forgiven of their sins.

The account of the Canaanite woman is also remarkable (Matt 15:21–28). Jesus discouraged her from approaching him since she wasn't an Israelite, and the disciples entreated Jesus to send her away. Nevertheless, she kept pressing Jesus to act on behalf of her daughter, and Jesus healed her daughter. Jesus highlights her great faith (15:28), showing that this is the fundamental requirement in our relationship with God.

Another story in Luke is worth examining, even though the word faith isn't mentioned. Jesus told the parable of the Pharisee and tax collector (Luke 18:9–14). The parable is important because we find the word "justified" (*dikaioō*) used in a soteriological context (18:13). The story is well-known, so there isn't any need to rehearse it in detail here. What stands out is that the Pharisee isn't justified in the end, despite his attention to religious ritual (18:12). Instead, the Pharisee was condemned before God because he trusted in his own righteousness and exalted himself (18:9, 14). The tax collector, however, was obviously a sinner, one who belonged in the same category as the "greedy, unrighteous," and "adulterers" (18:10). But in the end he was declared righteous because he humbled himself, because he admitted his sin, and because he pleaded with God to show him mercy (18:13–14). Though the word "faith" isn't found here, the parable certainly fits with the notion of justification by faith alone, for the tax collector wasn't justified by his works but solely through God's mercy. I. Howard Marshall says, "Jesus' lesson is precisely that the attitude of the heart is ultimately what matters, and justification depends on the mercy of God to the penitent rather than upon the works which might be thought to earn God's favour."[3] And Joseph Fitzmyer comments, "One achieves uprightness before God not by one's own activity but by a contrite recognition of one's own sinfulness before him."[4]

The importance of faith is underscored in the Synoptic Gospels, for

---

3.   I. H. Marshall, *The Gospel of Luke* (NIGTC; Grand Rapids: Eerdmans, 1978), 681.

4.   Joseph A. Fitzmyer, *The Gospel According to Luke X-XXIV* (AB; New York: Doubleday 1985), 1185.

entrance into the kingdom is for those who believe (Mark 1:15). Jesus often reproaches his hearers or disciples for their little faith (Matt 6:30; 8:26; 14:31; 16:8; 17:20; Luke 12:28), but even worse are those who are unbelieving (Matt 13:58; 17:17; Mark 6:6; 9:19, 24; Luke 9:41; 12:46; 24:11, 41). Even faith as a mustard seed suffices (Matt 17:20; Luke 17:6), though faith that is temporary doesn't save (Luke 8:13; cf. 18:8; 22:32). The little ones who belong to God are characterized by their believing (Matt 18:6; Mark 9:42).

Believing in the Gospel of John

The centrality of believing in the Gospel of John is evident, for John uses the verb "believe"(*pisteuō*) ninety-eight times. It isn't my purpose here to examine the usage of the verb in detail, but we will consider a few examples to appraise how John uses the word and to confirm its importance. We begin with the purpose of the gospel: "Jesus performed many other signs in the presence of His disciples that are not written in this book. But these are written so that you may believe Jesus is the Messiah, the Son of God, and by believing you may have life in His name" (20:30–31). John informs us that he included the signs in his gospel so that the readers of the gospel might believe. This belief has a specific content and profile, for John wants the readers to believe that Jesus is the Messiah and God's Son. Scholars debate whether John refers to initial faith or ongoing faith here, but the issue isn't decisive for our purposes, for in either case faith is necessary for eternal life.

The importance of faith is relayed in another story. In John 6 many disciples were forsaking Jesus, for they were scandalized by what he was saying, especially when he insisted that one must eat his flesh and drink his blood (John 6:52–59). Jesus asked the remaining disciples if they wanted to leave him as well. Peter responded, "We have come to believe and know that You are the Holy One of God" (6:69). Those who belong to Jesus believe that he is God's holy one, God's chosen one. We see the same kind of response from Martha after her brother died. In the midst of a conversation with Jesus, she confesses, "I believe You are the Messiah, the Son of God, who comes into the world" (11:27). Martha's words reflect the purpose of the gospel (20:30–31), which we looked at earlier.

The belief John calls for here is centered on Jesus: one must believe in Jesus (John 16:9) and that God sent him into the world (16:27, 30; 17:8, 21). Given the narrative of the gospel as a whole, this includes belief in

Jesus' death as the Lamb of God (1:29, 36), the conviction that he gave his life for his sheep (10:11, 15), that he gave his life so that his people would not perish (11:50), and that his flesh was given for the world's life (6:51). People must believe in his death—that is, eat his flesh and drink his blood to enjoy eternal life (6:52–58). They must believe that God sent his Son (3:16) in order to enjoy forgiveness of sins (20:23).

Belief is not optional or secondary. Only those who believe will enjoy life in the age to come (20:30). The notion that one must believe is central to the entire narrative. The children of God are limited to those who believe in Jesus' name (1:12), and thus those who don't believe are excluded from God's family. All who believe have eternal life (3:15; 6:40, 47), so that those who believe in the Father who sent the Son already possess the life of the age to come (5:24; cf. 11:25–26). By contrast, those who refuse to believe are condemned (3:18) and stand under God's wrath (3:36). They will die in their sins for refusing to believe in Jesus (8:24).

John not only emphasizes the importance of believing, he also contrasts faith with works, believing with doing. We have the fascinating exchange between Jesus and the crowd in John 6. They asked, "What can we do to perform the works of God" (6:28). They are fixated on what they must do, what they must perform. Surely, they must do some remarkable deeds to find favor with God. But Jesus rejects such notions entirely, saying, "This is the work of God—that you believe in the One He has sent" (6:29). They want to do and perform and work, but what they must do is believe and trust. Believing is a receptive activity; it is compared to coming and to eating and drinking (6:35). One eats and drinks to sustain life, and in the same way those who believe in Jesus do so to live. When we consider the role of good works in a later chapter, the fullness of what John means by believing will be investigated further. Suffice it to say here that believing in John is dynamic and full-orbed. It can't be confined to mental assent to truths. True belief dominates a person's life and changes dramatically how he or she relates to God.

Faith in Acts

In reading the NT it is important to realize that various documents have different purposes. Acts records the spread of the Christian faith in the Roman Empire, and thus its purpose is not to discuss in any detail the matter discussed in this book. Still, we can learn some things from Acts that support the primacy of faith. For instance, early Christians are often designated as "believers" (2:44; 4:32; 5:14; 15:5; 19:18), indicating that trust or belief is characteristic or fundamental to Christian experience. The proper response to the message proclaimed by the apostles was belief or trust in the message and in the Lord. Note the following texts.

"But many of those who heard the message believed" (4:4).[5]

"They believed Philip, as he preached the good news about the kingdom of God and the name of Jesus Christ (8:12).

"Many believed in the Lord" (9:42).

"All the prophets testify about Him that through His name everyone who believes in Him will receive forgiveness of sins" (10:43).

"We believed on the Lord Jesus Christ" (11:17).

"A large number who believed turned to the Lord" (11:21).

"The proconsul...believed" (13:12).

"Everyone who believes in Him is justified" (13:39).

"All who had been appointed to eternal life believed" (13:48).

"A great number of both Jews and Greeks believed" (14:1).

"They committed them to the Lord in whom they had believed" (14:23).

"By my mouth the Gentiles would hear the gospel message and believe" (15:7).

"Believe on the Lord Jesus, and you will be saved—you and your household" (16:31).

"He brought them into his house, set a meal before them, and rejoiced because he had believed God with his entire household" (16:34).

"Many of them believed, including a number of the prominent Greek women as well as men" (17:12).

"Some men joined him and believed, including Dionysius the Areopagite, a woman named Damaris, and others with them" (17:34).

"Crispus, the leader of the synagogue, believed the Lord, along with his whole household. Many of the Corinthians, when they heard, believed and were baptized" (18:8).

"He greatly helped those who had believed through grace" (18:27).

"They should believe in the One who would come after him, that is, in Jesus" (19:4).

---

5.   When I document many Scriptures in a series, even if the citation doesn't begin with a capital letter, a capital is used to begin the citation.

"How many thousands of Jews of there are who have believed" (21:20).

"The Gentiles who have believed" (21:25).

"Those who believed in You" (22:19).

The references above make it abundantly clear that faith, belief, and trust are characteristic of Christians. What it means to be a Christian is to believe in Jesus Christ and the apostolic message. One must believe in Jesus to be: saved (Acts 15:11; 16:31; cf. 14:9); receive forgiveness of sins (10:43); be justified (13:39); cleansed (15:9). At the same time, of course, those who heard the message were summoned to repent (2:38; 3:19; 5:31; 8:22; 11:18; 13:24; 17:30; 20:21; 26:20).[6] Faith and repentance were closely aligned, and genuine faith always includes repentance. For example, Acts 20:21 speaks of "repentance toward God and faith in our Lord Jesus."

Through a quotation of Jesus that Paul repeats, he describes the aim of his ministry as including faith and repentance: "to open their eyes so they may turn from darkness to light and from the power of Satan to God, that by faith in Me they may receive forgiveness of sins and a share among those who are sanctified" (26:18). We should not interpret this to mean that repentance is another thing a person has to do to receive salvation in addition to faith. Rather, genuine faith includes repentance. Faith that doesn't include repentance is false faith, for those who truly believe turn away from evil. Simon the sorcerer serves as the example of a false faith in Acts, for he allegedly believes (8:12) but shows by his subsequent behavior that he has no inheritance among the people of God (8:21). He remains "poisoned by bitterness and bound by iniquity" (8:23), so that he needs to repent (truly believe!) to be right with God (8:22).

Two passages in Acts warrant further comment relative to the theme of faith alone. Paul's proclamation of the gospel in Pisidian Antioch includes near the conclusion these fascinating words: "Therefore, let it be known to you, brothers, that through this man forgiveness of sins is being proclaimed to you, and everyone who believes in Him is justified from everything that you could not be justified from through the law of Moses" (13:38–39). Here we read that forgiveness and justification cannot be obtained through the law of Moses. We aren't given a full explanation as to why this is so, and part of the reason is likely salvation historical—the era of the Sinai covenant had ended. But it is also likely that the argument

---

6. "Turning" toward the Lord is another way of describing repentance (see Acts 3:19; 9:35; 11:21; 14:15; 15:19; 26:18, 20).

is anthropological, especially since Luke was a companion of Paul, and this is a Pauline speech. People don't receive forgiveness and justification through the Mosaic law since they have failed to obey its precepts. Their sin and disobedience exclude them from life. Forgiveness and right standing with God are only given through faith. On this basis, it seems fair to conclude that justification comes by faith alone and not on the basis of human works. Such a reading fits with the parable of the Pharisee and tax collector we looked at earlier in Luke's gospel (Luke 18:9–14). There, too, we saw that the tax collector was justified by faith alone.

Peter's words at the so-called Apostolic Council in Acts 15:7–11 point us in the same direction. Controversy erupted in the early church over whether circumcision and observance of the rest of the Mosaic law was required for salvation (15:1, 5). In the midst of the discussion Peter stood up and reminded the hearers of his previous encounter with Cornelius and his friends (10:1–11:18). Cornelius was uncircumcised, and hence was probably a God-fearer. Since he was uncircumcised, he wasn't considered part of the Jewish people. Still, Cornelius and his friends clearly became Christians when they heard Peter's preaching because God gave them the Holy Spirit, the identifying sign that one has become a Christian (15:8; cf. Rom 8:9; Gal 3:1–5). Peter's point is that Cornelius and his friends did not enter the people of God by virtue of their obedience to Torah.

Indeed, Peter proclaims that the law is a "yoke ... that neither our ancestors nor we have been able to bear" (15:10). The law can't save because human beings can't sustain it (i.e., they are unable to keep it). Instead, human beings "are saved through the grace of the Lord Jesus" (15:11). Salvation isn't obtained through works but through grace. Grace accords with faith, for God "[cleansed] their hearts by faith" (15:9). In this remarkable text, the law and works are opposed to grace and faith. Salvation is through grace alone and by faith alone, and obedience to the law is excluded as the way to salvation. Though there are only a few explicit references, we see that the necessity of faith to enjoy forgiveness of sins is a prominent theme in Acts.

Faith in Paul

In a previous chapter I noted in Paul the contrast between faith and works for salvation and justification, but a few more comments on faith in Paul should prove clarifying. First, I will make some observations on faith and believing in Paul. Second, we will investigate the nature of faith in

Paul. Then, in the next chapter, the meaning of the phrase "faith of Jesus Christ" will be briefly explored.

Statistics alone demonstrate the centrality of faith and trust in Paul: the word "faith" (*pistis*) occurs 142 times, and the verb "believe" (*pisteuō*) 54 times.[7] For Paul, what it means to be a Christian is to believe, for often Paul describes his readers as those who believed[8] or those who have faith.[9] Paul declares that "salvation" is given "to everyone who believes" (Rom 1:16; cf. 1 Cor 1:21; 15:2; Eph 2:8), and to those who believe in the gospel he proclaimed (1 Cor 15:11; Eph 1:13; cf. Rom 10:8). We are not surprised to learn that "faith comes from what is heard" (Rom 10:17), for one can scarcely believe in the gospel without knowing its content (10:14–16). Similarly, Christians put their faith "in the truth" (2 Thess 2:13), and the truth here is almost certainly the truth about Jesus. Faith is directed toward the gospel message, but the gospel centers on Jesus Christ (cf. Rom 1:1–2), particularly his death and resurrection, which secured forgiveness of sins and justification (Rom 4:25; 1 Cor 15:1–4).

Believing in the gospel isn't optional. It is imperative, for those who don't put their trust in Jesus will face eschatological humiliation (Rom 9:33; 10:11). Conversely, believers are the children of Abraham (Gal 3:6; cf. 3:8) and therefore the children of God (3:26). They belong to God's family and are members of the true Israel of God (6:16). Those who place their trust in the gospel receive the Spirit (3:14) and eternal life (1 Tim 1:16; cf. Col 2:12) by faith. The reception of the Spirit signifies that they have received the blessings of the new covenant (Jer 31:31–34; Ezek 36:26–27); the promises of the age to come are now theirs in Jesus Christ (cf. Rom 2:28–29; 2 Cor 3:1–6; Phil 3:3).

For the purposes of our investigation, we want to look specifically at those passages that say that righteousness is granted to those who believe,[10] a theme that Paul reiterates often. As noted earlier, in such contexts righteousness by faith is opposed to righteousness by works. This supports the truth that right standing with God is by faith alone since Paul contrasts "working" with "believing" (Rom 4:5); this demonstrates that justification

---

7. According to a search of NA[28] in Bible Works. Paul also uses the word "faith," especially in the Pastorals, to refer to "the faith," a body of doctrine or teaching that believers confessed (e.g., 1 Tim 3:9, 13; 6:10; 2 Tim 4:7).

8. E.g., Rom 3:22; 4:11; 10:4, 14; 13:11; 1 Cor 3:5; Gal 3:22; Eph 1:19; Phil 1:29; 1 Thess 1:7; 2:10, 13; 2 Thess 1:10; Titus 3:8.

9. Rom 1:8, 12, 17; 1 Cor 2:5; 15:14, 17; 2 Cor 5:7; 8:7; 13:5; Phil 2:17; 1 Thess 3:6; 2 Thess 1:3, 4; 3:2; 1 Tim 1:5, 19; 2 Tim 1:5; Titus 1:1.

10. Rom 1:17; 4:5, 9, 11, 12, 13; 5:1; 9:30, 32; 10:6; Gal 3:8, 11, 24.

is not granted to those who work *for* God but to those who trust *in* God. This righteousness is "credited to us who believe in Him who raised Jesus our Lord from the dead" (4:24), that is, to those who confess Jesus is Lord and believe God raised him from the dead (10:9–10). If righteousness is by faith and human activity and human works are excluded, we can safely conclude that righteousness is by faith alone.

We should, however, note that the faith that saves us is not just any faith. What makes faith salvific is the *object* of faith. Paul emphasizes that Abraham's faith was in God (Rom 4:17), but the God that Abraham trusted is not just any God. He is the God "who gives life to the dead and calls things into existence that do not exist" (4:17). Saving faith is directed to the creator God, the God who made the world and intervenes in it, the God who gives life where there is death.

The faith that saves trusts in God's promises, just as Abraham trusted that his offspring would be as many as the stars of the sky (Gen 15:6; Rom 4:18). Faith must not be confused with wish-fulfillment, nor do we find faith in faith itself. Abraham's hope was circumscribed by God's promise. Still, that promise was astonishing and beyond the capacity of Abraham and Sarah to fulfill themselves since they were well beyond the years where they could have children (Rom 4:19). Faith doesn't turn a blind eye toward human weakness; it faces the facts and acknowledges that humanly speaking, the fulfillment of the promise is impossible. Faith puts its hope in God instead of the human subject (4:18). Indeed, faith glorifies and honors God, for it confesses that God can do what he has promised (4:20–21).

Paul unpacks for us the faith that is counted for righteousness (Rom 4:22). It is a faith that stakes its life on God's promises, a faith that puts its hope in God when everything seems to oppose what he has pledged. This is why Christians are those who believe their sins are forgiven (4:25), even though the evidence and proof of that forgiveness isn't evident to anyone in the world. Nothing in life points to Christians as those who are specially favored by God, for they face suffering and the same kinds of difficulties that strike unbelievers. Still, believers trust that Jesus' death and resurrection secure their forgiveness and justification (4:24–25).

The faith that saves, then, is dynamic and powerful. It is a faith that expresses itself in love, for a living faith produces love, and such love functions as evidence that faith is genuine and vital. We see the same idea when Paul speaks of the "work of faith" (1 Thess 1:3; 2 Thess 1:11), for in the context that phrase clearly means the work that is the result or fruit of faith. Yes, salvation is by faith alone, but such faith is not inert. Faith that is real leads to works—it displays itself in a new kind of life. Hence, Paul speaks of the obedience of faith (Rom 1:5; 16:26), which likely refers to the obedience that comes from faith. At the same time it also indicates that we are called upon to obey the gospel (10:16). Those who truly believe, then, stand in the faith and persevere in the faith (Rom 11:20; 1 Cor 16:13; 2 Cor 1:24), for those who continue as Christians continue to exercise faith and trust (1 Thess 3:5). Hence, Paul prays that Christians would experience by faith Christ dwelling in their hearts (Eph. 3:17). Christ already indwells believers by his Spirit, and yet the beauty and power of his presence must be experienced afresh and anew by believers.

Conclusion

The NT writings aren't systematic documents, but the prominence of faith indicates that it is fundamental to one's relationship with God. In the Synoptics Jesus commends people for their faith and regularly declares that their faith has saved them. The centrality of faith is obvious in John, for the verb "believe" pervades the gospel, and in John's purpose statement he declares that life is obtained by believing that Jesus is the Christ, the Son of God. The apostles in Acts call on people to repent and believe to be saved. Indeed, both the Gospel of John and Acts stress that faith saves, suggesting that faith *alone* saves. We also see that Paul emphasizes the necessity of faith for salvation and justification. What it means to be a Christian is to be a believer, one who trusts in God and in his Son, Jesus Christ. Since righteousness is by faith, works are ruled out as a basis for salvation. Though we have covered much territory in looking at the prominence of faith in the NT, there remains one matter left to consider. There is a particular debate today over the phrase "faith of Jesus Christ" in Paul, and before we wrap up our discussion we will consider this phrase in the next chapter.

CHAPTER 9

Faith in Jesus Christ

> "And we have believed in Christ Jesus so that we might be
> justified by faith in Christ and not by the works of the law."
> —*Galatians 2:16*

There is an intense debate today in scholarly circles over the phrase
pistis Iēsou Christou ("faith of Jesus Christ") in Paul's letters.[1] Those
who read their English Bibles may not be aware of the dispute, since
virtually all English versions render the controversial passages as "faith *in*
Jesus Christ." But the NET Bible, a more recent English translation, provides a clue to the other interpretive option that has been proposed. You
will notice in the table below the translation of this phrase from various
passages of Scripture in both the NET Bible and the Holman Christian
Standard Bible (HCSB).

Versus	NET	HCSB
Rom 3:3	the **faithfulness** of God	God's **faithfulness**
Rom 3:22	the righteousness of God through the **faithfulness** of Jesus Christ for all who believe	God's righteousness through **faith** in Jesus Christ, to all who believe
Rom 3:26	so that he would be just and the justifier of the one who lives because of Jesus' **faithfulness**.	so that He would be righteous and declare righteous the one who has **faith** in Jesus
Gal 2:16a	no one is justified by the works of the law but by the **faithfulness** of Jesus Christ	no one is justified by the works of the law but by **faith** in Jesus Christ

---

1. For a recent book that includes arguments from both sides, see *The Faith of Jesus Christ: Exegetical, Biblical, and Theological Studies* (ed. Michael F. Bird and Preston Sprinkle; Peabody, MA: Hendrickson, 2009).

124

Versus	NET	HCSB
Gal 2:16b	And we have come to believe in Christ Jesus, so that we may be justified by the **faithfulness** of Christ and not by the works of the law	And we have believed in Christ Jesus so that we might be justified by **faith** in Christ and not by the works of the law
Gal 2:20	I live because of the **faithfulness** of the Son of God, who loved me and gave himself for me	I live by **faith** in the Son of God, who loved me and gave Himself for me
Gal 3:22	But the scripture imprisoned everything and everyone under sin so that the promise could be given—because of the **faithfulness** of Jesus Christ	But the Scripture has imprisoned everything under sin's power, so that the promise by **faith** in Jesus Christ might be given to those who believe
Eph 3:12	in whom we have boldness and confident access to God because of Christ's **faithfulness**.	In Him we have boldness and confident access through **faith** in Him
Phil 3:9	not because I have my own righteousness derived from the law, but because I have the righteousness that comes by way of Christ's **faithfulness**–a righteousness from God that is in fact based on Christ's **faithfulness**	not having a righteousness of my own from the law, but one that is through **faith** in Christ—the righteousness from God based on **faith**.

There are other texts besides these listed that are contested, but the examples I provide in the table should help English readers see what is at stake. Let me make two introductory comments. First, we have already seen in chapter 8 that righteousness is by faith in a number of texts. Hence, the truth of righteousness by faith stands, even if the alternative rendering "faithfulness of Jesus Christ" is preferred. The question before us is one of emphasis since elsewhere in Scripture we see that faith in Christ is necessary for justification. Second, I must warn you that the discussion has become quite technical and drawn out. For the purposes of this book, I can only sketch in briefly the main issues. Why does it matter? The issue is whether Scripture and Paul in particular put a particular emphasis on faith in Christ. Yes, faith is still called for even if these verses are translated as the "faithfulness of Jesus Christ." But the emphasis on faith in Jesus Christ is diminished if the alternative rendering is accepted. I will argue here that

Paul speaks of *faith in Jesus Christ*, and this is important because we are saved not by what we do but by putting our trust in Jesus himself.

Faith in Christ in Other Texts

Before launching into the debate itself, let's note a number of texts where Paul emphasizes faith in Christ where the grammatical construction is not under dispute.

Eph 1:15	"I heard about your faith in the Lord Jesus"
Col 1:4	"we have heard of your faith in Christ Jesus"
Col 2:5	"the strength of your faith in Christ"
2 Tim 3:15	"the sacred Scriptures, which are able to give you wisdom for salvation through faith in Christ Jesus"
Phlm 5	"I hear of your love and faith toward the Lord Jesus"

I mentioned earlier that there are a number of verses that teach that righteousness comes by faith regardless of what one does with the disputed "faith of Jesus Christ" constructions. The verses just listed, however, are distinct in that they mention faith in Christ, even though righteousness by faith isn't included. In other words, we have another piece of evidence that faith in Jesus Christ is a significant element in Paul's thought.

Support for Faithfulness of Christ

Having said all the above, I will now argue that the traditional reading "faith *in* Jesus Christ" is the most persuasive interpretation of the phrase. In order to make the case, some of the reasons presented for the alternative reading, "faithfulness of Jesus Christ," must also be presented.[2] First, we need to recognize that the construction is in the genitive "faith of Christ" (*pistis Christou*),[3] so that both "faithfulness of Christ" and "faith in Christ" are grammatically feasible.[4] A number of arguments are often presented in support of the rendering "faithfulness of Christ."

---

2.   E.g., Luke T. Johnson, "Rom 3:21–26 and the Faith of Jesus," *CBQ* 44 (1982): 77–90; Sam K. Williams, "Again *Pistis Christou*," *JBL* 49 (1987): 431–47; Richard B. Hays, *The Faith of Jesus Christ: An Investigation of the Narrative Substructure of Galatians 3:1–4:11* (2nd ed.; Grand Rapids: Eerdmans, 2002), 139–91; Ian G. Wallis, *The Faith of Jesus Christ in Early Christian Traditions* (SNTSMS 84; Cambridge: Cambridge University Press, 1995).

3.   The genitive after "faith" (*pistis*) varies from "Jesus Christ" (*Iēsou Christou*—Rom. 3:22; Gal. 2:16; 3:22), "Christ" (*Christou*—Gal 2:16; Phil. 3:9), to "Jesus" (*Iēsou*—Rom. 3:26).

4.   But see the recent analysis of Stanley E. Porter and Andrew W. Pitts. They argue that semantically and grammatically the objective genitive should be preferred. "*Pistis* with a Preposition and Genitive Modifier: Lexical, Semantic and Syntactic Considerations in the *pistis Christou* Discussion," in *The Faith of Jesus Christ* (ed. Bird and Sprinkle), 33–53.

1. In Rom 3:3 "the faith of God" (*tēn pistin tou theou*) clearly means "the faithfulness of God," as both the NET and HCSB demonstrate in the table above, and thus it is natural to translate the phrase in question in the other texts as "the faithfulness of Christ."

2. In Rom 4:12 the phrase refers to "the faith of our father, Abraham" (*pisteōs tou patros hēmōn Abraam*), and so the phrase in other instances should be rendered as "the faithfulness of Jesus."

3. A number of scholars have argued on the basis of grammar that the genitive is most naturally translated as subjective, so that the faith in view relates to the person named, whether Paul speaks of the faithfulness of Abraham, the faithfulness of God, or the faithfulness of Jesus Christ. For a subjective genitive the faith is produced by the person named with the genitive noun. In other words, the argument is that the Greek is most naturally translated *the faithfulness of Christ*, not *faith in Christ*.

4. It is superfluous for Paul to speak of "faith in Christ" in a number of key texts (e.g., Rom 3:22; Gal 2:16; Phil 3:9), for the importance of faith in Christ is already conveyed in a *verbal* clause in the immediate context. We see in these texts, where Paul compactly sets forth his theology, that righteousness is ours because of the faithfulness of Jesus *and* the need for personal faith. Let's take a closer look at one example. The NET Bible translates Gal 2:16 as follows, "And we have come to believe in Christ Jesus, so that we may be justified by the faithfulness of Christ and not by the works of the law." Notice that the verb "believe" is followed by the clause "in Christ Jesus." Thus, we already have the idea that we believe in Jesus in the clause with the verb *believe,* and so (it is argued) it would be redundant to speak of believing in Jesus again in the noun clause ("the faithfulness of Jesus Christ"). Paul has already said with the verb *believe* that we trust in Jesus, and he makes a distinct and new point in referring to the faithfulness of Christ.

5. The "faithfulness of Jesus" fits with and is another way of speaking of Jesus' obedience that achieved salvation (Rom 5:19; Phil 2:8). Our righteousness and salvation do not depend on what we do, even on our faith, but on the faithful obedience of Jesus Christ.

6. The coming of "faith" in Gal 3:23–25 cannot refer to personal faith, for Abraham already believed in the OT (Gen 15:6). Faith is described here as an objective reality, as a redemptive-historical entity,

and this fits far better with the faithfulness of Jesus Christ rather than faith in Christ.

7. Such a reading accords with Paul's theology, for Paul emphasizes God's work in Jesus Christ, not the human response. Salvation is God's work accomplished by the faithfulness of Jesus Christ and cannot be ascribed to the human response of faith. If salvation is due to the faithfulness of Jesus Christ, God gets all the glory for our salvation, for salvation depends on his faithfulness, not on weak human faith.

Faith *in* Christ Is More Persuasive

Despite these good arguments supporting *faithfulness of Christ*, there are convincing reasons to prefer an objective genitive (where the genitive is the object of the action of the first noun), so that Paul refers to "faith *in* Christ."[5]

1. The genitive object with "faith" is clear in some instances (Mark 11:22; Jas 2:1).[6] Thus we should not be surprised if we would find such a construction here. So, in Mark 11:22 Jesus exhorts his hearers, "Have faith in God." Jesus isn't talking about the faithfulness of God here but the importance of putting one's faith and trust *in God*.

2. We saw above that Paul uses other prepositions and constructions to denote faith in Christ, but we must recognize that Paul denotes faith in Christ with a variety of expressions, and we must not straitjacket his usage. This is another way of saying that Paul describes the importance of faith in Christ in a variety of ways.

3. A genitive object with other verbal nouns shows that an objective genitive (where the genitive receives the action of the previous verb)

5.   See, e.g., James D. G. Dunn, "Once More *Pistis Christou*," in SBLSP 1991 (ed. E. H. Lovering Jr.; Atlanta: Scholars, 1991), 730–44; Moisés Silva, "Faith Versus Works of Law in Galatians," in *Justification and Variegated Nomism: Volume 2–The Paradoxes of Paul* (ed. D. A. Carson, Peter O'Brien, and Mark A. Seifrid; Grand Rapids: Baker, 2004), 217–48; Debbie Hunn, "*PISTIS CHRISTOU* in Galatians 2:16," *TynBul* 57 (2006): 23–33; Barry Matlock, "Detheologizing the *PISTIS CHRISTOU* Debate: Cautionary Remarks from a Lexical Semantic Perspective," *NovT* 62 (2000): 1–23; idem, "'Even the Demons Believe': Paul and *pistis Christou*," *CBQ* 64 (2002): 300–18; idem, "*PISTIS* in Galatians 3:26: Neglected Evidence for 'Faith in Christ'?" *NTS* 49 (2003): 433–39; idem, "Saving Faith: The Rhetoric and Semantics of *pistis* in Paul," in *The Faith of Jesus Christ* (ed. Bird and Sprinkle), 73–89.

6.   For this reading of Mark 11:22, see R. T. France, *The Gospel of Mark* (NIGTC; Grand Rapids: Eerdmans, 2002), 448. On James 2:1, see Douglas J. Moo, *The Letter of James* (Pillar; Grand Rapids: Eerdmans, 2000), 100–101.

with the verbal noun is common grammatically: e.g., "knowing Christ Jesus" (*tēs gnōseōs Christou Iēsou*, Phil 3:8).[7] If Jesus is the object of knowledge, as he certainly is here, he could also be the object of faith in other passages. Hence, it follows that those who insist that the genitive *must* be subjective are incorrect. It makes perfect sense grammatically to speak of *faith in Christ* and accords with what Paul does with other nouns to use Christ as the object of the noun faith

4. We saw above that those who support the subjective genitive think that the objective genitive reading is superfluous and redundant in texts where we have the verb *believe* already. Why include faith *in* Christ after already mentioning believing in Christ? Such an argument could be right, but it isn't obviously correct. After all, Paul could use both the verbal and the noun construction *to emphasize* faith in Christ, and I believe that is exactly what he wants to do.[8] Faith in Christ is massively important, and thus Paul highlights it. The least complex interpretation should be favored, and such a reading supports an objective genitive. Paul hits the reader again and again with the truth that righteousness comes by faith. Furthermore, it actually isn't the case, even when a verbal idea is included, that the two phrases are exactly synonymous. There is an overlapping synonymy, but there are also distinctions. In several passages Paul says righteousness is given to those who believe and to those who have faith in Christ (Rom 3:22; Gal 2:16; 3:22). Note that the two ideas are not precisely the same: one speaks of believing in general, but the other specifies faith in Christ. We see the same phenomenon with the two nouns in Phil 3:9 — one speaks of faith in general but the other specifies faith in Christ. So, the two notions are closely connected (they both refer to faith or belief), but only one of them specifies faith in Christ.

5. Another significant problem with the subjective genitive is the train of thought in Paul's letters. It is difficult to believe that Paul refers to "faithfulness" in Gal 3:2, 5, when the next verse (3:6) uses the

---

7. Harrisville shows from a number of Greco-Roman writers that an objective genitive with "faith" (*pistis*) was common in classical Greek authors. Roy A. Harrisville III, "Before *PISTIS CHRISTOU*: The Objective Genitive as Good Greek," *NovT* 41 (2006): 353–58.

8. Matlock argues that rhetorical features in the text support an objective genitive as well. R. Barry Matlock, "The Rhetoric of *pistis* in Paul: Galatians 2.16, 3.22, and Philippians 3.9," *JSNT* 30 (2007): 173–203. For instance, one of the striking features of the verse is that it is characterized by redundancy regardless of one's view of "faith of Christ" here (193).

verb "believed."[9] We see the same kind of thing in Romans 3 as
well. If *pistis* means "faithfulness" in 3:22 and 3:26, it is difficult to
understand the transition to our faith, to our believing, in 3:27–31.
Indeed, some of those who support the subjective genitive revert to
the faith of human beings in 3:27–31. But on what grounds? If the
referent is to Jesus' faithfulness in 3:22 and 3:26, then it is natural
to see the same in 3:27–31. Some scholars, however, argue for this
very thing, seeing a reference to Jesus' faithfulness throughout. But
this approach runs into a significant problem in chapter 4, and all
agree that chapter 4 is closely related in content to 3:27–31. For Paul
clearly ascribes Abraham's justification to his "believing" (*pisteuō*,
4:4–5), and *hē pistis autou* clearly should be translated "his faith"
(4:5), for it follows hard on the heels of the verb "believing." In case
readers have gotten lost following all this, here is the point: if Paul
clearly refers to Abraham's faith in Romans 4 and if Romans 4 is
closely related to Romans 3, the similar construction in Romans 3
should be interpreted similarly. Throughout the entire argument Paul
describes the faith of human beings.

6. Paul often contrasts works and human faith in his theology. In
   other words, the contrast is between two human activities: doing
   or believing. Such a judgment is verified by other Pauline texts. For
   instance, in Rom 9:30–33 Paul contrasts righteousness by works with
   righteousness by faith. Israel didn't obtain righteousness by works. It
   is clear in the context that Israel stumbled because they failed to put
   their faith in Jesus (9:33). Indeed, the subsequent context clarifies
   that Israel's righteousness by faith (10:6, 17) is obtained by believing
   in Jesus Christ (10:4, 8–11, 14, 16). Certainly this fits with what
   Paul says in Eph 2:8, for salvation by faith is contrasted with salvation
   by works. There is nothing in the context of Ephesians 2 to suggest
   that faith here denotes the faithfulness of Jesus Christ. Some might
   object that the evidence here is superfluous since the genitive "Jesus
   Christ" is lacking. I am not claiming that this argument alone estab-
   lishes the case, for the argument is cumulative. But the point still
   stands: when Paul uses *pistis* elsewhere and contrasts it with works,
   he speaks of human faith. This lends credence to the notion that

---

9. See Silva who makes this point, observing that "one would need extraordinarily persuasive evidence to the contrary" ("Faith Versus Works," 235).

when he contrasts works and faith with the genitive "Jesus Christ," he means "faith in Jesus Christ."

7. We saw above that Paul often contrasts human works with faith, which inclines me to think that the contrast between works and faith refers to faith in Jesus Christ. What strengthens this argument even further is the fact that Paul nowhere uses the word "faith" (*pistis*) or "faithful" (*pistos*) to describe Jesus Christ's obedience (outside of the disputed passages). This observation is remarkable since he clearly refers to Christ's obedience (Rom 5:19; Phil 2:8), but we have no clear or undisputed texts where Paul identifies Jesus as faithful in terms of his faithful obedience to God.

8. The redemptive-historical argument isn't as persuasive as it seems to be at first glance. Clearly, Gal 3:23, 25 describes the coming of faith at a certain time in redemptive history. At first glance this seems to support the objective genitive, for obviously people (like Abraham!) believed before the arrival of the Messiah. But the redemptive-historical argument doesn't rule out faith in Christ. In fact, it fits well with such a notion. For Paul teaches that faith in Jesus Christ became a possibility at the time he entered history — after his ministry, death, and resurrection. Here we have an example where redemptive history and human response coalesce. The new age, the fulfillment of God's promise, has come in Jesus Christ, and because of this, those who belong to God put their faith in him.

9. Some have said that the emphasis on faith in Christ is Pelagian and smacks of works-righteousness. Such accusations fall under the umbrella of a kind of hyper-Calvinism. Certainly, salvation is the work of the Lord, but the Lord's saving work doesn't circumvent or preclude human response. Instead, it secures the response of the human being. Ephesians 2:8–9 declares that faith too is a gift of God. But the gift of faith does not preclude the summons to repent and believe. The indicative of what God gives us in Jesus Christ should never be played off against the imperative of what he demands from us, as if the former rules out the necessity of the latter.

Conclusion

Why is this debate over faith in Jesus Christ important? After all, we saw that other texts already indicate that faith is necessary, even faith in Christ, for right standing with God. Still, the dispute is important because it reveals the emphasis in Paul's thinking. In other words, if these texts say that one must believe in Jesus Christ for righteousness, such a theme is incredibly pervasive and forceful in Paul's letters. He reminds his readers again and again that they must put their faith in Jesus Christ to stand in the right before God, to be saved on the last day. Such a notion fits with the idea that we are saved by faith alone and not by our accomplishments.[10]

---

10. A few scholars have taken the genitive as a genitive of source (faith that comes from Jesus Christ). See, e.g., M. A. Seifrid, *Christ, Our Righteousness: Paul's Theology of Justification* (NSBT 9; Downers Grove, IL: InterVarsity Press, 2000), 139–46; idem, "The Faith of Christ," in *The Faith of Jesus Christ* (ed. Bird and Sprinkle), 129–46. Such a reading is attractive, but it is doubtful in this context that Paul calls attention to the gift God grants. Indeed, even though Paul thinks faith is a gift of God (Eph 2:8–9), this is not a theme he includes often. Another possibility is that we have both a subjective and objective genitive here. Such a complex reading is unlikely. We have seen in some of the texts that Paul speaks of both *believing* and *faith in Jesus Christ*. So, we have a clue, even if one thinks Paul refers to the faithfulness of Jesus Christ, that believing is also important. But when it comes to Jesus' faithfulness or obedience, we don't find such a clue in the context in which the expression occurs. In other words, Paul doesn't indicate anywhere in the context that Jesus' faithfulness or obedience are integral to the theme at hand. So, we have no contextual evidence for a both-and notion. This judgment is strengthened when we realize that nowhere else in Paul does he speak of Jesus' obedience in terms of his faithfulness.

CHAPTER 10

The Importance of Justification in Paul

> "God made him who had no sin to be sin for us, so that
> in him we might become the righteousness of God."
> —*2 Corinthians 5:21 (NIV)*

Justification has been at the center of biblical and theological discussion since the time of the Reformation. Scholars have questioned whether it deserves the prominence it has been given. Has justification been unduly emphasized because of the Reformation? How should we assess its importance in Paul's theology in particular? A number of scholars have argued that justification has been wrongly elevated, while others continue to see it as vital. I will briefly survey the matter and argue for the latter.

Reasons for Questioning Its Importance

Scholars have long been interested in and have disputed the significance and meaning of the term justification in Paul. Albert Schweitzer famously declared that righteousness "is a subsidiary crater within the main crater of being in Christ."[1] Schweitzer didn't think justification should be central in Pauline thought since it didn't integrate well with ethics and life in the Spirit, so he set forward the mystical doctrine of dying and rising with Christ as vital.

The focus on participation rather than justification in Paul's thought is evident in the work of Michael Gorman.[2] Or, we can think of James Dunn,

---

1. Albert Schweitzer, *The Mysticism of Paul the Apostle* (New York: Holt, 1931), 225.

2. For a contemporary advocate of the notion that participation is central and that justification includes the notion of *theosis*, see Michael J. Gorman, *Inhabiting the Cruciform God: Kenosis, Justification, and Theosis in Paul's Narrative Soteriology* (Grand Rapids: Eerdmans, 2009), 40–104. Supporting the notion that justification includes the notion of deification, see Veli-Matti Kärkkäinen, *One with God: Salvation as Justification and Deification* (Collegeville, MN: Liturgical, 2004); idem, "Deification View," in *Justification: Five Views* (ed. James K. Beilby and Paul Rhodes Eddy; Downers Grove, IL: InterVarsity Press, 2011), 219–43.

who argues that Luther's understanding of justification by faith represents a significant deviation from Paul's understanding of justification.[3] Another critic of what he calls justification theory is Douglas Campbell.[4]

The notion that righteousness is not central in Pauline thought has attracted many adherents. Scholars from the beginning to the end of the twentieth century, such as William Wrede,[5] Krister Stendahl,[6] and Georg Strecker,[7] have insisted that righteousness wasn't important in Paul's theology. The term appears in polemical letters like Romans and Galatians, where he resists opponents. Wrede even argued that Paul's theology could be explicated without mentioning the doctrine. Stendahl says that Paul's primary concern was the inclusion of the Gentiles, not justification, so that justification becomes a means to an end—the folding of Gentiles into the church.

While N. T. Wright and Dunn do not demote justification to the same extent as Stendahl, they argue that justification is fundamentally ecclesiological instead of soteriological.[8] N. T. Wright, in particular, emphasizes ecclesiology: "Justification is not how someone *becomes* a Christian. It is the declaration that they *have become* a Christian."[9] Justification has to do with who belongs to God's people and not how one gets saved. Strecker points out that justification isn't even mentioned in what he thinks is Paul's first letter (1 Thessalonians). E. P. Sanders and W. D. Davies think justification is one metaphor among several others designating salvation and is subservient to participation in Christ.[10]

---

3. See James D. G. Dunn, "The Justice of God: A Renewed Perspective on Justification by Faith," *JTS* 43 (1992): 1–22. But see the moderation of his position in Dunn, *The New Perspective on Paul*, 1–97.

4. Douglas A. Campbell. *The Deliverance of God: An Apocalyptic Rereading of Justification in Paul* (Grand Rapids: Eerdmans, 2009).

5. William Wrede, *Paul* (Lexington, KY: American Theological Library Association, 1962), 122–23.

6. Krister Stendahl, *Paul among Jews and Gentiles and Other Essays* (Philadelphia: Fortress, 1977), 1–23.

7. Georg Strecker, *Theology of the New Testament* (trans. M. E. Boring; Louisville: Westminster John Knox 2000), 148–49.

8. Dunn, "The Justice of God," 8–9.

9. N. T. Wright, *What Saint Paul Really Said: Was Paul of Tarsus the Real Founder of Christianity?* (Grand Rapids: Eerdmans, 1997), 125. "What Paul means by justification, in this context, should therefore be clear. It is not 'how you become a Christian,' as much as 'how you can tell who is a member of the covenant family'" (ibid.). Cf. also idem, *Justification: God's Plan and Paul's Vision* (Downers Grove, IL: InterVarsity Press, 2009), 116, 131–32. Wright says that we ought not to detach ecclesiology from soteriology (ibid., 132–33), but he continues to define justification fundamentally in terms of ecclesiology, not soteriology (ibid., 132–34). In actuality, he enforces a division between soteriology and ecclesiology, despite his protestation here.

10. E. P. Sanders, *Paul and Palestinian Judaism: A Comparison of Patterns of Religion*

My purpose here is not to defend the notion that justification is the center of Paul's theology. Scholars like Eberhard Jüngel, Oswald Bayer, and Mark Mattes think it takes pride of place among Christian doctrines and rules and judges all other doctrines.[11] Instead of contending for justification as the central doctrine of Paul's theology, it is sufficient to say that it plays a *crucial* role in his theology. Michael Allen rightly critiques those who give justification hermeneutical sovereignty over all other doctrines; he defends a more credible position, namely, that justification is crucial since it interlocks with so many important Christian doctrines, such as salvation (which includes sin, death, covenant, Christ's death and resurrection, both God's holiness and ours), grace, sacrifice, and the glory of God.[12]

In particular, the theme of grace and the glory of God call for special comment here. As Michael Allen points out, justification heralds the freeing grace of God, the truth that he loves and forgives us, even though as sinners we deserve judgment. The stunning grace of God also highlights the glory of God. The God who grants us his grace in justification receives all the glory for our salvation, for justification is his work. God is glorified, for in justification we see both his holiness and his love, both his justice and his mercy. As Ps 85:10 says, "righteousness and peace kiss each other" (ESV).

Defense of Its Importance

Even though I am not arguing that justification is the center of Paul's theology, it is necessary to give several brief responses to critics and scholars who have assigned it a diminished role in Paul's thought. J. Gresham Machen once wrote that Paul doesn't merely proclaim justification by faith so that Gentiles might be included in the circle of God's people. Rather, he proclaims justification by faith because it is the truth.[13] Against those who

---

(Philadelphia: Fortress, 1977), 502–8; W. D. Davies, *Paul and Rabbinic Judaism: Some Rabbinic Elements in Pauline Theology* (4th ed.; Philadelphia: Fortress, 1980), xxvii, 221–23.

11. Eberhard Jüngel, *Justification: The Heart of the Christian Faith: A Theological Study with an Ecumenical Purpose* (trans. Jeffrey F. Cayzer; Edinburgh: T&T Clark, 2001), see e.g., 47–48; Oswald Bayer, "Justification as the Basis and Boundary of Theology," in *Justification Is for Preaching: Essays by Oswald Bayer, Gerhard O. Forde, and Others* (ed. Virgil Thompson; Eugene, OR: Pickwick, 2012), 31–50; Mark C. Mattes, *The Role of Justification in Contemporary Theology* (Lutheran Quarterly Books; Grand Rapids: Eerdmans, 2004). Mattes reviews the justification theology of Eberhard Jüngel, Wolfhart Pannenberg, Jürgen Moltmann, Robert Jenson, and Oswald Bayer. He critiques the others and endorses Bayer's construal. Cf. also Oswald Bayer, *Theology the Lutheran Way* (ed. and trans. Jeffrey G. Silcock and Mark. C. Mattes; Grand Rapids: Eerdmans, 2007).

12. Allen, *Justification and the Gospel*, 3–19.

13. J. Gresham Machen, *The Origin of Paul's Religion* (Grand Rapids: Eerdmans, 1925), 278–79.

would argue that justification in Paul is merely a means to an end, I would suggest that we should grant Paul some respect as a thinker and conclude that he took his own ideas seriously. Paul was not merely a pragmatist.

In addition, it isn't convincing to dismiss the theme because it appears in polemical contexts. In many respects all of Paul's letters are polemical, for he defends the gospel often against opponents or false understandings. If we were to restrict Paul's theology to texts that were nonpolemical, we wouldn't have much left! Furthermore, Paul's ardent defense of justification in polemical contexts reveals that he thinks it is vital. If we become passionate about something in an argument, it is typically because we think the matter is important. Certainly, Paul applied his theology to various situations, and his theology developed and matured over the years. Nevertheless, his letters didn't begin to be written until he had been a missionary fifteen or twenty years, and by then his thought had matured through regular preaching and debate with opponents.

In the case of Romans, it is particularly unpersuasive to dismiss one of its major themes as merely polemical. Saying that Romans was written to address a particular situation is probably correct, and yet at the same time it should also be acknowledged that Paul carefully articulates his theology in the letter. Though Romans is not the whole of Paul's theology, at the same time it is a fuller presentation of his theology than any other letter. The theme of justification in Romans cannot simply be dismissed as polemical.

N. T. Wright avers that justification has ecclesiological implications and is not equivalent to salvation, and this is certainly true. Still, justification is fundamentally a matter of soteriology and by implication ecclesiology.[14] I will argue that the term means that one stands in the right before God, so that the very meaning of the word is soteriological, speaking to whether one is condemned or acquitted before God. Yes, there are ecclesiological ramifications to being right with God, but the main idea is soteriological. We will also see in defense of the soteriological character of justification that it is closely aligned with salvation and the forgiveness of sins. Saying this does not lead to the conclusion that justification should be *defined* as salvation or forgiveness, for both of these words have their own definitions. But simply saying that the words have distinct meanings doesn't rule out overlap among the terms. Reconciliation and redemption, for instance,

---

14. Rightly, Stephen Westerholm, *Justification Reconsidered: Rethinking a Pauline Theme* (Grand Rapids: Eerdmans, 2013), 1–22; Paul A. Rainbow, *The Way of Salvation: The Role of Christian Obedience in Justification* (Waynesboro, GA: Paternoster, 2005), 104, n. 22.

don't mean the same thing as justification, but both of these terms have soteriological significance as well.

I would also counter that those who claim that justification is peripheral to Paul's thought overstate their case. The term appears in nonpolemical contexts and in confessional-type statements, signifying its importance.[15] For instance, in 1 Cor 1:30 Paul declares that Christ is "our righteousness, sanctification, and redemption." Paul emphasizes that Christ is our righteousness to counteract boasting and pride (1:29, 31) and to give God the credit for our calling as believers (1:26). If Paul brings in justification as an antidote to pride, it then relates to ethics, for the fundamental sin, the root sin of the human race, is pride. All other sins, according to Paul, are rooted in the rejection of God's lordship in our lives, in the de-godding of God (cf. Rom 1:18–25).

We should also consider several features of 1 Cor 6:11. "But you were washed, you were sanctified, you were justified in the name of the Lord Jesus Christ and by the Spirit of our God." First, notice how all three of the terms here—washed, sanctified, and justified—have a soteriological character. The Corinthians are new in Christ, for they are in the realm of the holy (sanctified); they are right before God (justified), and they are baptized (washed clean). There is no evidence here that Paul brings up justification for polemical reasons. He *naturally* turns to it as one way, and a very important way, of expressing salvation in Jesus Christ. Apparently Paul doesn't agree with those who think that justification is severed from ethics, for in context he says that those who are justified will no longer live as they did before (6:9–10).

Another text with confessional character in 1 Corinthians is 1 Cor 15:1–4. Paul summarizes the gospel he proclaims in these verses, and though he doesn't mention justification, his words bear a close relationship to justification. Believing the gospel is what saves the Corinthians, a statement comparable to saying that justification is by faith. The gospel heralded by Paul is that "Christ died for our sins" (15:3). By this he almost certainly means that Christ died so that our sins would be forgiven. Paul goes on to speak of Christ's burial and resurrection, and it is the latter theme that is emphasized in the subsequent verses. It seems fair to say that the death and resurrection of Jesus Christ were the basis for forgiveness of sins. We find a similar statement regarding justification in Rom 4:25, where we are told that Jesus "was delivered up for our trespasses and raised

---

15. For the importance of justification in Paul's letters generally, see Seifrid, *Christ, Our Righteousness*, 77–93.

for our justification." In 1 Corinthians 15 the death and resurrection of Christ are necessary for the forgiveness of sins, while in Rom 4:25 they are necessary for our justification.

Another important text is 2 Cor 5:21, a text that will be investigated in more detail later. In a context where Paul refers to being a new creation and being reconciled (5:17–20), he brings in the notion of justification. "God made him who had no sin to be sin for us, so that in him we might become the righteousness of God" (5:21, NIV). Again, there is nothing in the context that demands a reference to justification, but Paul turns to it quite naturally in the course of his exposition.

Nor is this the only reference to justification in 2 Corinthians. In a fascinating passage Paul contrasts the Spirit and the letter and the superiority of his ministry to Moses (2 Cor 3:6–18). In the midst of this discussion he contrasts his ministry to that of Moses, describing it as "the ministry of righteousness" over against "the ministry of condemnation" (3:9). Here we have two of the more overtly theological texts from this letter, and in both cases justification surfaces. This suggests that it is more important in Paul's thought than dissenters have claimed.

Paul's letter to Titus is composed mainly of practical advice, but Paul grounds his advice in the grace of God (Titus 2:11–14). In 3:7 he writes, "so that having been justified by His grace, we may become heirs with the hope of eternal life." The soteriological nature of what is described here is striking, for those who are justified are "saved," washed, and renewed (3:5). In no uncertain terms we are told that salvation doesn't come by the righteous works we have done. Believers have the sure hope of "eternal life." The emphasis here is not on ecclesiology but our final salvation on the last day. When Paul turns to what God has done for believers in Jesus Christ, he quite naturally includes justification.

Insights from Parallel Passages

New Testament scholars today recognize the limitations of a word study approach, yet there are still things we can learn from careful study of the words and their associated terms. Conceptually, justification is closely related to and overlaps with forgiveness and salvation, as well as other terms like redemption and reconciliation. To be clear, this is not to say these terms are identical or that they all denote the same thing. Yet they do reveal that soteriology was crucial to Paul's thought, and not just in his polemical letters.

If this point is conceded, we find something like justification in what many think is Paul's earliest letter. In 1 Thess 1:9 something close to a "definition" of conversion is given. The Thessalonians "turned to God from idols to serve the living and true God." In v. 10 we read about "Jesus, who rescues us from the coming wrath." In other words, those who have been converted will be delivered from God's wrath on the final day, which is not far from saying that those who are converted will be declared by God to be in the right on the day of judgment.

First Thessalonians 5:9 is similar. "For God did not appoint us to wrath, but to obtain salvation through our Lord Jesus Christ." Paul doesn't use the word justification here, but the notion is similar. Those who belong to Jesus Christ will enjoy eschatological salvation instead of facing the wrath of God. Most recognize that Paul's letters were shaped by the circumstances and situation of his readers, and yet the soteriological safety of his readers and escape from God's eschatological wrath play a major role in two verses of a confessional nature in this early letter.

Though typically 2 Thessalonians isn't mentioned in discussions of justification, and Paul doesn't address the matter directly in this letter,[16] it is striking to note how many words he uses from the righteousness word group (words with the Greek root *dik-*): "God's righteous [*dikaias*] judgment" (1:5); "it is righteous [*dikaion*] for God to repay" (1:6); "taking vengeance [*ekdikēsin*] ... on those who don't know God" (1:8); "These will pay the penalty [*dikēn*] of eternal destruction" (1:9). In 2:10 Paul refers to those who "perish" and will not be "saved" because they refuse the truth, and thus they will be "condemned" (2:12). Again, even though Paul doesn't explicitly refer to justification, he uses *dik-* words in this letter to denote its opposite: condemnation. By implication, his readers are those who will not be judged and condemned on the last day. Note too that Paul says in 2:13 that the Thessalonians will experience "salvation." The notion of justification is not only present in direct statements, it is implied by the antonyms used with reference to unbelievers.

Even though Paul doesn't often speak of forgiveness of sins, the concept of forgiveness is also closely aligned with justification. This is apparent in Rom 4:6–8. "David also speaks of the blessing of the man God credits righteousness to apart from works: How joyful are those whose lawless

---

16. Many scholars claim that 2 Thessalonians is pseudonymous. I don't find such a view convincing. For a review of the arguments and a defense of Pauline authorship, see Donald A. Hagner, *The New Testament: A Historical and Theological Introduction* (Grand Rapids: Baker, 2012), 464–66.

acts are forgiven and whose sins are covered! How joyful is the man the Lord will never charge with sin!" David is here credited with righteousness (v. 6), and this is explained in vv. 7–8 in terms of forgiveness of sins. Paul glides easily from justification to forgiveness of sins. Again, I am not saying that forgiveness and justification mean exactly the same thing, but they overlap significantly.

I would finally note that there is no need to play justification off against participation. As Michael Allen has rightly argued, justification is the ground of our fellowship with God and participation with God is its goal.[17] Another way to put this is to say that justification is the ground of sanctification.[18] This is certainly Paul's argument in Romans 6. Those who are justified have also died with Christ. The verdict of being right with God is an effective one, and thus the forensic is the basis of the transformative.

Conclusion

Over the last century scholars have regularly questioned how vital justification is in Paul's thought. This questioning has continued in recent years with the New Perspective on Paul. In this chapter, I am making a modest argument that justification should not be pushed to the periphery in Paul's thought. It is not difficult to see that it is closely tied to the gospel he proclaims and that it plays a crucial role in Romans, where Paul develops his gospel most fully. Furthermore, we cannot limit our understanding of justification to the word itself. NT scholars now recognize that a concept should not be limited to a particular word, and the truth of justification is also expressed in texts where Paul speaks of deliverance from God's wrath on the final day, in his celebration of the forgiveness of sins, and in texts where he exposits his gospel.

Douglas Campbell's Deliverance of God

Doug Campbell has recently written a long book in which he attacks what he calls justification theory.[19] The God of justification theory punishes retributively and sacrifices his Son for our salvation, but the God Paul preaches, says Campbell, is benevolent and loving. The contractual God of justification theory contrasts strongly with the unconditional love of the God who liberates sinners by his grace. Justification theory is ominous in Campbell's eyes

17. Allen, *Justification and the Gospel*, 33–70.
18. Ibid., 127–51.
19. Campbell, *Deliverance of God*.

since it could lead to atheism, may offer support for the Holocaust, endorses a rejection of and punishment of homosexuals, and supports Constantianism and perhaps even Christian Fascism!

The bulk of the book is devoted to a detailed exposition of Romans 1–4 since, according to Campbell, these chapters are the "textual citadel" for justification theory. Campbell argues that traditional readings of this text are inadequate. Fundamental for his project is his reading of Rom 1:18–32. He contends that these verses do not represent Paul's own view. Rather, they represent the view of those who opposed Paul. Campbell typically uses the singular "Teacher" to characterize the perspective of Paul's opponents. The view of the Teacher, which must not be equated with Judaism but Paul's Jewish Christian adversaries, is sprinkled throughout Romans 1–4. Hence, readers must carefully observe textual clues to discern where Paul articulates his own view and where he presents and rebuts the view of the Teacher. The notion that God punishes retributively is identified as the theology of the Teacher. Paul, on the contrary, maintains that God is benevolent, forgiving, and loving.

What does Paul mean when he uses the word justification? Campbell argues that the term is not merely forensic but also denotes God's liberation of sinners. Justification theory cannot, says Campbell, explain the connection between forgiveness of sins and life in the Spirit and Christian ethics. If justification is understood in terms of God's liberation of sinners so that God's justifying work is also effective and transformative, the breach between justification and new life in the Spirit is filled in a more satisfying way. Hence, the critical paragraph in Paul (Rom 3:21–26) does not teach that God's justice is satisfied in the cross of Christ. Instead, it heralds the truth that believers are liberated from sin by Christ's work on the cross.

Campbell admits that justification theory is a formidable opponent, but he has misstated the theory historically[20] and misreads so-called contemporary advocates.[21] Campbell's construal stands on the basis of his own exegesis, and a detailed response to his own proposal cannot be offered here. A fundamental problem with

---

20. See the severe criticisms of Allen, *Justification and the Gospel*, 42–43, n. 29.

21. See the devastating review by Barry Matlock, "Zeal for Paul but Not According to Knowledge: Douglas Campbell's War on 'Justification Theory,'" *JSNT* 34 (2011): 115–49. Cf. also Douglas J. Moo, "Review Article: *The Deliverance of God: An Apocalyptic Rereading of Justification in Paul* by Douglas A. Campbell," *JETS* 53 (2010): 145. His entire review is insightful as well (see 143–50).

Campbell's reading is that he privileges love over justice when both notions are part of Paul's thought.[22] Campbell argues that justification is liberative and not forensic, but he doesn't support this claim with a careful study of the usage of the word; in other words, one of the central themes of his book is asserted rather than demonstrated. The failure to support his understanding of justification lexically is all the more surprising given the length of the book.

The notion that Rom 1:18–32 reflects the view of the Teacher rather than Paul is improbable. Such a reading is convenient for Campbell's view, for then the theology of retribution in Rom 1:18–32 isn't Pauline. The text, however, doesn't give any clear indication that we are hearing a voice other than Paul's. Indeed, the repetition of the word "revealed" in 1:18 (following on the heels of the same word in 1:17), and "for" (*gar*) connecting vv. 17–18 speaks against this notion. Also, the ascription of praise to God in 1:25 constitutes an exceedingly strange statement if Paul summarizes the view of an opponent.[23] What the so-called Teacher says in forbidding homosexuality concurs with Paul's view elsewhere (1 Cor 6:9; 1 Tim 1:10). Furthermore, the OT and Second Temple Jewish literature unanimously indict homosexuality, so why should we think Paul would disagree with his ancestors and contemporaries?

We remember the error of historical Jesus research: Campbell's Paul sounds like a contemporary twenty-first-century American—a lot like Doug Campbell. In any case, clear contextual evidence for the notion that Paul cites an opponent in 1:18–32 is lacking, nor are the parallels adduced from 1 Corinthians truly comparable. In the latter instance, citations from opponents are brief and marked more clearly. Furthermore, the interpretation of 1 Corinthians does not change dramatically even if all the alleged citations in the letter are from Paul. What Campbell proposes in the case of Romans is much more radical, and something that few interpreters, ancient or modern, have proposed. If Campbell is wrong here, and he almost certainly is, his textual "citadel" collapses.

It is also somewhat surprising that Campbell, in his presentation, which goes against almost all interpreters both ancient and modern, seems to adopt a modernist confidence in his reading of

---

22. So Westerholm, *Justification Reconsidered*, 89–93.

23. For the textual weaknesses of Campbell's case, see Matlock, "Zeal Not According to Knowledge," 140–42. Moo remarks that Campbell's understanding of Rom. 1:18–32 constitutes "one of the book's most breathtaking maneuvers" ("Review Article," 147). Moo also notes other problems with Campbell's argument (147–48).

Paul. He claims confidently that he has solved "all" the interpretive problems, and seems to think his own interpretation is not guilty of seeing only part of the elephant.[24] All of us can learn from reading Campbell, but I suspect that what he calls justification theory (rightly interpreted) will long outlast his own reading of Paul.

---

24. Campbell, *Deliverance of God*, 932.

CHAPTER 11

God's Saving Righteousness

> "Lord, I seek refuge in You; let me never be disgraced.
> Save me by Your righteousness."   —*Psalm 31:1*

> "I am bringing My justice near; it is not far away, and My
> salvation will not delay. I will put salvation in Zion, My
> splendor in Israel."   —*Isaiah 46:13*

In the next several chapters we will examine the meaning of both the noun "righteousness" and its verbal forms; in this chapter our focus will be on the noun "righteousness" in the OT Scriptures. Since this isn't an exhaustive study, I will largely concentrate on the uses of the word relevant to our study, in particular, the plural uses of the noun, the singular use of righteousness in salvific contexts, the relationship between righteousness and covenant, and the question as to whether righteousness represents conformity to a norm. I will also add that we won't be rehearsing the teaching of justification as it unfolds in the story line of the Bible. Brian Vickers has already done this in his helpful book.[1]

Plural Uses in the Old Testament

In order to understand the meaning of the term righteousness, we must examine how it is used. We begin with the plural noun *ṣidqôt*, which could be translated "righteous acts" or "saving acts." Deborah and Barak sing about "the righteous acts" of the Lord after their great victory over Sisera (Judg 5:11), which clearly denotes God's rescuing the Israelites from their enemies. In 1 Sam 12:7 Samuel rebukes the people because they have forgotten the Lord's "righteous acts" on their behalf, and then he recounts God's saving deliverance, including the exodus and his deliverance of the

---

1. Brian Vickers, *Justification by Grace through Faith: Finding Freedom from Legalism, Lawlessness, Pride, and Despair* (Phillipsburg, NJ: Presbyterian & Reformed, 2013).

people down to Samuel's day (12:6–11). Micah reminds the people of the Lord's "righteous acts" "from the Acacia Grove to Gilgal," rehearsing for them the Lord's deliverance in bringing them into the land of Canaan (Mic 6:5).

Yahweh's righteous acts in Ps 103:6 are described in terms of the salvation the people experienced under Moses when he delivered them from Egyptian slavery (103:7–8). Daniel petitions the Lord to have mercy on Israel despite their sins and rebellion, asking him to show mercy to Israel in accord with "all [his] righteous acts" (Dan 9:16). The word ṣidqôt, then, denotes God's saving acts for his people—the goodness he displays in delivering his people. At the same time, the word retains its association with what is right, the concept of righteousness (cf. Ps. 11:7; Isa 45:24). God's saving acts are righteous and right, and translating the expression as "righteous acts" fits well with the meaning of the term.

Singular Uses in the Old Testament

The noun ṣĕdāqâ ("righteousness") is often used in an ethical sense, denoting the right thing to do (e.g., Gen 18:19; 2 Sam 8:15; 1 Kgs 3:6), but those examples are not what concern us here. An important reference is in Gen 15:6, where Abraham's faith is counted as righteousness. This means that he is counted as standing in the right before God. Of particular interest are the texts where righteousness is parallel to other terms denoting God's salvation. Let me cite some of the relevant texts.

> "LORD, I seek refuge in You; let me never be disgraced. Save me by Your righteousness" (Ps 31:1).
> "Spread Your faithful love over those who know You, and Your righteousness over the upright in heart" (Ps 36:10).
> "I did not hide Your righteousness in my heart; I spoke about Your faithfulness and salvation; I did not conceal Your constant love and truth from the great assembly" (Ps 40:10).
> "In Your justice [righteousness], rescue and deliver me; listen closely to me and save me" (Ps 71:2).
> "Will Your faithful love be declared in the grave, Your faithfulness in Abaddon? Will Your wonders be known in the darkness or Your righteousness in the land of oblivion?" (Ps 88:11–12).
> "The LORD has made His victory [salvation] known; He has revealed His righteousness in the sight of the nations. He has remembered

His love and faithfulness to the house of Israel; all the ends of the earth have seen our God's victory [salvation]" (Ps 98:2–3).

"LORD, hear my prayer. In Your faithfulness listen to my plea, and in Your righteousness answer me" (Ps 143:1).

"Heavens, sprinkle from above, and let the skies shower righteousness. Let the earth open up so that salvation will sprout and righteousness will spring up with it. I, Yahweh, have created it" (Isa 45:8).

"I am bringing My justice near; it is not far away, and My salvation will not delay. I will put salvation in Zion, My splendor in Israel" (Isa 46:13).

"Pay attention to Me, My people, and listen to Me, My nation; for instruction will come from Me, and My justice for a light to the nations. I will bring it about quickly. My righteousness is near, My salvation appears, and My arms will bring justice to the nations. The coastlands will put their hope in Me, and they will look to My strength. Look up to the heavens, and look at the earth beneath; for the heavens will vanish like smoke, the earth will wear out like a garment, and its inhabitants will die like gnats. But My salvation will last forever, and My righteousness will never be shattered. Listen to Me, you who know righteousness, the people in whose heart is My instruction: do not fear disgrace by men, and do not be shattered by their taunts. For the moth will devour them like a garment, and the worm will eat them like wool. But My righteousness will last forever, and My salvation for all generations" (Isa 51:4–8).

The Meaning of the Term

In each of the verses cited above the concept of righteousness is parallel to salvation and deliverance, God's faithful love (*ḥesed*), God's truth or faithfulness (*'ĕmûnâ*), and his justice (*mišpāṭ*). Of course, as was pointed out in the last chapter, this is not to say that righteousness and salvation mean precisely the same thing, or that righteousness and faithfulness are equivalent. The overlapping of words does not mean they are synonyms. The parallels in the verses listed demonstrate that righteousness frequently designates the saving righteousness of God. When God unveils his righteousness, Israel will be saved and delivered and God's promises will be fulfilled. This does not mean that the term righteousness is synonymous in every respect with salvation. For example, there is also the notion that God's deliverance of his people is *right*, that it accords with justice and righteousness. God exercises his righteousness in vindicating his people.[2] God displays his righteousness in saving them from their enemies.

We should also note that righteousness often has a forensic meaning. We see evidence for this in Isaiah. The noun righteousness (*ṣĕdāqâ*) in Isaiah has the same orbit of meaning as the verb (*ṣādaq*). And the verb in Isaiah 40–55 signifies vindication and acquittal, as the following examples demonstrate.

> "Let them bring in their witnesses to prove they were right, so that others may hear and say, 'It is true'" (Isa 43:9 NIV).
>
> "Set forth your case, that you may be proved right" (Isa 43:26 ESV).
>
> "All the descendants of Israel will be justified and find glory through the LORD" (Isa 45:25).
>
> "The One who vindicates Me is near; who will contend with Me? Let us confront each other. Who has a case against Me? Let him come near Me!" (Isa 50:8).

These examples are instructive because the legal context in these passages is clear. The situation is one in which courtroom witnesses are summoned to testify in court. People are summoned to present their case; opponents are invited to present their case in contrast to the case that will be brought by Yahweh. The forensic and legal character of the verb is undeniable. At the same time, the verbal forms, especially in Isa 45:25 and 50:8, cast light on the meaning of the noun (cf. 45:8; 51:4–8), where God says his righteousness will become a reality.[3] It follows, then, that God's saving righteousness means that he will vindicate his people. They will be acquitted and stand in the right before their judge.

Righteousness and the Covenant

The verses cited above raise the question of the relationship between God's saving righteousness and his covenant. Some scholars disavow any relationship between righteousness and covenant since the words aren't

---

2. In defense of such a view in Isaiah 40–55, see Douglas J. Moo, "Justification in Galatians," in *Understanding the Times: New Testament Studies in the 21st Century: Essays in Honor of D. A. Carson on the Occasion of His 65th Birthday* (Wheaton, IL: Crossway, 2011), 174.

3. Rightly, ibid., 172.

often found together.[4] They contend that righteousness belongs with creation rather than covenant. Recognizing the creational dimension of righteousness is an important insight, for God's saving work fulfills his intentions in creating the world. Paul even describes God's saving work in terms of new creation (e.g., 2 Cor 4:6; 5:17; Eph 2:10).

Nevertheless, segregating righteousness entirely from the notion of covenant isn't convincing. Relying on a word study approach to determine the matter is an inadequate basis for assessing whether righteousness and covenant are related. It is difficult to believe that God's saving righteousness isn't integrally related to covenant, for the covenant plays a major role in OT thought, and the covenants promise that God will deliver Israel (e.g., Gen 12:1–3; 15:7–21).[5] For instance, when God rescues Israel from Egyptian bondage, this deliverance is in fulfillment of the covenant (Exod 2:23–25; 6:2–8). In addition, God says he will fulfill his covenant in returning Israel from exile (Lev 26:40–45). The Lord also made a covenant with David in promising him an unending dynasty (2 Sam 7:1–29), and through the Davidic king God's covenant promises with Israel would become a reality. Similarly, the new covenant (Jer 30–33; Ezek 36–37) promises forgiveness of sins and return from exile. The covenant promises, then, are another way of describing God's saving righteousness, for God's saving righteousness includes the return from exile and the fulfillment of God's covenant promises. We see this clearly in Isaiah 40–66, where God's righteousness means deliverance from enemies, the fulfillment of his saving promises, and return from exile.

Describing the precise relationship between the covenant and righteousness is not easy, and some make the mistake of defining righteousness *as* covenant faithfulness.[6] Yet this is similar to the mistake one makes in describing the relationship between salvation and righteousness. Two closely related terms are merged and defined as if they say the same thing.[7] Yet while covenant and righteousness are closely aligned, it does not follow that righteousness should be *defined as covenant faithfulness*. With this

---

4.   Mark A. Seifrid, "Righteousness Language in the Hebrew Scriptures and Early Judaism," in *Justification and Variegated Nomism: Volume 1 — The Complexities of Second-Temple Judaism* (ed. D. A. Carson, Mark A. Seifrid, and Peter T. O'Brien; Grand Rapids: Baker, 2004), 415–42.

5.   For a full defense of the centrality of covenant in biblical theology, see Peter J. Gentry and Stephen J. Wellum, *Kingdom through Covenant: A Biblical-Theological Understanding of the Covenants* (Wheaton, IL: Crossway, 2012).

6.   So Wright, *Justification*, 64–71. Against this, see Seifrid, "Righteousness Language in the Hebrew Scriptures and Early Judaism," 415–42; idem, *Christ, Our Righteousness*, 38–45.

7.   Moo rightly notes that covenant membership and justification may be closely related without being identical ("Justification in Galatians," 175).

definition the concept of covenant swallows up the word righteousness, and the notion of doing what is right is absent from the definition. It is better to say that God's saving righteousness *fulfills* the covenant instead of saying that it should be *defined as* covenant faithfulness.[8]

We can see the same thing when it comes to salvation. Salvation should not be defined as covenant faithfulness, but God's salvation fulfills what he promised in the covenant. In the same way, God's righteousness in saving his people demonstrates that he has made good on his covenant promises, but it doesn't follow that righteousness *means* covenant faithfulness. Again, this is an easy and somewhat natural mistake to make since righteousness is so integrally tied to the covenant, but the distinction must be maintained so that we can determine what righteousness truly means.

Along the same lines John Piper defines God's righteousness as his unswerving allegiance to God's glory.[9] Here Piper falls into the same mistake as those who define God's righteousness as his covenant faithfulness.[10] Here the definition offered has stripped out of the word the notion of doing what is right. God's glory effectively swallows up the word righteousness. It doesn't make much sense to say that righteousness by faith means God's unswerving allegiance to his glory by faith. Yet Piper has a vital insight here, one that must not be lost. God's saving righteousness does bring him glory and honor, but that is not the same thing as saying that God's righteousness *is* God's unswerving allegiance to his glory.

Righteousness as a Norm

It has become common to define God's righteousness in terms of salvation and to reject the idea that God's righteousness also includes his judgment.[11] It is often said that righteousness has to do with relationship within the covenant instead of conformity to a norm.[12] The use of the term

---

8. Bird rightly critiques Seifrid, who separates righteousness altogether from the covenant, but Bird goes too far in defining righteousness as covenant faithfulness (*Saving Righteousness of God*, 35–39).

9. John Piper, *The Future of Justification: A Response to N. T. Wright* (Wheaton, IL: Cross, 2007), 62–71; idem, *The Justification of God: An Exegetical and Theological Study of Romans 9:1–23* (2nd ed.; Grand Rapids: Eerdmans, 1993), 111–18.

10. Wright correctly critiques Piper at this point (*Justification*, 66–68).

11. For a very helpful study of the word righteousness, see Westerholm, *Justification Reconsidered*, 51–74.

12. See, e.g., Gerhard von Rad, *Old Testament Theology* (trans. D. M. G. Stalker; 2 vols.; New York: Harper & Row, 1962, 1965), 1:370–83; James D. G. Dunn, *Romans 1–8* (WBC; Dallas: Word, 198), 40–43; idem, "The Justice of God," 16–21; J. A. Ziesler, *The Meaning of Righteousness in Paul: A Linguistic and Theological Enquiry* (SNTSMS 20; Cambridge: Cambridge University Press, 1972), 34–43; P. R. Achtemeier, "Righteousness in the NT," *IDB* 4:91–99.

in the life of Tamar is frequently introduced to defend the idea that righteousness is covenantal instead of having to do with a norm. Judah declares that Tamar "is more in the right than I" (Gen. 38:26), even though she had sexual relations with Judah, for Judah had not given her his third son in marriage as was expected in the culture of that day. Righteousness is defined as appropriate action within the covenant since both of them did what was morally wrong. Tamar is vindicated, on this reading, because she did what was fitting covenantally. Despite the popularity of this interpretation, it is probably incorrect insofar as it strips the word righteousness of moral norms.[13] If righteousness were simply faithfulness to the covenant, Tamar would be completely in the right. But Judah doesn't defend Tamar as being completely in the right. He merely acknowledges that "she is more in the right." In other words, she was closer to the norm than Judah, but even Tamar didn't meet the standard absolutely.

In the same way, Jacob says to Laban his brother-in-law, "In the future when you come to check on my wages, my honesty ("righteousness," *ṣidqā tî*) will testify for me" (Gen 30:33). Certainly, we have conformity to a moral norm here: Jacob isn't a thief! He is a righteous person. Along the same lines, Saul acknowledges that David was more righteous than he was (1 Sam 24:17, 19). It seems evident that these references have to do with conformity to a norm, for Saul was trying to kill David, and David refused to put Saul to death when he had a similar opportunity. There is no evidence that David and Saul were in covenant with one another; it is more natural to see this in reference to conformity to a norm.

We see that righteousness has to do with conformity to a norm for the law requires "just balances, just weights, a just ephah, and a just hin" (Lev. 19:36, ESV; the word for "just" is *ṣedeq*). Weights and measures must meet the standard; they must be fair and right. Similarly, those with legal authority judge righteously when they conform to the law, to the standard articulated through Moses (Deut 1:16; 16:18). Justice (*ṣedeq*) is the standard (Deut 16:20), and hence favoritism to either the poor or the rich is prohibited (Lev 19:15, 36; Deut 16:19). Giving a poor person his garment is counted as righteous because it adheres to the standard God requires (Deut 24:12–14). Yes, it is a covenant obligation, but it doesn't follow that this replaces the notion of conformity to a norm. Noah wasn't a covenant member of Israel, and yet he is designated righteous (Gen 6:9;

---

13. See Seifrid, "Righteousness Language in the Hebrew Scriptures and Early Judaism," 415–24; idem, *Christ, Our Righteousness: Paul's Theology of Justification* (NSBT 9; Downers Grove, IL: InterVarsity Press, 2004), 38–45.

7:1), which suggests that he lived according to the standard God mandated. The righteousness God requires constitutes a norm of behavior that kings (2 Sam 22:21, 25; 1 Kgs 3:5; 10:9; 1 Chr 8:14; 2 Chr 9:8; Jer 22:3, 15) and all people are required to carry out (Job 27:6; Ps 106:3; 112:3, 9; Prov 8:20; 10:2; 11:5; 15:9; Isa 5:7; 28:17; 33:15; 59:14; Ezek 14:14; 18:5; 33:12).

If righteousness signifies conformity to a norm, to the standard that God requires—a standard that matches and conforms to God's character[14]—then we are not surprised to read that God judges those who fail to do what he has required.[15] God's righteousness is not just a saving righteousness, it is also a judging righteousness. Such an observation may seem obvious, but it is often denied.[16] Still, the evidence that God exercises his righteousness in judging the wicked is pervasive. In the judgment of Sodom and Gomorrah, for instance, he will not judge the righteous (Gen 18:23–26), signaling that judging the wicked is righteous. The same suggestion is evident when we read that the Lord repays every person for "his righteousness" (1 Sam 26:23; cf. 2 Chr 6:23). When Rehoboam and the people abandoned the Lord, they confessed that he was "righteous" (2 Chr 12:6) in punishing them. Nehemiah also acknowledges that the Lord was "righteous" in all the judgments that had come upon Israel because of their apostasy (Neh 9:33).

God's judging righteousness is apparent in the words, "God is a righteous judge and a God who shows His wrath every day" (Ps 7:11). The heavens shall "proclaim" God's "righteousness," for "God is the Judge" (50:6; cf. 96:13). God's righteousness means that he vindicates the righteous and judges the ungodly (9:4; 35:24; 37:6; 71:2). Psalm 99 declares that God is righteous (99:4) in a context that features God's holiness (99:3, 5, 9), and God's judging righteousness is clearly in view, for he is "an avenger of their sinful actions" (99:8). We see the same theme in Psalm 129. Those "who hate Zion" will "be driven back in disgrace" (129:5) since they have attacked and oppressed Israel (129:1–3). The Lord "is righteous" in cutting "the ropes of the wicked" (129:4).

---

14. Piper says that righteousness isn't conformity to a norm because the standard isn't always distributive justice (*Justification of God*, 105–8). Such a statement is correct, but the standard is God's own character, so that God's character is the norm.

15. Bird posits a both–and, so that righteousness means both right relationship within the covenant and conformity to a norm (*Saving Righteousness of God*, 10–12). Such an answer isn't so much incorrect as it is incomplete, for it doesn't answer the question about the foundation of the norm in the covenant relationship. It is here that we must say that it is God himself—his character and being are the norm for all human activity.

16. Rightly, Piper, *Justification of God*, 108–11.

Similarly, when God's people are thrust into exile, it is due to the judgment of God, and the "holy God is distinguished by righteousness" (Isa 5:16; cf. 10:22) in judging his people. Daniel also confesses God's righteousness in judging Israel and sending them into exile (Dan 9:7, 14). We see the same acknowledgment of God's righteousness in Lamentations, where the writer rehearses the reasons for Israel's exile (Lam 1:18). Jeremiah identifies God's righteousness with his judgment of the wicked (Jer. 11:20; 12:1). There is abundant evidence, then, that God's righteousness can't be limited to salvation but also includes his judgment, his punishment of those who practice evil.

Conclusion

In the OT, the plural form of the word righteousness (*ṣidqôt*) designates God's saving righteousness, his deliverance of his people. The singular noun (*ṣĕdāqâ*) is often used with parallel terms like "faithful love," "truth," and "salvation." Still, God's righteousness shouldn't be collapsed into these other terms, as if they all mean exactly the same thing. There is still the notion of "rightness" and "righteousness" in the term, even when it describes God's saving righteousness. Most scholars see righteousness as a covenantal and relational term, and we should not deny the covenantal dimensions of the word. The covenant plays a central role in the OT, and it is hard to imagine God's righteousness being separated from the covenant. Still, it doesn't follow from this that God's righteousness *is* his covenant faithfulness. It is better to say that God's saving righteousness fulfills his covenant promises.

Along the same lines, those who have focused on the covenantal and relational dimensions of righteousness have overemphasized their insight, for when we examine the use of the word, the idea of conformity to a norm can't be washed out of the word. We don't have a case of a norm above God here—the norm is God's own character. It is *his* justice and holiness that are expressed in the norms that are laid down. Hence, it isn't surprising to find that righteousness in the OT also has to do with God's judging righteousness. God pours his wrath out righteously on those who turn away from him, from those who reject his rule in their lives.

CHAPTER 12

Righteousness Is Eschatological

"The doers of the law will be declared righteous."
—*Romans 2:13*

"God is the One who justifies." —*Romans 8:33*

The Biblical Evidence

When does justification occur? Is it a past event? Or something in the future? And what significance does this have for our understanding of justification? Before we attempt to define the word righteousness in Paul's thought, we need to investigate the temporal horizon of justification. In this chapter, I hope to demonstrate that justification in Paul is fundamentally eschatological. I begin with the eschatological nature of justification in Paul because it is crucial for understanding his gospel. In what follows I will defend the notion that God's righteousness is eschatological, and the forensic nature of eschatological justification will be brought out more clearly in subsequent chapters.

At first glance, the time when justification occurs isn't easy to decipher. In some texts it is definitely future.

"The doers of the law will be declared righteous" (Rom 2:13).
"God is the One who justifies" (Rom 8:33).[1]
"For I am not conscious of anything against myself, but I am not justified by this. The One who evaluates me is the Lord. Therefore
don't judge anything prematurely, before the Lord comes, who
will both bring to light what is hidden in darkness and reveal the
intentions of the hearts. And then praise will come to each one
from God" (1 Cor 4:4–5).[2]
"No one is justified by the works of the law but by faith in Jesus

---

1. It seems clear in the context that the verse relates to the final judgment.
2. I included both verses, for the context makes it plain that the final judgment is in view.

Christ. And we have believed in Christ Jesus so that we might
be justified by faith in Christ and not by the works of the law,
because by the works of the law no human being will be justified"
(Gal 2:16).[3]

"But if we ourselves are also found to be 'sinners' while seeking to be
justified by Christ" (Gal 2:17).

"For through the Spirit, by faith, we eagerly wait for the hope of
righteousness" (Gal 5:5).

"And be found in Him, not having a righteousness of my own from
the law, but one that is through faith in Christ—the righteousness from God based on faith" (Phil 3:9).[4]

In other cases justification is something in the past. Several texts that
speak of righteousness by faith refer to a past justification (Rom 3:22; 4:3,
5, 6, 9, 11, 13, 22; 9:30; 10:4, 6, 10; Gal 3:6), denoting a righteousness
that is now enjoyed by faith.

"If Abraham was justified by works" (Rom 4:2).

"Since we have been declared righteous by faith" (Rom 5:1).

"Since we have now been declared righteous by His blood" (Rom 5:9).

"Those who receive the overflow of grace and the gift of righteousness" (Rom 5:17).

"And those He called, He also justified; and those He justified, He
also glorified" (Rom. 8:30).[5]

"But it is from Him that you are in Christ Jesus, who became God-
given wisdom for us—our righteousness, sanctification, and
redemption" (1 Cor 1:30).

"But you were washed, you were sanctified, you were justified in
the name of the Lord Jesus Christ and by the Spirit of our God"
(1 Cor 6:11).

"He made the One who did not know sin to be sin for us, so that we
might become the righteousness of God in Him" (2 Cor 5:21).

Jesus "was vindicated by the Spirit" (1 Tim 3:16, NIV).

---

3.   The first two instances are vague and could denote the past or the present, but the last
clause suggests the future. This reading is strengthened by the next verse where justification is
clearly future.

4.   The reference to being found in him clearly shows that the last judgment is in view.

5.   The aorist tense doesn't necessarily denote past time, but in this context the past is likely
in view.

"So that having been justified by His grace, we may become heirs with the hope of eternal life" (Titus 3:7).[6]

Still other texts are vague about the time.

"No one will be justified in His sight by the works of the law" (Rom 3:20).

"They are justified freely by His grace through the redemption that is in Christ Jesus" (Rom 3:24).

"So that He would be righteous and declare righteous the one who has faith in Jesus" (Rom 3:26).

"A person is justified by faith apart from the works of the law" (Rom 3:28, NIV).

"Since there is one God who will justify the circumcised by faith and the uncircumcised through faith" (Rom 3:30).

"To the one who does not work but trusts God who justifies the ungodly" (Rom. 4:5, NIV).

"Now the Scripture saw in advance that God would justify the Gentiles by faith" (Gal 3:8).

"No one is justified before God by the law" (Gal 3:11).

"The law, then, was our guardian until Christ, so that we could be justified by faith" (Gal 3:24).

"You who are trying to be justified by the law are alienated from Christ" (Gal 5:4).

Can we draw any conclusions from these texts about the timing of justification? Certainly some of the verses could arguably be in a different category. Yet it is hard to ignore the existence of different time periods in Paul's thinking. Still, most scholars today agree that Paul's theology is thoroughly eschatological, and I won't attempt a full defense of this perspective here.[7] Suffice it to say that justification fits into this eschatological framework, and as we saw above, the term is used to denote the verdict on the last day. Justification means that one is declared to be in the right by God as the divine judge. And the declaration as to who is acquitted and who is condemned will take place on the day of judgment, the final day. Paul considers the future judgment, and he is confident that believers will be vindicated and justified on the final day (Rom 8:33–34). He looks

---

6. This verse is likely past, but it is certainly debatable.

7. See, e.g., G. K. Beale, *A New Testament Biblical Theology: The Unfolding of the Old Testament in the New* (Grand Rapids: Baker, 2011).

forward with confidence to the declaration that he will be declared to be in the right (Gal 5:5). Those who believe will be "found" before the divine court to be in the right (Gal 2:17; Phil 3:9).

The Resurrection and the Eschatological Nature of Justification

Yet another piece of evidence points to the eschatological character of justification. The Bible speaks of Jesus Christ being "justified" or "acquitted" at his resurrection (1 Tim 3:16).[8] The resurrection demonstrated that Jesus wasn't a deluded messianic figure. No one could possibly be the Messiah if his life ended as a crucified criminal, but Jesus' resurrection demonstrates that the verdict "guilty" declared by the world has been overturned by God. The resurrection of Jesus reveals that he has been acquitted by God. At the same time, the resurrection communicates that the last days have arrived, that the eschaton has invaded history (Isa 26:19; Ezek 37:13–14; Dan 12:1–3). The resurrection of Jesus, therefore, is an eschatological event, demonstrating that the last days have arrived. Death has been defeated, and Jesus' resurrection testifies that he has been vindicated as the Messiah and the Son of God.

Believers in Jesus Christ are "not guilty" by virtue of Jesus' death and resurrection (Rom 4:25). Since they are "in Christ" (Eph 1:3–14) and united to him by faith, they are no longer in Adam (Rom 5:12–19; 1 Cor 15:21–22). Hence, Jesus' vindication at his resurrection is their vindication, his status is their status. Believers, even now, enjoy by faith the status of the resurrected one. In other words, in the resurrection of Jesus the last times have invaded history.

We see, then, how justification can be both future and past. Believers are now justified by faith (Rom 5:1) because they are united to Jesus Christ as the risen one, as the one who reigns at God's right hand. The end-time declaration has been pronounced in advance by the death and resurrection of Jesus Christ. This means that every text that speaks of past justification is also an eschatological text, for justification belongs to believers inasmuch as they are united to Jesus Christ as the crucified and risen Lord. The future is revealed and announced in the present. We shouldn't be surprised, then, to find that a number of texts are vague as to the timing of justification.

---

8.   On this theme, see particularly G. K. Beale, "The Role of the Resurrection in the Already-and-Not-Yet Phases of Justification," in *For the Fame of God's Name: Essays in Honor of John Piper* (ed. Sam Storms and Justin Taylor; Wheaton, IL: Crossway, 2010), 190–213.

Believers in Jesus Christ are now justified through faith in Jesus Christ. They are justified by faith alone by virtue of Christ's death for their sins and his resurrection for their justification (Rom 4:25). Still, they look forward to the day when the declaration will be announced *publicly* and to the entire world. In this sense, as many scholars attest, justification is an already but not yet reality. Presently, believers may doubt their justification, for it is theirs by faith and God hasn't publicly revealed their status to the entire world. Indeed, the truth that Jesus is ruling and reigning has been hidden from the world, and thus his role as resurrected Lord is doubted and rejected. But the day is coming when God will reveal to all that Jesus is the risen Lord and Christ, and then he will announce to all that those who have put their trust in Jesus are acquitted of all their sins.

Conclusion

In this chapter I have maintained that justification is an eschatological reality. We are already justified, but we await the not yet when our justification will be publicly announced to the world. This doesn't simply mean that our justification is a future event, because, as we have seen, the last days have arrived in the death and resurrection of Jesus Christ. The verdict of the final judgment is declared in advance for those who belong to Jesus Christ, and on the day of judgment that verdict will be proclaimed to the world. What is remarkable is that believers enjoy now the end-time verdict. Believers have assurance of salvation by faith alone because the verdict of the final day is already theirs! Here is one of the problems with the Roman Catholic view of justification, for in denying assurance of salvation, they fail to see that the end-time verdict has been declared in advance to those who trust in Jesus and are united to him by faith.

CHAPTER 13

Righteousness Is Forensic

> "For just as through one man's disobedience the many
> were made sinners, so also through the one man's
> obedience the many will be made righteous."
>
> —*Romans 5:19*

> "Now it is clear that no one is justified before God by the
> law, because the righteous will live by faith."
>
> —*Galatians 3:11*

We continue to ask the question: What does Paul mean by the word "righteousness"? We've looked at the various forms of the word as it used in the OT and NT, and we've considered the temporal dimensions of the concept. In this chapter we will consider whether God's righteousness is transformative or forensic.[1]

For those who are new to this discussion, it can be rather complicated. I'll be proceeding through the argument one step at a time. I will begin by giving a brief summary of the arguments for a transformative understanding of righteousness in Paul. Then I will review the prominence of a forensic reading of righteousness in the OT before turning to Paul's own writing. Why turn to the OT first? Because it was Paul's Bible. I am not claiming that the OT evidence presented here *proves* that righteousness is

---

1. Some argue that the verb form of righteousness is forensic in Paul and the noun is transformative, and that there is no reason why both forms need to bear the same meaning. I will argue that such a solution doesn't fit the evidence, though I would agree in principle that the verb and noun don't necessarily have the same meaning. In addition, I would point out that everyone agrees that Paul uses the word "righteousness" (*dikaiosynē*) on occasion to designate one's ethical righteousness (e.g., Rom 6:13, 16, 18, 19, 20; 2 Cor 6:7, 14; 9:9, 10; 11:15; Eph 4:24; 5:9; Phil 1:11; 1 Tim 6:11; 2 Tim 2:22). There isn't any debate over the meaning of the term in these instances. The issue in question is what Paul means by "the righteousness of God" or by the term "righteousness" in those texts where Paul refers to the saving righteousness of God given to human beings. The ethical use of the term in some contexts doesn't necessitate the conclusion that the term isn't forensic in other Pauline texts (rightly, Moo, "Justification in Galatians," 176). The key for determining the meaning of a word is the context in which the term is used.

forensic in Paul. I'm simply saying that a forensic meaning is most probable in light of the OT evidence adduced here. After looking at some of the OT passages, we'll continue the thread of the argument by showing that righteousness is also forensic in Paul's writings.

We begin, then, with the case for the opposing view—that righteousness is transformative in Paul.

Defense of Transformative Righteousness

A number of arguments have been given to defend a transformative meaning of righteousness in Paul.[2] A transformative reading doesn't necessarily contradict the Reformation if the forensic is the basis for the transformative, and some of those who advance a transformative view may also see justification as forensic. Nonetheless, I will explain in due course why the transformative view is not convincing. So what arguments support a transformative reading of righteousness in Paul?

First, "the righteousness of God" (Rom 1:17) is said to be transformative because it is parallel with "the power of God" (1:16) and "the wrath of God" (1:18; pers. transl. in all cases). Just as the wrath of God and the power of God are effective, and thus transformative, so too the righteousness of God.

Second, God's righteousness is "revealed" (*apokalyptetai*, Rom 1:17) and "manifested" (*pephanerōtai*, Rom 3:21). Such expressions indicate that God's righteousness is not merely a gift but also a power. It is the apocalyptic unleashing of God's power that changes human beings.

Third, we read in Rom 5:19, "For just as through one man's disobedience the many were made sinners, so also through the one man's obedience the many will be made righteous." The verse indicates that, according to the transformative view, human beings aren't just declared to be righteous but are actually made righteous. Just as those in Adam are actually made sinners because of Adam's sin, so those in Christ are made righteous because of Christ's righteousness.

---

2. See Ernst Käsemann, "The Righteousness of God in Paul," in *New Testament Questions of Today* (trans. W. J. Montague; Philadelphia: Fortress, 1969), 168–82; Karl Kertelge, *Rechtfertigung bei Paulus: Studien zur Struktur und zum Bedeutungsgehalt des paulinischen Rechtfertigungbegriffs* (2nd ed.; NTAbh 3; Münster: Aschendorff, 1967); Peter Stuhlmacher, *Gerechtigkeit Gottes bei Paulus* (FRLANT 87; Göttingen: Vandenhoeck & Ruprecht, 1965); Bird, *Saving Righteousness of God*, 12–17. Closely connected to the transformative view is the notion that justification involves the gift of the Spirit and thus is a transforming reality. See the Pentecostal scholar, Frank D. Macchia, *Justified in the Spirit: Creation, Redemption, and the Triune God* (Grand Rapids: Eerdmans, 2010). Macchia rightly sees a close correlation between justification and life in the Spirit, but he makes the mistake of collapsing them together. Justification and life in the Spirit are inseparable, but they are also distinguishable.

Fourth, Rom 6:7 says, "anyone who has died has been set free from sin" (NIV). The verb translated "set free" is *dedikaiōtai*, from the verb "justify" (*dikaioō*). No English version translates the verb forensically. They all render it "set free," which indicates that they understand it in a transformative sense. Apparently, even the verb "justify" has a transformative meaning, so that those who are justified are free from sin. God's verdict is an effective verdict, creating a new reality.

Fifth, God's righteousness is transformative because justification includes both the death and resurrection of Christ (Rom 4:25).[3] Justification isn't limited to death and forgiveness but also includes resurrection and new life. Here we find a basis for ethics, since those who are justified are a new creation in that they are raised with Christ.

Finally, the parallel in 2 Cor 3:8–9 supports a transformative view. Verse 8 speaks of "the ministry of the Spirit" and verse 9 of "the ministry of righteousness." Those who enjoy the ministry of righteousness also enjoy the ministry of the Spirit, and the Spirit changes, renews, and transforms believers. The parallel between the Spirit and righteousness indicates that righteousness for members of the new covenant can't be limited to a forensic matter; righteousness includes the notion of being transformed by the Spirit.

Forensic Justification in the Old Testament

The evidence adduced above constitutes some of the arguments for justification being transformative, presented in abbreviated form. While they may appear convincing, I will show why a forensic understanding is more convincing in both the OT and in Paul. The term *forensic* is often used in judicial contexts (in law court contexts), where a declarative meaning is evident. What distinguishes the forensic from the transformative? The former has to do with declaration, while the latter has to do with transformation. Righteous judges, for example, don't *make* persons guilty or innocent. They assess the facts of the case and *declare* someone to be innocent or guilty. We see this understanding in the following verses.

"Stay far away from a false accusation. Do not kill the innocent and the just, because I will not justify the guilty" (Exod 23:7).

"When people have a dispute, they are to take it to court and the

---

3. See especially Richard B. Gaffin, *The Centrality of the Resurrection: A Study in Paul's Soteriology* (Grand Rapids: Baker, 1978); Bird, *Saving Righteousness of God*, 40–59 (though Gaffin doesn't espouse the transformative view).

judges will decide the case, acquitting the innocent and condemning the guilty" (Deut 25:1, NIV).

"[Absalom] added, 'If only someone would appoint me judge in the
land. Then anyone who had a grievance or dispute could come to
me, and I would make sure he received justice'" (2 Sam 15:4).

"When anyone wrongs their neighbor and is required to take an oath
and they come and swear the oath before your altar in this temple,
then hear from heaven and act. Judge between your servants,
condemning the guilty by bringing down on their heads what
they have done, and vindicating the innocent by treating them in
accordance with their innocence" (1 Kgs 8:31–32, NIV).

"May You judge Your servants, condemning the wicked man by
bringing what he has done on his own head and providing justice
for the righteous by rewarding him according to his righteousness" (2 Chr 6:23).

"Acquitting the guilty and condemning the just—both are detestable
to the LORD" (Prov 17:15).

Those who are evil "acquit the guilty for a bribe and deprive the
innocent of justice" (Isa 5:23).

In all of the texts above, it is clear that judges don't *make* someone
guilty or innocent. They *declare* or *pronounce* someone to be guilty or
innocent. Judges make their assessment based on the facts of the case and
the evidence presented. Those who are free from a crime are declared to
be innocent by a judge. Indeed, a judge who declares a wicked person to
be righteous or a righteous person to be wicked is evil.

The forensic and declarative character of righteousness is also apparent
in a number of other texts as well. We see this especially in the book of Job,
where Job insists that he would stand in the right before God (not guilty)
if he only could try his case in court (though he also complains that God is
unfair and thus Job would lose the case even though he deserves to win).
The legal and forensic nature of what Job desires is obvious in the following verses. He longs for a court case so God will declare him to be in the
right, but Job's friends retort that he is actually guilty and would lose the
case. Both Job and his friends understand righteousness as a declaration
of innocence and condemnation as a declaration of guilt. Neither party
defines righteousness as being made righteous.

"Yes, I know what you've said is true, but how can a person be justified before God?" (Job 9:2).

"Even if I were in the right, I could not answer. I could only beg my
Judge for mercy" (Job 9:15).

"Even if I were in the right, my own mouth would condemn me; if I
were blameless, my mouth would declare me guilty" (Job 9:20).

"And even if I am righteous, I cannot lift up my head" (Job 10:15).

"Should this stream of words go unanswered and such a talker be
acquitted?" (Job 11:2).[4]

"Now then, I have prepared my case; I know that I am right" (Job
13:18).

"What is man, that he should be pure, or one born of woman, that he
should be righteous?" (Job 15:14).[5]

"How can a person be justified before God?" (Job 25:4).[6]

"I will cling to my righteousness and never let it go. My conscience
will not accuse me as long as I live!" (Job 27:6).

"Job has declared, 'I am righteous, yet God has deprived me of
justice'" (Job 34:5).[7]

"Do you think it is just when you say, 'I am righteous before God'?"
(Job 35:2).

"Would you really challenge My justice? Would you declare Me guilty
to justify yourself?" (Job 40:8).[8]

It is clear in every instance that forensic righteousness is what is being
debated in the book. Job claims that he really is righteous, that he would
pass the test in court, and that God as the judge would declare him to be
innocent. Job's interlocutors hold a different perspective and are convinced
that God would declare that Job is guilty before him. In any case, the
entire discussion indicates that righteousness is forensic.

We see the forensic and legal character of righteousness in a number of
texts in the prophets as well.

"Who told about this from the beginning, so that we might know,
and from times past, so that we might say: He is right? No one
announced it, no one told it, no one heard your words" (Isa
41:26). God's prophetic words vindicate his holy character, showing that he is in the right.

---

4.   These are the words of Zophar.
5.   These are the words of Eliphaz.
6.   These are the words of Bildad.
7.   This verse and the next are the words of Elihu.
8.   These are the words of God.

"All the nations gather together and the peoples assemble. Which of their gods foretold this and proclaimed to us the former things? Let them bring in their witnesses to prove they were right, so that others may hear and say, 'It is true'" (Isa 43:9, NIV). Once again it is obvious that we have a law court setting here, and God is proved to be in the right in the universal court of opinion.

"Put me in remembrance; let us argue together; set forth your case, that you may be proved right" (Isa 43:26, ESV). The legal character of this verse is obvious, for the matter is clearly a court case.

"You will be righteous, LORD, even if I bring a case against You. Yet, I wish to contend with You" (Jer 12:1). Jeremiah contemplates bringing a court case against God, and knows that he will lose the case even if he prosecutes it since God stands in the right.

In all of these examples the verb clearly means declare righteous, for a judge with integrity would not *make* a defendant righteous. The judge would *declare* the person to be righteous if he or she were indeed righteous. Similarly, words for righteousness or right are often used, especially in Job and Isaiah, where there is a legal debate, a law court setting, where the righteousness of a human being or God is the issue. We see in Job that the issue is the justification of God, for God is shown to be in the right in his treatment of Job and all human beings. Recognizing the forensic meaning for righteousness in the OT prepares us for Paul's use of the term.

Forensic Meaning in Paul

When we come to the Pauline writings, we are prepared for a forensic and declarative understanding of the righteousness from the OT context. We need to remember that in Protestant thought the term has been understood forensically, while Roman Catholics have maintained that it means "make righteous." As we investigate the Pauline evidence, it is clear that the Protestant understanding isn't merely a tradition; rather, there are good exegetical reasons for seeing a forensic meaning of the word.

In Paul the forensic, law-court, meaning of the word is evident. For instance, we read in Rom 8:33, "Who can bring an accusation against God's elect? God is the One who justifies." Paul considers here the final day, the judgment day, when God will assess the life of every human being. The verb "justifies" here clearly means "declares righteous," for there is a contrast between bringing a charge (*enkalesei*) and condemning (*katakrinōn*, 8:34) and justifying. Obviously, "bring an accusation" and "condemn" don't mean "make wicked," for it would be terribly unjust for God to make someone wicked on the day of judgment! It follows, then, that "justify" doesn't mean "make righteous" but "declare righteous." We see the same phenomenon in 2:13, "For it is not the hearers of the law who are righteous before God, but the doers of the law who will be justified" (ESV). The doers of the law aren't made righteous but "declared to be righteous" by God on the last day by virtue of their works.

The claim that no one is justified by works of law or by the law should be interpreted similarly. Consider these texts.

> "For no one will be justified in His sight by the works of the law, because the knowledge of sin comes through the law" (Rom 3:20).
> "For we maintain that a person is justified by faith apart from the works of the law" (Rom 3:28, NIV).
> We know "that no one is justified by the works of the law but by faith in Jesus Christ. And we have believed in Christ Jesus so that we might be justified by faith in Christ and not by the works of the law, because by the works of the law no human being will be justified" (Gal 2:16).
> "Now it is clear that no one is justified before God by the law, because the righteous will live by faith" (Gal 3:11).
> "You who are trying to be justified by the law are alienated from Christ; you have fallen from grace" (Gal 5:4).

In these texts it is clear that "justify" means that no one is declared to be righteous by keeping the law. Earlier, I argued that the reason justification isn't obtained by the law is because of sin—human disobedience. If the law were kept, justification would be gained by works of law. Thus, if people did the works of the law, they would be declared righteous. They wouldn't be *made* righteous; God as the judge would *declare* them to be in the right because they obeyed the law. Paul's argument here is that no one is justified by works of law since all disobey. The word "justify" here clearly means "declare righteous," which indicates that the word is forensic rather than transformative.

We have already seen in the above texts that the verb is forensic, and there is no reason to think it has a different meaning in the texts that say that we are justified by faith.

> "The law, then, was our guardian until Christ, so that we could be justified by faith" (Gal 3:24).

"They are justified freely by His grace through the redemption that is
in Christ Jesus" (Rom 3:24).

"He [God] did it to demonstrate his righteousness at the present
time, so as to be just and the one who justifies those who have
faith in Jesus" (Rom 3:26, NIV).

"Since we have been justified through faith" (Rom 5:1, NIV).

It would be semantically unlikely to define "justify" (*dikaioō*) as
"declare righteous" in the clear examples given previously and then to
shift the meaning in these instances so that the verb means "make righteous" when justification is said to be by faith. Questions arise, of course,
as to how human beings can be declared to be righteous by faith, since we
haven't kept God's commands. We will delay a full discussion of this matter
until we take a closer look at imputation, where we find that righteousness
is by faith because believers enjoy the righteousness of Christ. What is
evident here is that human beings are declared to be righteous by faith.

Counted as Righteous

Another argument supporting a forensic understanding of justification
in Paul is language of being counted righteous by faith. Here we leave the
verb "justify" and find the noun "righteousness" (*dikaiosynē*). We often
find in Paul the expression that faith is credited or counted (*logizomai*) as
righteousness (*dikaiosynē*, Rom 3:28; 4:3, 5, 9, 10, 11, 22, 23, 24; Gal
3:6). The word "count" or "credit" may be used in two different ways.
Something may be counted to a person because it truly belongs to him.
Thus, Phinehas's action was counted as righteous because it was righteous
(Ps 106:31). But something can also be counted as true that is actually not
the case. Jacob's wives were counted as outsiders by Laban even though
they were actually his daughters (Gen 31:15). When we are told that faith is
counted as righteousness, it isn't because faith *is* our righteousness. Instead,
sinners who aren't righteous are counted as righteous and considered as
righteous, even though they are not righteous in themselves. They are
counted to be something that is not theirs inherently.

Such a conclusion is borne out by the context of Romans 4, for righteousness is counted (*logizomai*) to those who haven't performed the
necessary works (4:6), to those who are sinners (4:8). Now if righteousness
is reckoned to sinners, to those who have failed to do what God commands, then it seems that the term designates a status before God instead
of describing the transformation of the human being. Believers are counted

as righteous, not because of what they have done, but because of what God has done for them in Jesus Christ. They are counted righteous because they are united to Jesus Christ by faith.

Righteousness by Faith

I have given one argument as to why the noun "righteousness" (*dikaiosynē*) should not be interpreted transformatively in Paul; it denotes a status—something counted or credited to a person. In the instances considered above, we saw that faith is counted as righteousness. Paul often speaks of righteousness by faith (or a similar expression) as well, and the phrase strengthens the notion that the noun righteousness is forensic.

> "Righteousness through faith" (Rom 3:22).
> "Righteousness that he had by faith" (Rom 4:11).
> "Righteousness of faith" (Rom 4:13, ESV).
> "Righteousness that is by faith" (Rom 9:30, NIV).
> "Christ is the culmination of the law so that there may be righteousness for everyone who believes" (Rom 10:4, NIV).
> "The righteousness that is by faith" (Rom 10:6).
> "One believes with the heart, resulting in righteousness" (Rom 10:10).
> "For through the Spirit, by faith, we eagerly wait for the hope of righteousness" (Gal 5:5).
> "Not having a righteousness of my own from the law, but one that is through faith in Christ—the righteousness from God based on faith" (Phil 3:9).

The phrase righteousness by faith supports a forensic reading, for it suggests that righteousness is given to us, that righteousness is not inherent to the human being, which demonstrates that this righteousness is a gift of God. It is possible, of course, that Paul teaches that human beings are made righteous by faith. Such a conclusion seems less likely, however, since Paul speaks of our faith being counted as righteousness.

Righteousness by Law or Works

To be clear, the argument being made here is that the verbal phrase "justified by faith" and the noun phrase "righteousness by faith" (with all the diversity in the noun phrase) express the same idea. This is the most natural and common sense conclusion. An additional piece of evidence supporting this is the use of both the verb "justify" and the noun "righteousness" in near context to one another.[9] If, as I am suggesting, the two expressions are roughly synonymous, then "righteousness" refers to a righteous *status*. Paul isn't saying that human beings are transformed by faith; he teaches that they stand in the right before God by faith. Such an interpretation is also supported by the references to righteousness by law or righteousness by works:

> "But now, apart from the law, God's righteousness has been revealed" (Rom 3:21).
>
> "David also speaks of the blessing of the man God credits righteousness to apart from works" (Rom 4:6).
>
> "The people of Israel, who pursued the law as the way of righteousness, have not attained their goal" (Rom 9:31, NIV).
>
> "For Moses writes about the righteousness that is from the law: The one who does these things will live by them" (Rom 10:5).
>
> "If righteousness comes through the law, then Christ died for nothing" (Gal 2:21).
>
> "For if a law had been given that was able to give life, then righteousness would certainly be by the law" (Gal 3:21).
>
> "Regarding the righteousness that is in the law, blameless" (Phil 3:6).
>
> "Not having a righteousness of my own from the law" (Phil 3:9).

Just as there are many texts that speak of righteousness by faith, these verses show that there are a number that refer to righteousness by the law or works. Paul teaches often that righteousness isn't obtained by the law or by works. This is similar to the verbal construction we saw earlier where Paul denies that one could be justified by works or the law. The similarity to the verbal phrase is a powerful argument for the notion that the noun "righteousness" along with the verb "justify" are both declarative. In these noun phrases Paul teaches that a righteous status before God isn't achieved through works or through obeying the law.

Thus far, we have seen formidable arguments supporting the forensic view of righteousness. The verb is clearly forensic, meaning that one stands in the right before God. We have also seen that the noun "righteousness" is used in phrases that match the verbal phrases. The parallels suggest that the noun "righteousness" also refers to one's status before God. Such an interpretation is strengthened further by the notion that righteousness is counted to those who believe, to those who trust in God.

---

9. Moo makes this argument effectively in Galatians, and it applies to other Pauline letters as well ("Justification in Galatians," 165–67).

Two Unpersuasive Arguments

At this point, we should take note of a couple of objections to the view presented here. I mentioned earlier that Rom 6:7 could be used to support the transformative view, for there the verbal form "justify" is rendered "freed" in nearly all English versions, and almost all commentators agree that Paul speaks of liberation from sin. Yet this argument is not compelling for several reasons. Almost all scholars still agree that in the vast majority of cases the verb *is* forensic. One slice doesn't make a pie. So even if we have one example where the verb has a transformative meaning, such a conclusion should not be foisted on the other instances where the verb is clearly forensic. Words take their meaning in context, which explains why English translations render "justify" as "freed" here, but they do not do the same elsewhere.

We should also remain open to the possibility that the verb has a forensic meaning in Rom 6:7 as well. Such an interpretation would fit with the use of the verb elsewhere. If this is the case, the forensic declaration (justification) would function as the basis of the transformative (sanctification). Paul would then be teaching that all those who are justified are also sanctified. For these reasons, it is possible that we don't have an exception to the meaning of the verb here.

Another argument sometimes mentioned in support of the transformative view is the parallel between "the ministry of the Spirit" (2 Cor. 3:8) and "the ministry of righteousness" (*dikaiosynē*). The argument goes like this: since those who have experienced the ministry of righteousness also enjoy the ministry of the Spirit, then the ministry of righteousness must be transforming. This argument doesn't convince, however, for parallels should not be confused with equivalency. Yes, all those who are righteous are also transformed by the Spirit, but it doesn't follow logically or lexically that both words signal transformation. Transformation and forensic righteousness are inseparable, but they are also distinguishable. As Douglas Moo says, "The fact that Paul associates justification with transformation through participation in Christ in texts such as Galatians 2:15–21 does not mean that he identifies them."[10]

In fact, there is significant evidence in 2 Cor 3:9 that "righteousness" (*dikaiosynē*) is, indeed, forensic. Righteousness is contrasted with "condemnation" (*katakrisis*), and condemnation is a declarative term. In condemning people God doesn't make them wicked; he declares that they

---

10. Ibid., 175.

are wicked. Similarly, God doesn't make people righteous but declares that they are righteous. They are righteous, as we have seen, by faith alone. How that can be will be explained in due course.

Conclusion

In this chapter we have seen significant evidence supporting a forensic understanding of justification. We began with a look at several examples from the OT before turning to the writings of Paul. In looking at how Paul understands justification, we saw that the verb "justify" (*dikaioō*) is almost certainly forensic. In some contexts, it stands opposed to the word "condemned," and thus it clearly means "declare righteous" instead of "make righteous." Additionally, we saw that people aren't justified by works of law or by the law or by works, and in none of these cases does it make sense to render the verb "make righteous." Thus, it follows that when Paul says we are justified by faith, he means we are declared to be righteous, that we stand in the right before God, by faith.

The noun "righteousness" (*dikaiosynē*) in Paul is likely forensic as well. Like the verb it is found in contexts where its antonym is condemnation, and thus a forensic meaning is almost certainly correct. It is also notable that the noun "righteousness" and the verb "justify" appear in similar contexts, which suggests that the noun has the same forensic color as the verb. Even more important, just as we have verb phrases like "justify by works" or "justify by faith," so too we have noun phrases such as "righteousness by works" and "righteousness by faith." It is unlikely that the word "righteousness" has a different sense in the noun phrases, for the simplest meaning should be preferred instead of multiplying meanings. Hence, in both cases Paul speaks of our right standing before God by faith.

Though the case seems settled, one question yet remains. Noun phrases such as "righteousness by works" and "righteousness by faith" are forensic, but what about the phrase "the righteousness of God"? The phrase "righteousness of God" has played a key role in Pauline theology over the centuries. The question is whether this phrase is also forensic, or should we understand it in a different way? We turn to this subject in the next chapter.

CHAPTER 14

The Righteousness of God

"For in it [the gospel] God's righteousness is revealed
from faith to faith, just as it is written: The righteous will
live by faith."   —Romans 1:17

One of the most significant phrases in Pauline theology is the "righteousness of God." The phrase appears in some of the most important soteriological passages in Paul's writings. If we remember church history, we recall that Luther's understanding of justification turned on, among other things, his comprehension of "the righteousness of God" in Rom 1:17. We aren't surprised to learn, then, that the meaning of the phrase "righteousness of God" has been vigorously debated in recent years. After examining several of the key texts, I will argue here that the term includes the idea of right standing with God.

We have already seen one reason why such a conclusion is probable: when Paul uses the term "righteousness" in soteriological contexts, it denotes right standing with God. It would fit with our expectations, then, to find that Paul uses the phrase "righteousness of God" in soteriological contexts with a similar meaning. Before we investigate the phrase, let's take a look at the relevant verses. Some of these don't have the exact phrase "righteousness of God," but if the concept is present in some form (e.g., with a pronoun), they are included below.

> "For in it [the gospel] God's righteousness is revealed from faith to faith, just as it is written: The righteous will live by faith" (Rom 1:17).
> "But if our unrighteousness highlights God's righteousness, what are we to say? I use a human argument: Is God unrighteous to inflict wrath?" (Rom 3:5).
> "But now, apart from the law, God's righteousness has been revealed—attested by the Law and the Prophets—that is, God's

righteousness through faith in Jesus Christ, to all who believe, since there is no distinction" (Rom 3:21–22).

"God presented Him as a propitiation through faith in His blood, to demonstrate His righteousness, because in His restraint God passed over the sins previously committed. God presented Him to demonstrate His righteousness at the present time, so that He would be righteous and declare righteous the one who has faith in Jesus" (Rom 3:25–26).

"Because they disregarded the righteousness from God and attempted to establish their own righteousness, they have not submitted themselves to God's righteousness" (Rom 10:3).

"But it is from Him that you are in Christ Jesus, who became God-given wisdom for us—our righteousness, sanctification, and redemption" (1 Cor 1:30).

"He [God] made the One [Jesus] who did not know sin to be sin for us, so that we might become the righteousness of God in Him" (2 Cor 5:21).

"And be found in Him, not having a righteousness of my own from the law, but one that is through faith in Christ—the righteousness from God based on faith" (Phil 3:9).

God's Judging Righteousness

The phrase "God's righteousness" may refer to an attribute of God. In Rom 3:5 and 3:25–26, this is almost certainly the meaning, and the emphasis is on God's righteousness in judgment. God's righteousness will be displayed as an attribute of his character when he judges the world on the last day (Rom 3:5). God also demonstrated his righteousness (his holiness and justice) when his wrath was satisfied through Jesus' death on the cross (3:25–26).[1] We have further evidence here that righteousness includes the notion of God's judging righteousness. It can't be limited to his saving righteousness, for God's justice is satisfied in the cross of Jesus Christ. In the cross, then, the judging and saving righteousness of God meet (Rom 3:21–26): God is revealed to be both Savior and Judge, merciful and holy.

The righteousness of God is uniquely revealed in the gospel in that both the love and holiness of God are disclosed. That God's righteousness

---

1. The meaning of these verses is debated fiercely. For a defense of what is said here, see Schreiner, *Romans*, 191–98.

includes the idea of judgment is borne out by Rom 2:5, "But because of your hardness and unrepentant heart you are storing up wrath for yourself in the day of wrath, when God's righteous judgment (*dikaiokrisias*) is revealed." That God's righteousness includes the idea of holiness or justice is borne out by the reference to "propitiation" or the "mercy seat" (*hilastērion*, 3:25), where God both expiated and propitiated sins. This means that our sins were both wiped away and satisfied God's wrath at the cross. If God's wrath was appeased at the cross, then his righteousness, his holiness, is manifested. The sins of the world aren't swept under the rug. Instead, Jesus Christ took upon himself the punishment we deserved.

Justification of the ungodly, then, is the justification or vindication of God, for it vindicates his holiness and righteousness, while at the same time it discloses his mercy and love. God's righteousness is manifested in judgment, but the emphasis in Paul is on God's saving righteousness when he uses the term "righteousness of God." Even when the text denotes God's saving righteousness, the gift that he gives to human beings, the righteousness of God is also an attribute of God. In other words, it is both a genitive of source ("righteousness from God") and a genitive of description ("God's righteousness"). The gift God gives human beings is his own righteousness, his own character. The righteousness of God in Jesus Christ is, as we will see, *imputed* to believers. In the cross of Jesus Christ, then, both the saving and judging righteousness of God are revealed.

A Gift of God

So does the righteousness of God really refer to the gift of God, to one's status before God? The following arguments suggest that it should be interpreted in this way. First, several texts speak of a righteousness of God accessed by faith (Rom 1:17; 3:21–22; 10:3; Phil 3:9). We have already seen that Paul speaks of righteousness by faith. If *righteousness by faith* refers to a right standing with God by faith, which was argued previously, it is natural to think as well that the *righteousness of God* denotes the gift of righteousness from God by faith. The words "of God" in the phrase "righteousness of God" add a new thought that is compatible with "righteousness by faith," namely, the righteousness that belongs to believers by faith is *from God*. It is his gift to them.

Philippians 3:9 removes any doubt about this meaning by using the expression "righteousness from God [*ek theou*]." Here, Paul explicitly contrasts his own righteousness, which derives from the law, to the righteousness that is given to those who have faith in Christ. Our own righteousness is something we achieve if we fulfill the mandates of the law, but the righteousness of God is *from* him—it is a gift granted to those who believe. It is granted by faith alone!

The near context of Rom 3:21–22 points us in the same direction, for the noun clause speaks of a righteousness given by God through faith, and then the verbal clause in 3:24 says Christians "are justified freely by his grace." The clause in 3:24 emphasizes that justification is a gift of God, granted freely, and this fits nicely with the idea that God's righteousness is his gift given to believers in 3:21–22. We see something similar in 10:3, where Paul refers to the righteousness of God. In 10:4 he says righteousness belongs to those who believe and in 10:6 that "righteousness" "is by faith" (NIV). Again, it seems most likely that the expression "righteousness of God" and the use of the word "righteousness" have the same meaning, so that in both cases it denotes the gift God gives his people.

Another text supporting the notion that righteousness is a gift lacks the phrase "of God," yet in the context there is no doubt that the righteousness comes from God. In Rom 5:17 Paul is in the midst of an extended discussion where he contrasts and compares Adam and Christ (5:12–19). He says in 5:17, "Since by the one man's trespass, death reigned through that one man, how much more will those who receive the overflow of grace and the gift of righteousness reign in life through the one man, Jesus Christ." Of interest to us here is the phrase "the gift of righteousness" (*tēs dōreas tēs dikaiosynēs*). Certainly the righteousness in view here comes from God, but what is striking is that it is explicitly designated as a gift. It is something God gives to us in Jesus Christ, and this matches with the notion that the righteousness of God denotes the gift of righteousness God grants to believers.

Paul's reference to righteousness in 1 Cor 1:30 also indicates that righteousness is a gift of God. In Christ Jesus, Paul exclaims, believers are given wisdom, righteousness, sanctification, and redemption. Paul specifically says that "wisdom" is "from God" (*apo theou*), and obviously the phrase "from God" includes righteousness as well. Believers may only boast in the Lord because their righteousness is from him (1 Cor 1:31). It is his gift! Similarly, in 2 Cor 5:21 believers become "the righteousness of God" in Christ Jesus. They are given God's righteousness by virtue of Christ's sacrifice on the cross. We see, then, significant evidence that the righteousness of God is a *gift* of God, a gift that denotes a right standing with God granted to those who put their trust in Jesus Christ.

Parallels between Philippians 3 and Romans 10

The parallels between Philippians 3 and Romans 10 indicate that God's righteousness is the same in both instances, strengthening the idea that the righteousness of God is a gift of God. Philippians 3:2–11 recounts Paul's story and experience before and after his conversion, and we see in Rom 10:1–8 that unbelieving Israel replicated Paul's story as an unbeliever. Unbelieving Israel had a "zeal for God" (10:2), which was expressed in their devotion to the law. Similarly, Paul expressed his "zeal" in persecuting the church before he met Jesus Christ on the Damascus Road (Phil 3:6). Israel tried to "establish their own righteousness" by observing the law (Rom 10:3), and Paul attempted to secure and establish his own righteousness based on his law obedience (Phil 3:6, 9). In both texts Paul contrasts righteousness by law and righteousness by faith (Rom 10:4–8; Phil 3:9).

The remarkable similarities in subject matter that tie Romans 10 and Philippians 3 together strongly suggest that the definition of "righteousness of God" in Romans 10 is the same as the "righteousness from God" in Phil 3:9. In the latter text, righteousness clearly is a gift given to sinners—a declaration that those who have failed to keep the law but who have trusted in Jesus Christ stand in the right before God. In Philippians Paul emphasizes that righteousness is a gift *from God*. I would argue that the parallels and contextual similarities between Philippians 3 and Romans 10 suggest that "the righteousness of God" in Romans 10 shouldn't be interpreted differently from "the righteousness from God" in Phil 3:9. Paul doesn't have to use the preposition "from" (*ek*) in Romans 10 to say that righteousness is God's gift, for his syntax is full of variety and Paul doesn't write technically. This means that the righteousness of God in Rom 10:3 most likely refers to a righteousness *from God*—righteousness that is a gift of God. God's righteousness is not gained through keeping the law; it is given to those who put their faith in God.

We can go one step farther. It is unlikely that the "righteousness of God" in Rom 1:17 and 3:21–22 has a different meaning from what we have found in Romans 10. In all three texts we have similar contexts and similar subject matter. In every case the phrase occurs in a soteriological context, and thus all three passages almost certainly teach that righteousness is a gift of God given to believers.

A Response to Some Transformative Arguments

At this point, let me address a few other arguments that have been adduced to support a transformative understanding of justification. Some have asked: Doesn't the collocation "power of God," "righteousness of God," and "wrath of God" support a transformative view (Rom 1:18)? The argument here is rather imprecise, for this collocation of terms doesn't really help us define *what* righteousness is. The definition of the term must be established from the way the word is used and should be based on clear contextual indicators. Parallel phrases don't necessarily lead to the conclusion that the phrases have the same meaning or significance. The fact that "righteousness" sits next to the word "power" doesn't clearly lead to the conclusion that righteousness is a power that transforms us. It makes perfect sense to say that God's power in the gospel declares us to stand in the right before him since righteousness is a gift.

Romans 5:19 is also sometimes presented to support the transformative position: "For just as through one man's disobedience the many were made sinners, so also through the one man's obedience the many will be made righteous." Those who defend a transformative view maintain that sinners are truly made righteous in Christ, just as they were made sinners through Adam's disobedience. Even if this is the case, it doesn't necessarily follow that the righteousness discussed here is transformative. The verb translated "made" (*kathistēmi*) can be translated in a number of ways, but it especially bears the meaning "appoint" (cf. Matt 24:45; Luke 12:14; Acts 6:3; Titus 1:7; Heb 7:1, 28), which actually fits nicely with a forensic understanding of the verse.

Such a view seems to be borne out by considering the larger context in which Rom 5:18 is located. It seems fair to conclude from the contrast between Adam and Christ that pervades this passage (Rom 5:12–19), and from the insistence that sin and death come from Adam and that righteousness and life hail from Christ that the fundamental thought of the text is forensic. We can also say it this way: the forensic is the basis of the transformative. It is even possible that the future tense ("the many will be made [*katastathēsontai*] righteous") signifies that the righteousness spoken of here is eschatological. People truly become righteous by virtue of Christ's work, but that righteousness is future and won't be theirs fully until the eschaton. Thus, even if this text does say that believers are truly righteous in Christ in the present, it is likely that the forensic is the foundation of the transformative, and the verse doesn't decisively teach that God's righteousness is transformative.

God's Effective Verdict

One additional variant of this view is worth exploring before we move on.[2] Peter Leithart has argued that Yahweh's judgment isn't simply a legal verdict but is also effective and executive, that his justice for the poor isn't only a verdict but also involves deliverance: "He executes justice for the fatherless and the widow, and loves the foreigner, giving him food and clothing" (Deut 10:18; cf. Ps 68:5).[3] Similarly, the righteousness of the future messianic king (Ps 72:1–2) is also effective: "May he vindicate the afflicted among the people, help the poor, and crush the oppressor" (Ps 72:4). The idea in Isa 11:4 is similar, which is also a messianic text: "He will judge the poor righteously and execute justice for the oppressed of the land. He will strike the land with discipline from His mouth, and He will kill the wicked with a command from His lips." God's judgment on the wicked is a verdict that is carried out (Joel 3:12; Mic 4:3; cf. Ezek 7:3–5, 8–9). His word isn't an idle word but creates a new reality.

The notion that God's righteousness is effective is certainly correct. God's verdicts are never empty words; they create a new reality. Yet it doesn't follow from this that righteousness is transformative. Leithart argues that justification is both a verdict and forensic. The verdict is effective so that it "includes the deliverance of those who have been reckoned righteous."[4] Leithart points to Ps 35:22–28, where David's vindication and righteousness include his victory over his foes, his deliverance, suggesting that a forensic category, while true, is too limiting.[5] Similarly, Isa 54:11–17 pictures Israel's justification as its rebirth and restoration, so that once again we have the notion of deliverance.[6] The same notion of deliverance is evident in Paul, according to Leithart, for Paul draws on Psalm 143 in Rom 3:20, and in Psalm 143 righteousness includes the notion of deliverance.[7]

Leithart especially focuses on the implications of Jesus' resurrection for

---

2. See esp. Peter J. Leithart, "Justification as Verdict and Deliverance: A Biblical Perspective," *ProEccl* 16 (2007): 56–72; cf. also Mark A. Seifrid, "Righteousness Language in the Hebrew Scriptures and Early Judaism," in *Justification and Variegated Nomism; Volume 1: The Complexities of Second-Temple Judaism* (Grand Rapids: Baker, 2001), 415–42. I think, however, Seifrid's understanding of effectiveness is closer to mine, for he doesn't see the inherent transformation of human beings in justification.

3. For many of the examples here, see Peter J. Leithart, " 'Judge Me, O God': Biblical Perspective on Justification," in *The Federal Vision* (ed. Steve Wilkins and Duane Garner; Monroe, LA: Athanasius Press, 2004), 203–35.

4. Leithart, "Justification as Verdict and Deliverance," 59.

5. Ibid., 60–61.

6. Ibid., 62–63.

7. Ibid., 64–65.

justification (Rom. 4:25).[8] Jesus' resurrection was his justification (1 Tim 3:16), and it can't be a mere verdict (it can't be limited to the forensic, according to Leithart), for otherwise Jesus would still be in the grave. The verdict of God actually delivered Jesus from the domain of death and sin. Leithart sees this same truth in other texts we have considered, such as Rom 5:15–19; 6:7, and 8:1–4.[9]

Leithart makes a strong case for an understanding of righteousness that hearkens back to Augustine. Such an understanding differs from the Reformers, however, and ventures into Catholic territory, for righteousness now also has the meaning of *make righteous* and isn't limited to *declare righteous*. How should we respond to the evidence presented here? On the one hand, it is certainly correct to say that God's verdicts are effective. On the other hand, there is a danger of confusing terms, so that everything means everything. If a psalm speaks of righteousness, deliverance, victory, and the like, we shouldn't make the mistake of thinking that righteousness means victory or deliverance. As was argued earlier, words still have distinct meanings. So while it is certainly true that all those who are justified are also delivered, it doesn't follow from this that justified means deliverance. Too often, words that are associated with righteousness are used to define righteousness and thus the distinction between the words used is completely erased.

Still, there is truth to the notion that this forensic verdict is effective. God's vindication of Jesus was displayed in his resurrection. God's words are never empty; they do create a new reality. Nevertheless, despite Leithart's protestations, his reading ventures into the Augustinian definition "make righteous." If the verdict that we are justified or righteous is, indeed, an effective one, it would follow that Leithart is saying that we are not only declared righteous, but we are actually made righteous.

The problem with this line of thinking—that the effectiveness of the verdict means that we are made righteous—is that the term itself has a forensic meaning, as we showed earlier. Understanding either the noun or the verb to mean "make righteous" doesn't accord with the many texts we have examined. No one denies, of course, that those who are declared righteous are also changed by God's grace. The issue, though, is the precise meaning of the term before us. If the term means *make righteous*, then it seems that justification is progressive, for we aren't made perfectly righteous when we first believe. In other words, the effectiveness doesn't

---

8. Ibid., 65–67.
9. Ibid., 67–72.

go that far. This isn't to deny that the verdict is effective. It does mean, however, that we need to carefully define what we mean when we speak of an *effective* verdict.

I would suggest that what we mean when we say a verdict is effective is that sinners who trust in Christ are truly righteous before God, but the righteousness doesn't lie in themselves but in Jesus Christ. They are righteous because they are united to Jesus Christ, and he is their righteousness. This verdict of righteousness isn't a legal fiction, for believers are truly righteous because all that Christ is belongs to them. They are righteous because Christ's righteousness is imputed to them, and to that subject we turn in the next chapter. The imputation of Christ's righteousness is no legal fiction, but neither should it be defined in terms of transformation or the infusion of righteousness.

Conclusion

I have argued that the term "righteousness of God" should be understood forensically, to denote right standing before God. God's righteousness is a gift he gives to those who trust in him for salvation. Hence, believers are right before God by faith alone. The term also refers to the character of God, so that the genitive refers to a gift of God and an attribute of God. God gives his righteousness to human beings. The gift character of righteousness is evident from Rom 5:17; 1 Cor 1:30; and Phil 3:9. We also saw that the parallels between Phil 3:2–9 and Rom 10:1–8 demonstrate that God's righteousness is a gift in each instance.

The fact that "from" (*ek*) isn't repeated in Romans 10 is scarcely determinative, for Paul is flexible in his use of language. Context is the most important factor for assessing the meaning. If "righteousness of God" refers to God's gift in Romans 10, it almost certainly has that meaning in Rom 1:17 and 3:21–22 as well. Furthermore, Paul glides from "righteousness" in Rom 9:30–32 to "righteousness of God" in Rom 10:3, and it is likely that the term has the same meaning. The latter simply emphasizes that it comes from God. Some have argued that the effectiveness of the verdict means that righteousness is transformative. But such arguments don't overturn the normal meaning of the word. Yes, the verdict is effective: we really are in a right relationship with God since Christ is our righteousness and we are united to Christ by faith. We are truly right in God's sight by faith alone!

CHAPTER 15

Imputation of Righteousness

> "So then, as through one trespass there is condemnation
> for everyone, so also through one righteous act there is
> life-giving justification for everyone. For just as through
> one man's disobedience the many were made sinners, so
> also through the one man's obedience the many will be
> made righteous."　　　　　　　　　—*Romans 5:18–19*

The idea that Christ's righteousness is counted or credited to believers is known as imputation. Imputed righteousness has been the subject of controversy, but as we have seen in our journey through church history to the present day, such controversy is nothing new. During the Reformation, Roman Catholics rejected imputed righteousness. Richard Baxter and John Wesley both worried that the notion of imputation would lead to antinomianism. Today, two of the most prominent opponents of imputation are Robert Gundry and N. T. Wright.

Since this book is an introduction and a tour through the doctrine of justification—historically, biblically, and theologically—I can only cover some of the broad strokes of the issue. In this chapter, I will summarize the fundamental objections to the idea that Christ's righteousness is imputed to believers and then respond to them and show how this teaching is biblically grounded. I will argue that Christ's righteousness is imputed to us because we are united with Christ.[1] The central texts we will consider are those that state that faith is *counted* as righteousness (e.g., Rom 4:1–8; Gal 3:6; 2 Cor. 5:21; Phil 3:9; Rom. 5:12–19).

---

1. So Bird, *Saving Righteousness of God*, 60–87. Hence, in my judgment Bird's expression "incorporated righteousness" or Seifrid's notion that our righteousness is in Jesus Christ crucified and risen (*Christ, Our Righteousness*, 174–76) are simply different ways of expressing the truth of imputation. Imputation isn't grounded in the technical language of active and passive righteousness.

Arguments against Imputation

N. T. Wright is well known for his writing on justification. Wright agrees that justification is forensic and that it derives from the courtroom.[2] But he doesn't agree with the idea that righteousness is imputed, believing that imputation strays from the biblical text. Wright contends that in a courtroom when the judge declares the defendant to be righteous, he doesn't give his righteousness to the defendant. "If Paul uses the language of the law court, it makes no sense whatever to say that the judge imputes, imparts, bequeaths, conveys or otherwise transfers his righteousness either to the plaintiff or the defendant."[3] And, "Here we meet, not for the last time, the confusion that arises inevitably when we try to think of the judge transferring by imputation, or any other way, his own attributes to the defendant."[4] And, "When the judge in the lawcourt justifies someone, he does not give that person his own particular 'righteousness.' He *creates* the status the vindicated defendant now possesses, by an act of *declaration*, a 'speech-act' in our contemporary jargon."[5]

In his consideration of 1 Cor 1:30, Wright notes that imputation isn't a convincing way to understand this passage, for if one maintains that righteousness is imputed to us, then one also has to say that wisdom, sanctification, and redemption are imputed since all these benefits are listed together. Since no one claims that these other gifts are imputed, it doesn't work to say that righteousness alone is imputed.

Wright also rejects any notion of imputation in 2 Cor 5:21 ("He made the One who did not know sin to be sin for us, so that we might become the righteousness of God in Him"). He finds three problems with interpreting the verse to support the notion that Christ's righteousness is imputed to believers.[6] First, the text speaks of God's righteousness, not Christ's.

---

2. Wright, *Justification,* 46, 69, 157–67, 206, 231–33.

3. Wright, *What Saint Paul Really Said,* 98. He goes on to say, "To imagine the defendant somehow receiving the judge's righteousness is simply a category mistake. That is not how language works" (ibid.).

4. Wright, *Justification,* 66. Wright declares, "The judge has not clothed the defendant with his own 'righteousness.' That doesn't come into it. Nor has he given the defendant something called 'the righteousness of the Messiah'—or, if he has, Paul has not even hinted at it. What the judge has done is to pass judicial sentence on sin, in the faithful death of the Messiah, so that those who belong to the Messiah, though in themselves 'ungodly' and without virtue or merit, now find themselves hearing the law court verdict, 'in the right'" (ibid., 206).

5. Ibid., 69. *"But the righteousness they have will not be God's own righteousness.* That makes no sense at all. God's own righteousness is his covenant faithfulness.... But God's righteousness remains his own property" (*What Saint Paul Really Said,* 99).

6. Wright, *Paul and the Faithfulness of God,* 881–84.

So how can people say that Christ's righteousness is imputed when Paul refers to *God's* righteousness? Second, Paul doesn't say that righteousness is reckoned or imputed to us but says we "become" God's righteousness. The verbal language hardly fits with imputation, for the language implies a process. And third, Paul discusses his own ministry here, and so it doesn't fit to inject the idea of imputation into the context.

First person plurals dominate the text (cf. 2 Cor. 5:11–6:13), and Paul distinguishes between himself as an apostle and his readers, identifying himself with the first person plurals and his readers with third person plurals (5:14–15, 19), second person plurals (5:11–13, 20; 6:1), or third person singulars (5:16–17). Hence, the first person plurals refer to Paul as an apostolic emissary. In other words, 5:21 teaches that Paul embodies in his apostolic ministry the covenant faithfulness of God.

Several years ago, Robert Gundry caused a stir in evangelical circles when he denied the positive imputation of Christ's righteousness.[7] Along with N.T. Wright, he believes in what is sometimes called negative imputation: the idea that our sins are forgiven for Christ's sake but a rejection of any positive imputation of Christ's righteousness. Gundry raises a number of objections to this sense of positive imputation. He points out that texts used to support the imputation of Christ's righteousness actually speak of *God's* righteousness being given to us (e.g., 1 Cor 1:30; 2 Cor 5:21; Phil 3:9). Hence, these texts don't actually teach the imputation of *Christ's* righteousness. In addition, the "one righteous act" of Christ that grants justification refers to his work on the cross, not his lifelong obedience (Rom 5:18). Thus, there is no basis here to see that Christ's righteous life is credited to believers. Finally, when we look at texts like Rom 4:1–8, we read that faith is counted to believers as righteousness. The most natural way of reading this verse is to say that *faith is our righteousness.*[8] Gundry sees nothing in the text to support the idea that the righteousness of Christ is imputed to us when we believe. In fact, he has argued that we lack an explicit statement anywhere in Scripture that says Christ's righteousness is imputed to believers.

---

7.   See Robert H. Gundry, "Why I Didn't Endorse 'The Gospel of Jesus Christ: An Evangelical Celebration' ... Even Though I Wasn't Asked to," *Books and Culture* 7.1 (January-February 2001): 6–9; idem, "The Nonimputation of Christ's Righteousness," in *"Justification": What's at Stake in the Current Debates* (ed. M. A. Husbands and D. J. Trier; Downers Grove, IL: InterVarsity Press, 2004), 17–45.

8.   Gundry's reading is not new. Richard Baxter also held this view. See Boersma, *A Hot Pepper Corn*, 287; Clifford, *Atonement and Justification*, 25.

Arguments Supporting Imputation

At the outset, it should be said that the question of imputation is rather complex and nuanced. There are several excellent treatments of this topic that ably defend its biblical-theological credibility.[9] My aim here is to present some of the main arguments supporting imputation so you are familiar with them. Before we begin, I would point out that the discussion regarding imputation does not depend on the distinction commonly made between Christ's active and passive righteousness, though such terminology (rightly understood) conveys well what Paul teaches. Unfortunately, as has often been pointed, the meaning of the words active and passive is liable to misunderstanding.[10]

Still, we shouldn't restrict the notion of imputation to those who use the language of active and passive obedience. Martin Luther, for instance, certainly believed that all our righteousness was in Jesus Christ, and yet he did not use the language of active and passive obedience. Instead, he stressed that believers were married to Christ, that all of who Jesus is belongs to believers, and this includes their righteousness. If we wish to speak in Pauline biblical categories, we can say that believers are *in Christ*—they are united to him. In that sense Christ is, as 1 Cor 1:30 says, our wisdom, righteousness, sanctification, and redemption. Those who affirm that their righteousness is not in themselves but in Jesus Christ

---

9. Brian Vickers, *Jesus' Blood and Righteousness: Paul's Theology of Imputation* (Wheaton, IL: Crossway, 2006); John Piper, *Counted Righteous in Christ: Should We Abandon the Imputation of Christ's Righteousness?* (Wheaton, IL: Crossway, 2002); D. A. Carson, "The Vindication of Imputation: On Fields of Discourse and, of Course, Semantic Fields," in *Justification: What's at Stake in the Current Debates?* (ed. Mark A. Husbands and Daniel J. Treier; Downers Grove, IL: InterVarsity Press, 2004), 46–78.

10. John Murray remarks (*Redemption Accomplished or Applied* [Grand Rapids: Eerdmans, 1955], 21–22):

Neither are we to suppose that we can allocate certain phases or acts of our Lord's life on earth to the active obedience and certain other phases and acts to the passive obedience. The distinction between the active and passive obedience is not a distinction of periods. It is our Lord's whole work of obedience in every phase and period that is described as active and passive, and we must avoid the mistake of thinking that the active obedience applies to the obedience of his life and the passive obedience to the obedience of his final sufferings and death.

The real use and purpose of the formula is to emphasize the two distinct aspects of our Lord's vicarious obedience. The truth expressed rests on the recognition that the law of God has both penal sanctions and positive demands. It demands not only the full discharge of its precepts but also the infliction of penalty for all infractions and shortcomings. It is this twofold demand of the law of God which is taken into account when we speak of the active and passive obedience of Christ. Christ as the vicar of his people came under the curse and condemnation due to sin and he also fulfilled the law of God in all its positive requirements. In other words, he took care of the guilt of sin and perfectly fulfilled the demands of righteousness. He perfectly met both the penal and the preceptive requirements of God's law. The passive obedience refers to the former and the active obedience to the latter.

affirm what the Scriptures teach about imputation, and they agree on this fundamental issue.

Romans 5:12–19

One of the most important texts on imputation is Rom 5:12–19. The goal here isn't to provide a full exegesis. What is striking is the fundamental role of both Adam and Christ. Human beings are sinners because they are united with Adam, and they are righteous if they are united with Christ. Let's begin by citing the passage in full:

> [12]Therefore, just as sin entered the world through one man, and death through sin, in this way death spread to all men, because all sinned. [13]In fact, sin was in the world before the law, but sin is not charged to a person's account when there is no law. Nevertheless, death reigned from Adam to Moses, even over those who did not sin in the likeness of Adam's transgression. He is a prototype of the Coming One. [15]But the gift is not like the trespass. For if by the one man's trespass the many died, how much more have the grace of God and the gift overflowed to the many by the grace of the one man, Jesus Christ. [16]And the gift is not like the one man's sin, because from one sin came the judgment, resulting in condemnation, but from many trespasses came the gift, resulting in justification. [17]Since by the one man's trespass, death reigned through that one man, how much more will those who receive the overflow of grace and the gift of righteousness reign in life through the one man, Jesus Christ. [18]So then, as through one trespass there is condemnation for everyone, so also through one righteous act there is life-giving justification for everyone. [19]For just as through one man's disobedience the many were made sinners, so also through the one man's obedience the many will be made righteous.

The issue before us is whether this text teaches that Christ's righteousness is imputed or counted to us as believers. I would maintain that we see imputation in Rom 5:18, for Paul says that Christ's one act of righteousness brings justification and life to all who belong to him. The one act of righteousness probably focuses on Jesus' obedience at the cross, and yet Jesus' act of obedience in consenting to die would not have availed for us if he hadn't lived an obedient life. His single act of obedience shouldn't be segregated from the obedience that marked out his whole life.

How does this relate to imputation? The whole of Jesus' obedience — the entirety of his righteous life — is counted or credited to us when we are united to him. It should be noted that NT writers don't actually emphasize that Jesus obeyed the law, though imputation is often explained in these terms. Instead, they stress that he obeyed his Father, that he did everything the Father called him to do, for the Father mandated him to do many things that were not written in the law. Jesus, as the Son of the Father, did what his Father commanded on all occasions and in every circumstance, and so his obedience transcends keeping the Torah. Jesus' obedience is displayed supremely in the cross, his taking the punishment upon himself that human beings deserved. In any case, when we put our faith in Jesus, we are given the whole Christ, so that both his sin-bearing death and his obedience are counted to us.

If we look at the Adam–Christ parallel in Rom 5:12–19, it is evident that sin, death, and condemnation entered the world through Adam. Conversely, Jesus, in contrast to Adam, was the obedient one, and hence life and righteousness come through him. The issue of imputation, then, turns on the larger structure of the passage. All human beings enter the world as sons and daughters of Adam. They are sinners, dead and condemned because of Adam's sin, because they are united with Adam. By contrast, those who are in Christ enjoy life and righteousness because they belong to him. The doctrine of imputation, then, doesn't depend simply on a close reading of Rom 5:18 or even on detailed analysis of 5:19, though such readings are valuable. It is something we see when we take the passage as a whole. The larger context clearly teaches that human beings belong to either Adam or Christ. If one belongs to Christ, then one enjoys all that he is and all that he has for them. This is another way of saying that believers are righteous because they enjoy union with Christ. All of who Jesus is belongs to us and is counted to us — both in paying sin's penalty and in his obedience to the law.

Paul returns repeatedly in this passage to the truth that believers are righteous or justified in Christ (Rom 5:16, 17, 18, 19). The parallel with Adam is illuminating. All people are sinners and dead because of their solidarity with Adam, and conversely all believers, all those who have received "the gift of righteousness" (5:17), enjoy this righteousness by virtue of their union with Christ. Their righteousness doesn't lie in themselves but in Jesus Christ. Nor is there any reason to parcel Christ out, as if believers have only received forgiveness of sins. In receiving Christ they enjoy all that he is. Luther's picture of being married to Christ captures well what Paul teaches here.

Faith Unites to Christ

Another important issue for us to consider is what Paul means when he says that righteousness is ours by faith. We can certainly see why some think this means that faith *is* our righteousness. Paul doesn't answer our question directly, but again the larger context is helpful, supporting the notion that faith counts as our righteousness because it unites us with Jesus Christ in his death and resurrection (Rom 3:21–26; 4:25).[11] Paul emphasizes that the faith that justifies is apart from works and that faith justifies the ungodly (4:1–8). There is nothing in the human subject that brings justification. It is striking and illuminating that Paul's repeated emphasis on faith being counted as righteousness in Romans 4 is subsequent to his exposition of the death of Christ (3:21–26). *What saves believers is not ultimately their faith but the object of their faith.*[12] They believe in the God who has given over his Son to death and raised him from the dead (4:25). Faith saves, faith alone saves, because Christ as the crucified and risen one saves. The curse for human beings is only removed through the cross (Gal 3:13), and thus faith is the instrument that connects human beings to the one who redeems us from our sins (Eph 1:7; Col 1:14).

Some argue that defining faith as an instrument is a theological imposition on the text, but I would suggest that such a conclusion is exegetically reasonable and theologically sensible. First, no one reads texts with a blank slate. Everyone comes to texts with a theological map, and having such a map shouldn't be rejected as a disadvantage, as long as we recognize that we all come to the text with preconceptions. Those who believe they are reading the text historically and neutrally without any theological presuppositions are naïve and are deficient readers precisely because they think their reading is completely objective. A satisfying reading recognizes, at least in part (since none of us can succeed completely in this enterprise), our biases and theological preconceptions and then attempts to read the text afresh and anew, probing to see if the text reshapes and reconfigures our theology.

So is faith our righteousness? Or is faith an instrument whereby we receive Christ as our righteousness? Paul regularly says that our righteousness comes from God (Rom 10:3; Phil 3:9), and believers are righteous by faith because they belong to Jesus Christ. Another way of putting it is to say that righteousness doesn't come from the law but from the death

---

11. So also Rainbow, *The Way of Salvation*, 111, n. 38.

12. It is somewhat ironic that Clifford sees this point but denies imputation (*Atonement and Justification*, 176–77).

of Christ (Gal 2:21). The curse of the law is removed from those who put their trust in Jesus Christ, who became a curse for them (3:10–13). Redemption doesn't come from the obedience of human beings but from God's Son, who liberates those who were under the law (4:4–5). The only boast for believers is the cross of Jesus Christ, for their death to the world and the arrival of the new creation are theirs via the cross (6:14–15). Jesus gave himself so that those who trust in him experience a new exodus; they are delivered from the present evil age by his grace (1:4).

We see the same emphases in Romans—another letter where Paul emphasizes righteousness by faith. Believers are right before God by Jesus' redeeming work in which he satisfied the wrath of God through his blood (Rom 3:24–26). The righteousness of believers is outside of themselves and is located in the cross of Christ. Believers are forgiven and justified because of the death and resurrection of Jesus Christ (4:25). His vindication, received at his resurrection (1 Tim 3:16), is their vindication. This fits with what we saw above. Believers enjoy life and are righteous because they are in Christ instead of in Adam (Rom 5:12–19). They are no longer under the law because they have died with Jesus Christ (7:4), and thus there is no condemnation by virtue of Jesus' giving himself as a sin-offering, where he took upon himself the condemnation that human beings deserved (8:1–3).

The centrality of the cross in Paul, which we have touched on lightly and briefly, plays a fundamental role in the debate of whether faith is our righteousness. This debate can't be definitively settled, for Paul doesn't address directly the question we are asking, and we can understand why some make the claim that faith *is* our righteousness. Nevertheless, it seems more likely both theologically (given the centrality of the cross) and exegetically (since the righteousness of faith is in close proximity to expositions on the cross), that faith justifies because it unites believers to the crucified and risen Lord. Hence, the righteousness of believers is not in themselves, nor even in their faith. Faith justifies because God justifies the ungodly in Jesus Christ. It isn't our faith that saves us but the object of our faith.

2 Corinthians 5:21

Certainly one of the most important texts dealing with imputation is 2 Cor 5:21: "He made the One who did not know sin to be sin for us, so that we might become the righteousness of God in Him." If you recall,

Wright had several objections to interpreting this passage in support of imputation. For instance, how could this text refer to the imputation of Christ's righteousness since Paul speaks of the righteousness of God? I don't find this question persuasive, for even though Paul does speak of the righteousness of God, such righteousness is ours in and through Jesus Christ. The righteousness of God is "in Him."[13] Hence, God's righteousness, which is given to us as believers, becomes ours through union with Christ.

We have here what the Epistle to Diognetus calls the great exchange.[14] God made Jesus Christ who was free from all sin to be sin on our behalf. Saying that Jesus was made to be sin either means that Jesus was counted as a sinner, even though he was sinless, or it means that Jesus became a sacrifice of sin for our sake. It is difficult to decide exactly which is intended, and for our purposes we do not need to make a decision, for in both instances the sin of human beings was placed on Jesus so that as a substitute for sinners, he took on himself the penalty we deserved. This is the great exchange, for Jesus took on himself human sin, and believers receive the righteousness of God in and through Jesus Christ. God reconciles the world to himself in Christ by not counting our trespasses against us (2 Cor 5:19). Those who belong to Christ enjoy all that Christ is for their sake, so that the righteousness of God is theirs in Jesus Christ.

Wright thinks the verb "become" (*genōmetha*) can't be equative, that the verb carries the notion of "becoming." He doubts that imputation can be intended if we *become* the righteousness of God. But the verb "become" (*ginomai*) is flexible in Paul and can easily be taken as equative (cf. Rom 11:6; 12:6; 1 Cor 3:18; 4:16). And even if the verb means "become," it doesn't rule out imputation, for believers become something they weren't before ("righteous!") by virtue of union with Christ. They receive right standing with God as a gift.

Wright also doubts that imputation is present in 2 Cor 5:21, for he interprets the first person plural pronoun to refer to Paul and to his apostolic ministry. Seeing a reference to Paul is certainly understandable since first person plural pronouns dominate 5:11–21, and they refer often to Paul. Despite this evidence, Paul almost certainly refers to all Christians when he uses a first person plural pronoun in 5:21. When Paul uses pronouns, he is flexible and switches the referent back and forth frequently.

---

13. See here David E. Garland, *2 Corinthians* (NAC; Nashville: Broadman, 1999), 300–302; Murray J. Harris, *The Second Epistle to the Corinthians: A Commentary on the Greek Text* (NIGTC; Grand Rapids: Eerdmans, 2005) 454–56, and esp. n. 207 on pp. 455–56.

14. See the citation on p. 29 above.

For example, in 4:14 the first person plural clearly refers to Paul (and perhaps his coworkers), but in 4:16–5:10 the first person plural includes all Christians. In the same way, "we" in 3:18 refers to all Christians, but in 4:1 "we" focuses on Paul. When we turn to 5:11–21, most of the first person plurals in this section refer to Paul, but when he writes in 5:18 that God "reconciled us to Himself through Christ," the "us" should not be limited to just Paul and his coworkers. The reconciling work of God includes all believers.

Indeed, because of God's reconciling work on the cross, all are exhorted to be reconciled to God (2 Cor 5:20). So too in 5:21 Christ became sin for all believers, so that all those who are in Christ enjoy the righteousness of God by virtue of their union with Jesus Christ.[15] To sum up, 5:21 clearly teaches that God's righteousness is imputed to us in and through Jesus Christ. Because we are united to Jesus, all that he is and has is given to us, including his righteousness.

1 Corinthians 1:30

First Corinthians 1:30 has been another prominent text in the discussion of imputation. Clearly, the righteousness of believers is a gift of God, for it is righteousness "from God" (*apo theou*). It won't work to say that believers don't receive Christ's righteousness since Paul speaks of God's righteousness in this verse. The Father and the Son cannot be easily and neatly separated from one another, for the righteousness of God belongs to believers because they are "in Christ Jesus."

More compelling, however, is the objection that because this verse also refers to God's wisdom, sanctification, and redemption, how can we say that God's righteousness is imputed to us unless we are also willing to say that God's wisdom, sanctification, and redemption are also imputed? Though I would agree that this objection has some merit, ultimately it is not decisive. I won't argue here that this verse clearly and indisputably teaches the imputation of Christ's righteousness. Since interpretation is both an exegetical and theological endeavor, any interpretation of 1:30 will be colored (and rightly so) by how other texts are understood.

But this objection assumes that every item in the list (wisdom, righteousness, sanctification, and redemption) must be given to believers in the

---

15. In support of the notion that righteousness is a gift here, see Joseph A. Fitzmyer, "Justification by Faith in Pauline Thought: A Catholic View," in *Rereading Paul Together: Protestant and Catholic Perspectives on Justification* (Grand Rapids: Baker, 2006), 86–87.

same way—if one item in the list is imputed, then all have to be imputed. But this necessity doesn't follow logically, for each of the words has a different meaning. I would argue that the use of the word righteousness suggests imputation. It isn't necessary to assume that God's wisdom and righteousness are given *in the same way*, for the meaning of each term is also determined by the semantic range of the word selected. We have seen that when Paul uses the word righteousness, there are good reasons for thinking that he refers to the gift of righteousness, to an alien righteousness that is given to us in Christ. Again, though we can't prove imputation from this verse, imputation isn't ruled out by the collocation of terms either. Indeed, imputation fits plausibly with what Paul says about God's righteousness elsewhere.

The Courtroom

One final objection should be considered. Wright protests that no judge in a courtroom actually *gives* his righteousness to the defendant, and hence we should not conceive of God giving his own righteousness to believers. Wright falls into the mistake of limiting what Paul teaches because of the analogy he has used. Wright is correct in saying that judges don't grant their righteousness to defendants. But Paul's point is that the divine courtroom is radically different in some respects from a human courtroom! "Acquitting the guilty" is "detestable to the LORD" (Prov 17:15), and yet God justifies the ungodly (Rom 4:5)! Human judges should not acquit the guilty, but God justifies the ungodly by virtue of Christ's sacrifice. In ordinary courtrooms the judge doesn't declare a person to be innocent if someone else takes the punishment they deserved. If a typical judge made such a pronouncement, people would—and should—be outraged. But the cross is an entirely different affair, for God in his love sent his Son Jesus Christ who voluntarily and gladly came to suffer in the place of sinners. Jesus took upon himself the punishment sinners deserved. Just as God forgives sinners through the cross and resurrection of Jesus Christ, so too he grants them his righteousness through Jesus. Yes, this is quite different from a human courtroom. And thank God for that!

Conclusion

I have briefly argued here that there are good reasons for believing that Paul taught the imputation of Christ's righteousness. Again, Rom 5:12–19 is a decisive text. All human beings either belong to Adam or to Christ as their covenant heads; they are either condemned in Adam or righteous in Christ. Just as the sin of Adam is imputed to human beings, so the righteousness of Christ is imputed to believers. The most natural reading of 2 Cor 5:21 also supports imputation. Jesus became sin for us, and we receive the righteousness of God since we are united to Jesus Christ. The believer's union with Christ points strongly to imputation, for our righteousness doesn't lie in ourselves but in Jesus Christ as the crucified and risen one. Other texts, such as 1 Cor 1:30 and Phil 3:9, support imputation as well. When Paul says faith counts as our righteousness, he doesn't mean that faith *is* our righteousness. He means that faith counts as righteousness because through faith we are united to Jesus Christ. Justification is by faith alone, because it is achieved by Christ alone, and it is ours only through union with Jesus Christ.

CHAPTER 16

The Role of Good Works in Justification

> "What good is it, my brothers and sisters, if someone claims to have faith but has no deeds? Can such faith save them?" —*James 2:14 (NIV)*

W hen some hear the Reformation cry of *sola fide*—"Faith alone!"— they assume that it means that good works are an optional part of the Christian life or that they play no role at all in our final justification or salvation. Such a perspective radically misunderstands the NT witness, while also distorting the historical and biblical meaning of *sola fide*.[1] The NT clearly teaches that bare faith cannot save, and that works are necessary for final justification or final salvation. As we will see, this latter notion does not compromise or deny *sola fide* when it is properly understood.

Mental Assent Isn't Saving Faith

What do we mean when we speak of "bare" faith? By bare faith I refer to what is often called intellectual assent to a set of statements, doctrines, or beliefs. In other words, merely saying that one believes isn't the same thing as saving faith. As James says in Jas 2:14, "What good is it, my brothers and sisters, if someone claims to have faith but has no deeds? Can such faith save them?"[2] Obviously not! Faith without works, a faith without deeds, does not profit us. To put it another way, it doesn't deliver us from God's eschatological wrath. A "claiming" faith, a "saying" faith, an "assenting" faith without any accompanying works is not a saving faith.

Devils have bare faith. James gives what is probably the most powerful

---

1. It distorts the OT as well, but for space reasons we confine ourselves to the NT. See here Bird, *Saving Righteousness of God*, 155–78.

2. For a history of interpretation of how to reconcile Paul and James, see Clifford, *Atonement and Justification*, 221–39.

and telling example of such in the Scriptures. "You believe that there is one God. Good! Even the demons believe that—and shudder" (Jas 2:19 NIV). Ascribing to and endorsing orthodox doctrines should never be confused with genuine faith. Demons can confess monotheism, and yet their hearts are far from the one true God. Indeed, they hate him and all of his ways. Consider the reactions of the demons when they encountered Jesus during his earthly ministry. They acknowledged that he was "the Holy One of God" (Mark 1:24; cf. Luke 4:34), and in that sense, they "believed" in him and knew more about him at that stage in his ministry than most anyone, even Jesus' own disciples. But they certainly didn't love Jesus, and they didn't believe in him to the extent that they entrusted their lives to him. This leads me to conclude that there is a kind of faith, an intellectual understanding, that is "bare" and "empty." It subscribes to mental propositions but doesn't embrace and love Jesus, and in the final analysis it proves to be no faith at all.

Some in the movement known as the Free Grace movement claim that bare mental assent actually saves people.[3] They have come up with a novel interpretation of James 2, for they claim that the words "justify" (*dikaioō*) and "save" (*sōzō*) do not refer to eschatological salvation. James, they claim, isn't actually talking about end-time salvation, for that would contradict salvation by faith alone. Instead, James refers to a fruitful life on earth, to being saved from a life shorn of God's blessing and power.

The motive behind this interpretation is commendable, for those who espouse it long to celebrate the grace of God. They want to eliminate any notion that human works qualify us to stand before God. They want to preserve in all its power and beauty the notion that salvation is *sola fide*. Still, the gambit fails, for this is an example of desperate exegesis. It doesn't work to provide new definitions for the words "justify" and "save," definitions that aren't found in the rest of the NT.

We have every reason to think that the words "justify" and "save" refer to our final salvation. After all, James uses the same words Paul uses when discussing soteriology ("faith," "works," "justify," and "save"). Indeed, one of the most prominent verses that Paul appeals to in discussing justification (Gen 15:6; Rom 4:3; Gal 3:6) is cited in James (Jas 2:23). And James and Paul both discuss the same person—Abraham. Surely, the burden of proof is on the one who thinks the issue is salvation in Paul but an entirely different matter in James.

---

3.   See, e.g., Earl D. Radmacher, "First Response to 'Faith According to the Apostle James' by John F. MacArthur Jr.," *JETS* 33 (1990): 35–41.

Instead, the natural way to read these texts is to say that both James and Paul are addressing the same issue. The Free Grace interpretation looks like an expedient to defend and support one's theology. While Scripture interprets Scripture, at the same time we must ensure that we don't do violence to what texts say, for otherwise we are in danger of twisting the Scripture to fit our own preconceptions.

It is clear, then, that James is teaching that bare faith alone — simply agreeing that certain statements are true — does not save us. "Faith by itself" when "it is not accompanied by action, is dead" (Jas 2:17). Or, "faith without deeds is useless" (2:20 NIV). By this, James isn't denying *sola fide*; rather, he inveighs against an empty faith, a barren faith, an inactive faith — a dead faith. Genuine faith is a living and active thing, and it will inevitably produce results. We see this plainly in 2:22, "You see that his faith and his actions were working together, and his faith was made complete by what he did" (NIV). Faith and works belong together.

If I really trust my auto mechanic, I will trust him when he fixes my car instead of accusing him of cheating. If I trust my doctor's expertise and wisdom, I will take the medicine he or she prescribes. Faith is shown as genuine when it is brought to completion by our actions. As Prov 20:6 says, "Many claim to have unfailing love, but a faithful person who can find?" (NIV). People can *claim* to believe, but the reality of their faith is demonstrated in their actions. Their actions reveal whether they have a bare faith when they nod in mental agreement but nothing more.

Deficient Faith in Matthew, John, and Paul

Deficient Faith in Matthew

This notion of bare faith isn't limited to James. I will include some brief examples from Matthew, John, and Paul so that it will be evident that the New Testament speaks with one accord on this matter.

To begin, consider Jesus' interpretation of the parable of the Sower. In this parable, some of the soils show initial promise, but as time elapses they reveal that they weren't the types of soil that produce lasting fruit.

The seed falling on rocky ground refers to someone who hears the word and at once receives it with joy. But since they have no root, they last only a short time. When trouble or persecution comes because of the word, they quickly fall away. The seed falling among the thorns refers to someone who hears the word, but the worries of this life and the deceitfulness of wealth choke the word, making it unfruitful. But the seed falling on good soil refers to someone who hears the word and understands it. This is the one who produces a crop, yielding a hundred, sixty or thirty times what was sown. (Matt 13:20–23 NIV)

Only the last soil *truly* receives the seed. We learn from Jesus that some initially accept the word joyfully (they exercise a kind of faith), but they renounce it when troubles arise, which demonstrates their faith isn't genuine, for true faith is a *persevering* faith. These people don't have roots, and this shows that they weren't truly planted by God. Similarly, the troubles of life choke out the word falling on the third soil. The only proof of genuine faith, then, is fruitful faith—faith that perseveres and leads to a long-term bearing of fruit, a faith that leads to good works.

Deficient Faith in John

John's gospel has at least two additional examples of inadequate faith. Early in Jesus' ministry, when the crowds coming to see him were exploding in number because of his miracles, John gives us an extraordinary glimpse into what Jesus was thinking. "While He was in Jerusalem at the Passover Festival, many trusted in His name when they saw the signs He was doing. Jesus, however, would not entrust Himself to them, since He knew them all" (John 2:23–24). Jesus' signs had a remarkable effect, for people saw them and believed (*episteusan*) in him. John hints, however, that their belief was not genuine, for even though they believed in Jesus, the trust wasn't mutual. Jesus didn't believe in or entrust (*episteuen*) himself to them. Why would Jesus act in such a puzzling and even off-putting way? The clue is found in the last line in v. 24: Jesus knew what was in the human heart. He knew they were attracted by signs and wonders (cf. 4:48), and that they were amazed by the miracles Jesus had performed. Their "belief" in him wasn't genuine or lasting, and so Jesus didn't entrust himself to them. Jesus recognized that there is a kind of faith that is temporary, a faith that doesn't truly save.

To be clear, the problem wasn't that their faith was linked to Jesus' signs, for John himself in the purpose of the gospel tells us that Jesus performed signs so people would believe he is "the Messiah, the Son of God" (20:30–31). Signs themselves aren't intrinsically deficient; they are intended to lead us to faith. But the account in 2:23–24 warns us about a possible danger with miracles. People may get caught up in the excitement and the outward show and fail to truly commit themselves to Jesus. The crowds were happy that their stomachs were filled (6:26), but they didn't perceive that Jesus is the bread of life (6:35). One can be entranced by signs and fail to see what the signs point to. Some may appear to be disciples and believers, when in reality they are not.

Another vivid example of this phenomenon shows up in John 8:31–59, a story about inadequate belief. In this story, Jesus addressed those who "believed" (*pepisteukotas*) in him (8:31). But it quickly becomes apparent that their belief was not of the saving kind. As the conversation continues between the "believers" and Jesus, they turn on Jesus and try to kill him. Their "belief" in Jesus is revealed by the narrative to be superficial and inadequate, which shows us again that there is a kind of faith, a way of believing in Jesus, that isn't truly saving. So what was lacking in their faith?

Fundamentally, these "believers" weren't receptive to Jesus' teaching. In particular, they weren't willing to admit that they were slaves of sin and needed to be freed from their bondage (8:31–36). When Jesus had the nerve to point out their sins, they were filled with murderous rage. Genuine disciples, those who truly believe, are open to correction. They are humble, receiving and responding to the teaching of Jesus, even when he points out the sin that distorts and corrupts their lives.

We see a similar reality in 1 John. The church (or churches) that once were united had become divided, and some of those in the community had left and formed a new group, a new church. Those who left certainly appeared to be believers since they were part of the church, and indeed some of those who had left may have been leaders in the original church. John gives us his perspective on those who had abandoned the church, "They went out from us, but they did not belong to us; for if they had belonged to us, they would have remained with us. However, they went out so that it might be made clear that none of them belongs to us" (1 John 2:19). Though initially they had been thought to be believers, it became apparent by their leaving the church that they didn't truly belong, that they were not genuinely believers. John doesn't say that they have "lost" their salvation. He says that if they had truly belonged, they would have remained and persevered. This isn't a matter of losing what they once had; it reveals what was there all along. Genuine faith, then, has a persevering and abiding quality.

Deficient Faith in Paul

What we saw in Matthew and John's gospels is also present in Paul's writings. Paul doesn't explicitly say that there is a kind of belief that isn't genuine. Instead, we are given examples to demonstrate that there is an inauthentic faith. For instance, Paul tells us about a man named Demas, who was counted among those who believed and is listed among Paul's coworkers (Col 4:14; Phlm 24). But the last word we hear about Demas is not encouraging, since we are told that he "deserted" Paul because of his love for the world (2 Tim 4:10). Demas gave every indication of being a genuine believer initially, but his later actions called into question the authenticity of his faith. Another example is Hymanaeus (1 Tim 1:20; 2 Tim 2:17). Hymanaeus must have shown some promise as a leader in the church, for Paul gave him a position of responsibility. His later actions proved, however, that his faith wasn't genuine. These examples from Paul fit with what we read in Matthew and John. Both Demas and Hymanaeus exercised a kind of faith that wasn't true faith.[4]

A Living, Active Faith

As we just saw, the faith that saves us isn't a bare faith, a mere mental assent to ideas or truths. The faith that saves is living and active. We could demonstrate the vitality of faith from a number of places in the NT, but here we concentrate on John's gospel.

As noted earlier, John uses the verb "believe" (*pisteuō*) 98 times, though he also uses many other words to unpack what it means to believe. In most instances the verb designates what one must do to be saved, though there are a few cases where a false belief is indicted. John sets forth the dynamism and vitality of faith by portraying it in a variety of ways. For instance, faith is described as "receiving" (*lambanō*) Jesus. Those who trust in Jesus welcome him as the Messiah and Son of God (John 1:12; 5:43; 13:20; cf. 1 John 5:9). They receive his testimony and pay heed to his words (John 3:11, 32, 33; 12:48; 17:8). Faith welcomes and cherishes the words of Jesus and the witnesses that point to Jesus.

Faith also *obeys* Jesus. The parallelism in John 3:36 is most interesting, for disobeying (*apeitheō*) is contrasted with "believing" in him, which indicates that disobedience is an expression of unbelief. John cannot conceive of those who believe in Jesus but fail to obey him. Those who trust in Jesus keep (*tēreō*) his word and his commandments (8:51, 52; 14:15, 23, 24; 15:10); those who refuse to keep Jesus' commands do not truly love him. Jesus identifies his disciples as those who keep his word (17:6). Similarly,

---

4.   If true believers can lose or abandon their salvation, then the analysis here is flawed. Space is lacking to defend the notion that true believers will never apostatize. For a full discussion of these matters, see Thomas R. Schreiner and Ardel Caneday, *The Race Set before Us: A Biblical Theology of Perseverance and Assurance* (Downers Grove, IL: InterVarsity Press, 2001).

Jesus' disciples "follow" (*akoloutheō*) him (1:37, 38, 40, 43; 8:12; 12:26; 21:19, 22), just as sheep only follow their shepherd (10:4–5, 27). Those who refuse to follow Jesus don't truly believe in him and are not truly his disciples. We see the same theme in 1 John. Those who truly know Jesus keep his commands (1 John 2:3–6; cf. 3:22; 5:3). They are not sinless (1:7–2:2), but they don't persist in a life of sin (3:4–10; 5:18). Sin doesn't dominate their lives, and they do not give themselves over to evil.

Another way of putting this is that those who believe in Jesus "abide" or "remain" (*menō*) in Jesus (15:4, 5). Those who don't remain in Jesus will be cast aside and perish forever (15:6). True disciples continue in Jesus' words (15:7; 8:31); they remain in Jesus' love by keeping his commands (15:9–10). First John again teaches the same truth. Those who remain in Jesus live as he lived (1 John 2:6; cf. 3:24), and do not give themselves over to a life of sin (3:6). They continue in the light by loving brothers and sisters (2:10), by caring for the needy and indigent (3:17). Those who do not truly belong to the people of God demonstrate their inauthenticity by leaving the church, by failing to abide (2:19), whereas those who truly belong to God remain within the circle of apostolic teaching (2:24, 27). As 2 John says, disciples don't "progress" beyond apostolic teaching about the Christ but continue to uphold an orthodox Christology (2 John 9).

In John "hearing" (*akouō*) occasionally denotes obedience, in the sense that those who truly hear obey. Such a meaning for "hearing" derives from the OT, where hearing often has the idea of obeying. We see this meaning in the Gospel of John when Jesus says to his adversaries, "You cannot bear to hear my word" (8:43). In other words, they don't want to submit to what Jesus teaches. Conversely, the one who is of God "hears the words of God" (8:47). The sheep hear and heed the voice of the shepherd (10:3, 16, 27), but refuse to listen to false shepherds (10:8). Along the same lines we find in 1 John that those who belong to God listen to and therefore obey the apostolic message (4:6). A genuine hearing of Jesus' words provokes one to action so that the hearing has a practical effect in everyday life.

The richness of the Johannine conception of faith is confirmed by the many terms that express the outflow of faith. One of the most prominent is love (*agapaō*), which is naturally the antithesis of hate (*miseō*). Unbelievers are drawn toward the darkness and "love" it (3:19), while they "hate" the light since it exposes their evil (3:20); they love the approval of society more than the glory of God (12:43). Those who truly belong to the Father love Jesus (8:42) and demonstrate their love for him by keeping his commands (14:15, 21, 23, 24; 1 John 5:2).

The vigor and dynamism of faith is expressed with words of motion. I have already noted that John uses the word "follow" to denote the vitality of faith. Other verbs of motion are used as well, namely, "come," "enter," and "go." For instance, those who do evil do not "come" (*erchomai*) to the light, for they flinch at the appearance of the light (John 3:20). Conversely, believers, whose works have a divine origin, come to the light (3:21). People must come to Jesus to obtain life (5:40; cf. 6:35, 37, 44, 45, 65; 7:37; 14:6).

Similarly, faith is portrayed as going, as Peter said: "Lord, to whom shall we go? You have the words of eternal life" (6:68). Faith is also described as entering. Jesus uses the image of the door of the sheepfold, saying he is the door so that "if anyone enters by Me, he will be saved and will go in and out and find pasture" (10:9). John would not recognize as faith what many identify as faith today, for faith is never separated from activity.

The vivacity of faith is also conveyed by sensory metaphors. Faith "beholds" (*theaomai*) the Son, seeing and perceiving him for who he really is (6:40; cf. 12:45). The necessity of "seeing" Jesus is communicated particularly in the healing of the blind man (ch. 9; cf. 11:9). His physical healing represents the granting of spiritual sight as well, for the story concludes with his believing that Jesus is the Son of Man and worshiping him. Conversely, the Pharisees, who claim to see, are blind since they don't see that Jesus is the Christ. Indeed, those who give themselves to sin haven't really seen Jesus (1 John 3:6). The Greeks want to see Jesus (12:21), but they cannot truly perceive him apart from his death (12:24), his being lifted up on the cross (12:32). If one doesn't see that Jesus is the crucified Messiah and Son of God, then one doesn't truly grasp who he is.

Two other sensory metaphors for faith are "drinking" and "eating," which both convey the notion that faith invades and takes residence in a person. Those who believe in Jesus drink of the water he gives them so that he slakes their thirst forever (4:14; 7:37). So too, those who eat Jesus' flesh and drink his blood obtain eternal life (6:50, 51, 52, 53, 54, 55, 56). Only those who put their faith in Jesus' bloody death have life. Believing in Jesus is not a passive activity. Those who come to him and believe in him eat and drink of him, so that they ingest his life in themselves.

In John's writings, believing is a dynamic and vital reality. Believing that Jesus is the Christ and God's Son is necessary to enjoy eternal life. John uses many different terms and expressions to convey the nature of faith. Faith obeys, keeps, abides, follows, comes, enters, goes, eats, drinks, loves, hears, and sees. All that God requires for life is belief in the Son, but faith is no cipher for John. Faith "is the victory that has overcome the world" (1 John 5:4 NIV). Faith is a many-splendored thing; it is a living, breathing, and pulsating reality. Yes, salvation is by faith alone, but faith is dynamic, energetic, and life-changing.

Sola Fide Demands Good Works for Salvation

So how does a dynamic faith like the one we find in John's gospel correspond with the notion of *sola fide*, that our salvation is by faith alone? Good works are necessary for final salvation, and yet these works don't compromise salvation by faith alone. To show this, we will examine a few representative examples from the entire NT witness.[5] I will argue that faith alone isn't compromised because such works are the fruit of faith, the evidence of genuine faith. Though biblical writers don't always pause to say that such works are the fruit of faith, there is sufficient evidence to clarify that works are a vital expression of faith.[6]

Matthew

Examples could be given from all of the Synoptic Gospels, but for reasons of space I will limit myself to Matthew. False prophets are recognized by their fruit (Matt 7:15–20). Because they are bad trees, they produce rotten fruit. Their lives demonstrate that they haven't truly experienced the transforming power of the kingdom. Such an interpretation is confirmed by the next text in Matthew (7:21–23). Confessing that Jesus is Lord doesn't guarantee entrance into the kingdom, for the kingdom is restricted to "the one who does the will of My Father in heaven" (7:21). One might think that those who prophesy, perform exorcisms, and do miracles in

---

5. Rainbow (*The Way of Salvation*) rightly sees the necessity of good works and reminds us that some have failed to see this theme in Paul and in the Scriptures. Too often, however, he fails to clarify the role good works play, and thus his own contribution is somewhat confusing.

6. By way of contrast, N. T. Wright says that "future justification" is "on the *basis* of the entire life" (Wright, *What Saint Paul Really Said*, 129). Wright comments in an article on Romans 2, "Future justification, acquittal at the last great Assize, always takes place on the *basis* of the totality of the life lived" (N. T. Wright, "The Law in Romans 2," in *Paul and the Mosaic Law* [ed. J. D. G. Dunn; Grand Rapids: Eerdmans, 2001], 144). Wright seems to separate present justification by faith from future justification based on works. He says in his commentary on Romans, "It is present justification, not future, that is closely correlated with faith," but "future" justification "always takes place on the *basis* of the totality of the life lived." And on the same page he remarks, "Justification, at the last, will be on the basis of performance" (*The Letter to the Romans*, 440). And in another essay he remarks, "This declaration, this vindication, occurs twice. It occurs in the future, as we have seen, on the *basis* of the entire life a person has led in the power of the Spirit—that is, it occurs on the *basis* of 'works' in Paul's redefined sense" ("New Perspectives on Paul," in *Justification in Perspective: Historical Developments and Contemporary Challenges* (ed. Bruce L. McCormack [Grand Rapids: Baker, 2006], 260).

Jesus' name truly belong to him. Not necessarily. They will be excluded from the kingdom if their lives are given over to their own selfish will and to evil actions. Jesus will declare, "Depart from Me, you lawbreakers!" (7:23). Their evil demonstrates that Jesus never truly knew them (7:23).

The subsequent passage makes the same point in the Sermon on the Mount (Matt 7:24–27). Those who build their houses on the rock will withstand the storm unleashed on the judgment day, for they both heard and obeyed the words of Jesus. But those who erected their houses on sand will find their houses washed away when the thunder and lightning and floods come. They heard the words of Jesus but failed to put them into practice. The narrow gate in Matthew is the way of discipleship—a life of obedience to Jesus Christ (7:13–14). Matthew isn't talking about perfection here. Otherwise, he wouldn't include Jesus' petition to ask for forgiveness of sins (6:12; cf. 18:21–35). Still, those who are disciples of Jesus live in a new way—evil no longer dominates their lives.

One other text from Matthew should suffice. Matthew presents a memorable scene of the final judgment where Jesus sits on his glorious throne and all nations are presented before him (Matt 25:31–46). Jesus distinguishes between the sheep and the goats, inviting the sheep into the kingdom and casting the goats "into the eternal fire prepared for the Devil and his angels" (25:41). The goats suffer "eternal punishment" but the "righteous" enjoy "eternal life" (25:46). It is patently clear that one's eternal and final destiny is at stake. But what determines whether one suffers "eternal fire" or enjoys "eternal life"? Matthew tells us that it depends on what people did, on their actions. Those who don't give food and drink to hungry and thirsty disciples, who don't care for the stranger, clothe the naked, or visit the imprisoned will be banished from God's presence forever (25:41–45). Conversely, those who care for those in pain will be rewarded with eternal life (25:34–40). Matthew isn't talking about caring for the hurting in general, as wonderful as that it is, for he focuses on "the least of these" (25:40, 45), which refers to the disciples of Jesus.

Matthew clearly teaches that good works are necessary for eternal life, and he specifically teaches that those who lack such works will be excluded from the kingdom. Doesn't this contradict *sola fide*? We should recognize a tension in Matthew's teaching, for we saw earlier that he emphasizes the importance of faith, while in other texts he proclaims the necessity of works. Matthew himself doesn't explain how these two teachings cohere, but it seems fair to conclude that good works *are a result of and evidence of* a genuine faith; they are a result of the rule of the kingdom in one's life. The works aren't perfect since believers need to ask for forgiveness of sins, but the works that are done testify that those who believe in Jesus are members of the kingdom.

The Gospel of John and 1 John

While we are scratching the surface on our tour through these passage, my hope is that you are truly seeing the places we are visiting. Both the Gospel of John and 1 John emphasize the importance of good works for eternal life.[7] We already know that John features the importance of believing in Jesus Christ for eternal life (John 20:30–31), a theme I earlier highlighted. But this doesn't lead to the conclusion that good works are unnecessary or unimportant. Those who do evil flee from the light so that their deeds won't "be exposed" (3:20), while those who follow the truth demonstrate their works were accomplished by God (3:21). Indeed, John shows clearly that true belief issues in obedience, for those who trust in the Son have "eternal life," but those who don't "obey" him are under God's wrath (3:36). Those who love Jesus (which, as was shown earlier, is another way of speaking of those who believe in Jesus) keep his commands (14:15, 21–24). Those who don't love Jesus refuse to do what he says, showing that they don't truly belong to the Lord. Only those who keep Jesus' commands continue to remain in his love (15:10), for Jesus' friends keep his commands (15:14).

First John is even more emphatic about the necessity of obedience. Those who want to be ensured of their new life must keep Jesus' commands (1 John 2:3). If one claims to know Jesus Christ and to belong to him and yet he or she fails to do what he commands, they are liars and not truly part of the people of God (2:4). Again, we should recognize that John isn't talking about perfection, for he acknowledges that all Christians continue to sin (1:8, 10). Indeed, if one claims to be sinless, that person is outside the fellowship of God's people. True believers regularly confess their sins and walk in the light by acknowledging their sins (1:7, 9). John emphasizes both sides of the equation: believers still sin and need forgiveness for their transgressions. At the same time, those who truly know God live a new life. "The one who commits sin is of the Devil" (3:8), and "Everyone who has been born of God does not sin" (3:9).

Obviously, John doesn't mean that such persons are sinless, given what

---

7. I am not pausing here to defend Johannine authorship, though such is convincing to me. In any case, most scholars believe that both the Gospel of John and 1 John were written by the same author.

he said in 1 John 1:8, 10, but he does mean that sin no longer rules and reigns in their life. They show they are believers by their righteous lives. What it means to love God is "to keep His commands" (5:3). But John doesn't leave it at this. Where does the power to keep the commands come from? God's commands are not a burden because obedience flows from our faith (1 John 5:3–4). Obedience, as well as love, is the fruit of faith.

John is clear in his letter about the necessity of obedience, but we must understand that such obedience flows from faith, from believing that Jesus is the Christ. John specifically tells us that it is faith in Jesus Christ that conquers the world, showing that the ability to overcome flows from faith (1 John 5:5). The obedience that saves, then, doesn't qualify us to be members of the people of God. It indicates that we are truly trusting in Christ, that we are members of his people.

The Apostle Paul

We find this even more clearly expressed in Paul, who stresses that justification is apart from works of the law. We might be surprised, then, to see that Paul also emphasizes the necessity of good works for final salvation. God repays every person "according to his works" (Rom 2:6). Those who do evil will suffer "wrath and indignation" (2:8) and "affliction and distress" (2:9), while those who do good will enjoy "eternal life" (2:7, 10). Some have taken these verses to be hypothetical, but the conclusion to Romans 2 shows that the hypothetical reading isn't convincing, for we see that those who obey do so because of the work of the Spirit in them (2:26–29). Their obedience isn't self-generated but the result of the supernatural work of the Spirit in their lives. Hence, their obedience doesn't earn or merit eternal life but is the result of the new life they already possess, showing that God's grace has transformed them in Jesus Christ.

It is important to recognize that obedience isn't motivated by a desire to be accepted by God. Acceptance with God is by faith alone through the work of Christ alone and to the glory of God alone. Obedience, then, stems from joy, from a delight in God, from a desire to do what pleases him. Obedience is necessary, for those who don't obey reveal that they haven't truly been accepted by God and show that they don't know God's love. But the obedience of believers isn't animated by a desire to receive God's love. On the contrary, it is a response to his love. All Christian obedience enshrines the principle: "we love because he first loved us" (1 John 4:19). So too, we obey because we know his love. Obedience, then, flows out of our freedom and joy. Though it is required, it isn't simply a duty, it is a delight.

Paul is rightly famous as the theologian of God's grace in Jesus Christ, and perhaps no letter is more well known for this emphasis, and rightly so, than Galatians. Yet in Galatians, while exhorting believers to live in the Spirit instead of by the flesh (Gal 5:16–24), Paul recounts the works of the flesh (5:19–21). He concludes the list of these evil actions by declaring, "I tell you about these things in advance — as I told you before — that those who practice such things will not inherit the kingdom of God" (5:21). Justification is in Christ alone through grace alone to the glory of God alone, and yet the new life isn't an abstraction. Those who practice evil, those who give themselves over to the works of the flesh, won't enter God's kingdom. Those who sow to the flesh "will reap corruption from the flesh," but those who sow to the Spirit "will reap eternal life from the Spirit" (6:8). Sowing to the Spirit, then, is imperative to obtain eternal life, while those who sow to the flesh will experience the final judgment. We have seen in the two letters where Paul emphasizes justification by faith that good works are necessary; such a theme doesn't contradict justification by faith. Indeed, good works are a vital element in Paul's gospel since he includes the theme in two letters that proclaim the grace of God.

We could investigate several more texts in Paul but for our purposes here one more will suffice. He declares in 1 Cor 6:9 that the "the unrighteous will not inherit God's kingdom." Paul then lists the kind of behavior that excludes someone from the kingdom in vv. 9–10. An evil life does not accord with those who are washed, sanctified, and justified (1 Cor 6:11). Paul calls on the Corinthians to live in a way that pleases God, and yet the priority isn't assigned to ethics. What precedes the call to be new is the saving work of God in washing them of their sins and in setting them apart for the holy and in declaring them to be right before God.

Justification in Paul is by faith alone, but, as most Christians have seen throughout history, their faith is not alone. True faith manifests itself in a new way of living, in works that demonstrate the authenticity and reality of faith. Faith expresses itself in love (Gal 5:6), and those who don't love reveal that they lack genuine faith. Justification is by faith alone, but such faith is never alone; it always produces good works.

James

We could examine many other texts and authors in the NT to demonstrate the importance and necessity of obedience for final salvation. Nevertheless, our survey will conclude with James, for many have maintained that James contradicts Paul's teaching that justification is by faith

alone. After all, James specifically says that justification isn't by faith alone
(2:24)! I will try to explain here that James's teaching on the necessity of
good works for justification doesn't contradict Paul's teaching that justification is by faith alone.

We must begin by noting what James actually says. James asks whether
one can be saved by a "claiming" faith, whether one can saved if they *say*
they have faith but works don't accompany their faith (2:14). Can this
"saying" faith save someone on the day of judgment? Does it do them any
"good" when they face God's appraisal on the last day (2:14, 16)? The
answer is obvious. Such a faith does not and cannot save. Faith without
works is "dead" (2:17, 26) and "useless" (2:20). It is comparable to saying
to one who is cold and hungry, "I hope you are well," while not doing
anything to help the person. James puts it rather starkly: justification is by
works. Abraham was "justified by works" in sacrificing Isaac (2:21). So
too, Rahab was "justified by works" in protecting the Israelite scouts when
they spied on Jericho (2:25).

One can see why some scholars think that Paul and James contradict
one another, for Paul says justification is by faith and James says that it is
by works.[8] Paul says Abraham was justified when he trusted in God (Gen
15:6), but James says that he was justified when he sacrificed Isaac (Jas
2:21–23). Those of us who believe the Scriptures are a unified word reject
the notion that the Scriptures contradict, especially on a vital matter like
justification.

Roman Catholics have often resolved the problem by contending that
Paul and James operate with different definitions of works.[9] On this reading, James refers to moral works, to the virtuous actions human beings
are called by God to perform. Paul, however, has in mind the ceremonial
law. And this solution makes perfect sense if one accepts such exegesis.
Paul says we aren't justified by the Jewish ceremonial law, but James insists
that we must keep the moral law to be justified. But the problem with this
view, as I argued in chapter 10, is that this definition of works, when we
apply it to Paul's writings, fails. Paul doesn't restrict the term "works" or
even "works of law" to ceremonial works of the Jewish law. In fact, "works

---

8.   See e.g., Martin Hengel, "Der Jakobusbrief als antipaulinische Polemik," in *Tradition
and Interpretation in the New Testament: Essays in Honor of E. Earle Ellis for His 60th Birthday*
(ed. Gerald F. Hawthorne with Otto Betz; Grand Rapids: Eerdmans, 1987), 248–65.

9.   Luke Timothy Johnson maintains that works of law in Paul refer to circumcision and
ritual law (*The Letter of James* [AB; New York: Doubleday, 1995], 62). So also Peter H. Davids,
The Epistle of James [NIGTC; Grand Rapids: Eerdmans, 1982], 50–51. Davids mistakenly says
that works in Paul "are never moral prescriptions, but rather ceremonial rites added to the work
of Christ" (p. 50).

of law" include everything commanded in the law, including the moral commands. Furthermore, Paul often uses the term "works" without any reference to the law; thus the idea that he has in mind only the ceremonial law is exegetically insupportable. So we must look for another solution.

A popular Protestant solution, one argued by John Calvin and John Owen, suggests that the word "justify" means "proved to be righteous" or "demonstrated to be righteous" instead of "declare righteous."[10] In this understanding, Abraham and Rahab weren't declared to be righteous by works but were proven or shown to be righteous by works. This view is often accompanied by the notion that justification in James is before people instead of before God.

Theologically, this solution is on the right track, but lexically it isn't convincing. It is apparent that James isn't talking about righteousness before people. The citation of Gen 15:6 in Jas 2:23 shows that he was counted righteous by God. Indeed, there is no evidence that justification here relates to justification before people rather than God. When James uses the words "save" and "justify," he has in mind one's relationship with God. Also, the evidence for "justify" meaning "prove to be righteous" is limited, and the usual meaning of the verb "declare righteous" is most likely. James uses the same verb Paul does in a soteriological context, and the word almost certainly has the same meaning that we find in Paul (i.e., "declare righteous").[11]

Again, then, we return to the central question: How do we correlate what Paul and James teach about justification? To begin, it should be recognized that they are addressing different circumstances and situations. Paul responds to those who desire to keep the law to gain justification, whereas James responds to those who are antinomians—those who think faith without obedience is saving. Neither Paul nor James was writing a treatise on justification. Both were responding to issues facing the churches they addressed.

I believe the best solution recognizes that James discusses a notion of faith that differs from what Paul means when he says justification is by faith apart from works. In other words, James criticizes a notional faith, a faith that endorses doctrines, a faith that consists of mental assent.[12]

---

10. Davids, *James*, 51, 127; R. C. Sproul, *Faith Alone: The Evangelical Doctrine of Justification* (Grand Rapids: Baker, 1995), 166.

11. See here Douglas J. Moo, *The Letter of James* (Pillar; Grand Rapids: Eerdmans, 2000), 134–35.

12. Joachim Jeremias, "Paul and James," *ExpTim* 66 (1955): 370. Cf. also Moo, *The Letter of James*, 130–31; Davids, *James*, 50.

The faith that saves embraces Jesus Christ, so that faith is living and vital, for the person who believes gives himself or herself to God. James, then, doesn't deny that justification is by faith, nor does he deny that justification is by faith alone. James denies that a notional faith, a mental assent faith, saves. The faith that saves, in other words, has vitality and energy, so that works necessarily follow. True faith is completed by works (2:22), and it should never be confused with mere mental assent. Abraham and Rahab were justified because their faith expressed itself in works, which showed that their faith was genuine.

But how does what James teaches fit with Paul when James says that Abraham and Rahab were declared to be in the right by their works? I have argued that "justify" means to declare to be in the right. I believe we should see the works functioning as an evidence of the reality of their faith, for James also says that Abraham was counted as righteous because he believed (2:23; cf. Gen 15:6). Hence, justification by works, being declared to be right by works, ought not to be interpreted to say that works are the *basis* or *foundation* of one's relationship with God. Such a reading is improbable, for God demands perfection, as James himself teaches (Jas 2:10), and he also confesses that we all sin regularly (3:2). So, the works that justify are best understood to be the result and evidence of one's faith, showing that faith is genuine.[13] At the end of the day, James isn't really different from Paul, for Paul teaches that faith saves apart from works but also claims that works are a necessary fruit in the lives of those who have faith.

Conclusion

Justification is by faith alone, which means that our works don't warrant our justification. Still, this does not mean that faith is dead and lifeless. True faith always leads to works, to a changed life. There is no such thing as cheap grace in the Bible, as Dietrich Bonhoeffer rightly said. There is only costly grace, grace that is purchased at a cost and that is powerful to change us. Yet it is free grace because it is given to us in Jesus Christ. The faith that is ours expresses itself in works and manifests itself in works. Hence, justification is by faith alone, but it is a faith that expresses itself in good works. Good works aren't the basis of justification, but they are a necessary evidence and fruit of justification.

---

13. Timo Laato remarks, "Good works subsequently brought into effect the living nature of faith" ("Justification according to James: A Comparison with Paul," *TrinJ* 18 [1997] : 69). And he notes that faith "*only subsequently* (but nevertheless inevitably) will yield fruit" (70, italics his). So, he sees works as the fruit of faith (72). Cf. also the helpful reflections of Richard Bauckham on this matter (*James: Wisdom of James, Disciple of Jesus the Sage* [New York: Routledge, 1999], 120–27).

PART 3

Contemporary Challenges to Sola Fide

CHAPTER 17

Sola Fide and the Roman Catholic Church

> "No one can merit the initial grace which is at the origin of conversion. Moved by the Holy Spirit, we can merit for ourselves and for others all the graces needed to attain eternal life, as well as necessary temporal goods."
>
> —*Catechism of the Catholic Church*

Reflections on the Tour So Far

Before we launch into some contemporary discussions on justification, we should summarize where we are on our tour—that is, what has been presented so far in this book. I argued that the earliest fathers seemed to be in harmony with *sola fide*. They affirmed that justification was by faith apart from works. Some of them even declared that justification was "by faith alone." At the same time, they also emphasized that good works are necessary for salvation. In doing so they were faithful to the biblical testimony. They didn't work out the relationship between faith and works since it wasn't a matter of discussion.

During the Reformation the truth that justification was by faith alone was articulated clearly by Luther and Calvin. The Reformers agreed on this vital point over against Roman Catholics, who rejected *sola fide* at the Council of Trent. The Catholic position maintained that works were part of the basis of justification at the last judgment.

The Reformed understanding was restated and elaborated on in John Owen's treatise on justification by faith. Owen's work represents the mature Reformed articulation of the doctrine, formulated in response to Socianians and Roman Catholics. We see the same teaching in the work of Turretin. Baxter dissented from the Reformed understanding on this matter, but the mainstream teaching of the Reformed continued to uphold justification by faith alone.

The work of Edwards and Wesley on this matter is controverted, and Wesley is especially difficult to understand, since he seemed to go back and forth in his comments on the doctrine. I argued, however, that at the end of the day both Edwards and Wesley affirmed *sola fide* and the imputation of Christ's righteousness. They were both concerned about antinomianism, which represents a distortion of the teaching that justification is by faith alone, for true faith always manifests itself in good works.

After conducting a historical tour, we turned to an investigation of the biblical writings, concentrating on the NT witness. Here we found that the Scriptures teach justification by faith alone. Righteousness doesn't come via works of law or works but only and exclusively through faith in Jesus Christ. We considered what the Scriptures teach about justification and argued that righteousness is declarative instead of transformative. We aren't *made* righteous by faith but *pronounced* to be righteous.

Nor is it the case that faith itself saves us. Faith is the instrument that unites us to Jesus Christ, and he is our righteousness. His righteousness is imputed to us, so our righteousness doesn't lie in ourselves but in Jesus Christ our Lord. The faith that saves, it must be said, is vital, living, dynamic, and active. True faith should not be confused with mental assent, where one simply agrees with certain doctrines or teachings. True faith embraces Jesus Christ and finds satisfaction and hope in him.

When we understand the nature of saving faith, the necessity of good works for salvation is clarified, for true faith always expresses itself in works. If works don't follow faith, it is evident that faith isn't genuine. So, good works are necessary for justification, but these good works aren't the basis of justification. How could they be since our works are imperfect and stained with sin? The good works we do are a necessary fruit and evidence of our justification. They don't contradict faith alone as defenders of *sola fide* have always said, for the motto is that justification is by faith alone, but true faith is never alone — good works always follow.

As we now look at contemporary challenges to *sola fide*, the preceding material must be kept in mind. There is inevitably some overlap here since the issues examined today aren't new but have been discussed in previous eras. I also will look at some of the newer challenges from different angles, and hence the New Perspective is discussed in more than one place below.

A Word about Where We Are Going

At this juncture in our journey through history and the Scriptures, we enter the modern world, though for lack of space the work of many scholars will be bypassed.[1] Here we will consider two contemporary challenges to the doctrine of *sola fide*. The first half of this section will look closely at some of the recent discussions between Protestants and Roman Catholics relative to justification. We must understand what Roman Catholics mean by justification and then look at some of the notable dialogues between Catholics and Protestants on the doctrine.

First, we will investigate the new Catholic Catechism to discern its teaching on justification by faith. Second, the Joint Declaration on Justification between Lutherans and Roman Catholics has received much press, and the significance of what was accomplished will be examined in light of the Reformed view of justification defended in this book. Third, the agreement on justification in the document Evangelicals and Catholics Together will be discussed and evaluated. Finally, in the next chapter I will present and assess Frank Beckwith's understanding of justification, for his conversion out of evangelicalism back to Roman Catholicism has received considerable attention in recent years.

In the second half of part 3, I turn my attention to the movement commonly known as the New Perspective on Paul, with a particular focus on the scholarly work of N. T. Wright. Though Wright is not the only scholar who has written on the doctrine of justification, he is one of the most popular and widely known. The two chapters that conclude this volume are an extended dialogue and critique of Wright's understanding of justification.

Have Things Changed with the New Catholic Catechism?

Many years have passed since the 1500s and the disagreements and debates the Reformers had with the Roman Catholic Church. The Council of Trent and the words of Luther and Calvin were written long ago. Has anything changed in the past five hundred years? Are the disagreements of the past still relevant today? Are Protestants and Catholics still at odds over their understanding of justification?

---

1. For a history of the doctrine, which is especially helpful for more recent discussion, see Mark W. Elliott, "Judaism, Reformation Theology, and Justification," in *Galatians and Christian Theology: Justification, the Gospel, and Ethics in Paul's Letter* (ed. Mark W. Elliott, Scott J. Hafemann, N. T. Wright, and John Frederick; Grand Rapids: Baker, 2014), 143–55.

Lane argues that past differing definitions of justification between Protestants and Catholics (forensic for Protestants and transformative for Catholics) do not necessarily indicate a theological divide, since Protestants also believe in transformation. They just use other terms to express this reality.[2] And it has often been pointed out that the condemnations of Trent directed at the Reformers may have been directed against notions of justification that they didn't espouse. This potentially leaves room for some compromise and possible consensus today. Catholics don't renounce Trent, but they may understand it in a new way, so that the old condemnations don't apply to Protestants who uphold justification by faith alone today.

Justification as Inner Renewal

Certainly the Roman Catholic Church has changed in dramatic ways since the Reformation. Today, Protestants are identified as separated brethren instead of being damned with anathemas. But our interest here is not in efforts at ecumenical unity. We are particularly interested in what the new Catholic Catechism teaches about justification.

The Catechism defines justification as the forgiveness of sins, but in contrast to Reformation understandings, it is also said to include "the sanctification and renewal of the inner man" (1989; cf. 2019).[3] Here we find the Augustinian teaching that justification means not only to declare righteous but also to make righteous. The Catechism goes on to say that justification "frees from the enslavement to sin" and "heals" (1990). In justification believers are given God's righteousness (1991), which has been merited by Christ (1992), and thus justification is God's gracious gift (1996). Personal faith isn't necessary for justification since it is granted in baptism (1992). At the same time, justification is a cooperative enterprise between God's grace and human freedom (2002). Human beings must choose with their own free will the grace being offered to them (1993). In choosing and working, human beings are responding to the mercy of God (2001).

This seems to fit awkwardly with the notion that justification occurs at baptism, but in the Catholic understanding justification is an ongoing process that entails "the *sanctification* of his whole being" (1995, emphasis original). Hence, cooperation refers especially to the ongoing process of justification, and in Roman Catholic theology the process is integrated especially with the sacraments.

---

2. Lane, *Justification by Faith in Catholic-Protestant Dialogue*, 152–58.
3. *Catechism of the Catholic Church* (rev. ed.; New York: Random House, 2012). The numbers in parentheses represent the paragraph number in the Catechism.

The Role of Merit

The Catechism speaks of merit, understanding it as a reward or recompense (2006). At the same time, it is acknowledged that strictly speaking, human beings can't merit God's favor (2007). Any merit accrued is itself from God's grace and a fruit of his goodness (2008–2009, 2011). Merit is ascribed to God's grace first of all and then "secondly to man's collaboration" (2025). The catechism states, "No one can merit the initial grace which is at the origin of conversion. Moved by the Holy Spirit, we can merit for ourselves and for others all the graces needed to attain eternal life, as well as necessary temporal goods" (2027).

This use of the word "merit" is something that continues to separate Catholics and Protestants. While it is true that the Catechism says there is no merit apart from grace, the role of the human being in choosing is still given a prominent place, and human beings play a role in meriting eternal life. Protestants who are the theological children of Luther and Calvin will continue to find such notions to be unbiblical, for the notion of free will and merit held by Catholics contradicts the biblical witness. Instead, the Scriptures teach that human beings only choose God by virtue of his electing grace, and the good works they do aren't the basis of eternal life. Indeed, their good works are the result of God's grace in the human heart and can't ultimately be ascribed to the free will of the human being.

The cooperation between human beings and God that we find in the Catholic scheme is contrary to the Reformers understanding of grace, where God frees our hearts from the bondage of sin, God regenerates those whom he elects, and God grants faith to those whom he has given new life. God receives all the glory in salvation, since it is his work alone that saves. There is thus no room for merit, for salvation is of the Lord.

Imputed Righteousness

At this point a crucial difference between Roman Catholics and Protestants surfaces. Protestants believe in *imputed* righteousness, but Catholics in *imparted* righteousness.[4] Here, the old divide between Catholics and Protestants resurfaces. The new Catechism fails to bridge this divide, for these understandings differ fundamentally on the definition of justification.[5] The Catechism tells us that Roman Catholics see

---

4. Lane, *Justification by Faith in Catholic-Protestant Dialogue*, 158–59. We have to add immediately that some Protestants today reject the notion that righteousness is imputed instead of imparted. Many argue that it is imputed *and* imparted.

5. For a vigorous exegetical and theological defense of a traditional Catholic view, see Sungenis, *Not by Faith Alone*.

justification and sanctification as two different ways of describing the same reality, whereas for Protestants they are inseparable, yet still distinguishable from one another. The Catechism continues to see justification as a process, which fits with the sacramental understanding of salvation in Roman Catholicism. But for evangelicals justification is an event, a declaration, not a process. Those who trust in Christ are justified, declared to be in the right before God.

Though five hundred years have passed since the Reformation, the Catholic Catechism doesn't seem to break new ground relative to justification. While it is wonderful that the Catechism isn't filled with anathemas toward Protestants and has an entirely different tone, the view of justification defended at Trent hasn't changed substantially. Justification is still renovative instead of forensic. It is still a process instead of just being an event. Merit still plays a role, even though the grace of God is acknowledged. It is difficult to see how there can be any real progress toward a common understanding on this doctrine, given the teaching of the Catechism. And yet, in recent years some significant discussions among Protestants and Catholics have taken place, and we now turn to two of those discussions.

The Joint Declaration on Justification

Over the past five centuries Protestants and Catholics have tried to bridge the gap that separates them, to come to a consensus on justification. And a fair number of documents on justification have been produced by Protestants and Roman Catholics.[6] These discussions and agreements have delighted some and frustrated others. My purpose here is not to examine all the discussions that have taken place, nor will I discuss the consultations in detail. As I mentioned earlier, anything said or written on justification begets book after book and article after article! Here I simply want to take note of two contemporary discussions on justification that are helpful to understanding the ongoing relevance of *sola fide* for today's Protestant church: the Joint Declaration and the discussion between evangelicals and Roman Catholics.

On October 31, 1999 (Reformation Day), the Lutheran World Federation and Roman Catholic Pontifical Council for Promoting Christian Unity ratified a Joint Declaration of the Doctrine of Justification

---

6.   For a survey, see Lane, *Justification by Faith in Catholic-Protestant Dialogue*, 87–126.

in Augsburg, Germany.[7] The Joint Declaration is not an *ex cathedra* statement by the Roman Catholic Church, though it is accepted as a magisterial document. In other words, the document isn't the official position of Catholicism and is subject to critique and revision. Some prominent Roman Catholics affirmed the document, but this should not be confused with the idea that the Declaration represents Roman Catholic theology.

The Catholic Church raised questions about an earlier draft of the document in 1998, which suggested to many its displeasure. But an Annex was added to the document, and the document was signed in 1999. Significantly, Cardinal Ratzinger, who went on to become Pope Benedict XVI, played a major role in the ratification of the document, verifying that the document was not merely the work of outliers. Remarkably, we see an acceptance of the motto *sola fide* in the document by Roman Catholics, and Pope John Paul II seemed to endorse its contents, even though it never received an official endorsement by Roman Catholicism.[8]

The Joint Declaration represents more than thirty years of dialogue and discussion between Lutheran and Catholic scholars, and thus the rapprochement between the two theological traditions is significant, indicating that many of the recriminations and divisions of the last five hundred years had been healed.[9] A common understanding of justification through faith in Jesus Christ is trumpeted (5),[10] although Lutherans and Catholics understood the Declaration differently, presumably in accord with their own traditions.[11] Still, the consensus reached means, according to some, that the recriminations and condemnations issued by both communities in the past don't apply to the changed circumstances of today's world since they found common ground on the basic truths of justification. Susan Wood says that the Joint Declaration means that the condemnations of the past don't apply today, not because the two communities have departed from the teachings of the past, but because Lutherans and Catholics "do

---

7. The document can be accessed at www.vatican.va/roman_curia/pontifical_councils/ chrstuni/documents/rc_pc_chrstuni_doc_31101999_cath-luth-joint-declaration_en.html. One can also find this document in published form: *Joint Declaration on the Doctrine of Justification: The Lutheran World Federation and the Roman Catholic Church* (Grand Rapids: Eerdmans, 2000).

8. See Lane, *Justification by Faith in Catholic-Protestant Dialogue*, 122.

9. At least it was healed for those who participated in the discussion, for as we will see below, the statement generated controversy.

10. The numbers in parentheses represent the paragraphs in the Joint Declaration.

11. Susan K. Wood, "Catholic Reception of the Joint Declaration on the Doctrine of Justification," in *Rereading Paul Together: Protestant and Catholic Perspectives on Justification* (Grand Rapids: Baker, 2006), 45.

not today hold the positions that are condemned in the way that they were condemned in the sixteenth century."[12] In other words, the differences between Lutherans and Catholics in the past were due in part to misunderstandings.[13]

We must beware of being overly simplistic here, for others vigorously contested the content of the Joint Declaration, maintaining that it distorts the biblical witness.[14] Over 240 German Lutheran theologians objected, seeing the document as a compromise of the gospel.[15] Nevertheless, the signing of such a new document reveals that new winds are blowing, that the anathemas hurled in former times are being withdrawn in some quarters. Interestingly, the Joint Declaration also harmonizes with the new Finnish view of Luther noted above, which has been promulgated by a number of theologians, especially Tuomo Mannermaa.[16]

Content of the Joint Declaration

The agreements reached in the Declaration are significant, particularly as we consider the contemporary relevance of *sola fide*. In the document, both Lutherans and Roman Catholics affirm that Christ is our righteousness and that justification is "by grace alone," not by our merits (15).[17] Human beings don't obtain justification through their own abilities or freedom or merit, for it is entirely a work of God's grace (19). Justification is through Christ alone and is received by faith, which is trust in Christ's saving work (16, 25). Justification is celebrated as "essential" and as "an indispensable criterion" for all the truths of the faith (18). Even though Lutherans and Catholics differ in some respects, they agree that justification plays a special role in our salvation.

The Joint Declaration says that justification is by faith (11–12), and it is even affirmed that it is by faith alone (26). Justification is fundamental to one's relationship with God, and it must be understood as a work of grace accessed by faith (27). Such a teaching does not preclude the necessity of

---

12. Ibid., 46.

13. Ibid.

14. For a sympathetic but critical analysis, see Henri A. Blocher, "The Lutheran-Catholic Declaration on Justification," in *Justification in Perspective: Historical Developments and Contemporary Challenges* (ed. Bruce L. McCormack; Grand Rapids: Baker, 2006), 197–217.

15. See the discussion in Lane, *Justification by Faith in Catholic-Protestant Dialogue*, 121–22.

16. See David G. Truemper, "Introduction to the Joint Declaration on the Doctrine of Justification," in *Rereading Paul Together: Protestant and Catholic Perspectives on Justification* (Grand Rapids: Baker, 2006), 39.

17. We think here of Oden who says, "There is a textually defined consensual classic Christian teaching on salvation by grace through faith" (*Justification Reader*, 16).

good works but distinguishes between faith and good works. Faith and works, then, are distinguishable while also being inseparable. Along the same lines, justification is defined both as forgiveness of sins and "liberation from the dominating power of sin and death" (11). The language of liberation signals that justification isn't construed to be only forensic; it also frees one from sin. It seems, then, that justification is understood in Augustinian terms, so that it doesn't merely mean "declare righteous" but also "make righteous." Roman Catholics continue to defend the notion that justification means that one is made righteous and renewed by God's grace (27). It seems here that the Lutherans who signed the Joint Declaration agree with the Roman Catholic definition.[18]

Roman Catholics see justification as entirely by grace, but at the same time they think human beings can cooperate with grace, though this ability to cooperate is itself a work of grace (20). Good works are not the basis of justification nor do they merit it (according to the Roman Catholics, 25). Good works are, according to both sides, the fruit and result of justification (37). When Catholics say good works are meritorious, they are not denying that they are the result of God's grace but are affirming that God rewards those who do his will (38).

Roman Catholics, however, in contrast to Lutherans, see growth and progress in justification, whereas Lutherans see justification as a gift given at salvation that is not increased (38–39). Lutherans and Roman Catholics continue to have distinct views of sin (29–30), for Lutherans confess *simul iustus et peccator*, so that, even though believers are righteous before God since they are united to Christ, they continue to be sinners until the day of their death. Roman Catholics, by contrast, do not see concupiscence as sin in the same sense. The notion that righteousness is imputed in the Protestant sense is omitted.[19]

Evaluation of the Joint Declaration

In one sense the agreements reached in the Joint Declaration are striking. Both Lutherans and Catholics agree that justification is by faith alone

---

18. See here the criticisms of the Lutheran Church, Missouri Synod: "*The Joint Declaration on the Doctrine of Justification in Confessional Lutheran Perspective*," accessed at www.lcms.org/Document.fdoc?src=lcm&id=339 on December 2, 2013. The Missouri document also observes that justification is not made "the criterion" for faith, which opens up the door for Rome's sacramental theology. But it is questionable whether justification should be made *the criterion* for the Christian faith (see Lane, *Justification by Faith in Catholic-Protestant Dialogue*, 140–49).

19. Lane, *Justification by Faith in Catholic-Protestant Dialogue*, 126; Blocher, "The Lutheran-Catholic Declaration on Justification," 203.

and that good works are the fruit of justification. Merit doesn't represent independent human activity but is the consequence of God's grace. It is also acknowledged that some differences remain in terms of the continuing presence of sin in believers and the sacramental system of Roman Catholics.

Certainly *some* progress has been made, but the Joint Declaration does not accomplish as much as is advertised. The fundamental problem with many ecumenical documents is their ambiguity. Both parties read the agreement in a way that accords with their theological tradition. In other words, both Catholics and Lutherans could sign off on the Joint Declaration without changing their theology in any significant way. The ongoing sacramental theology of Roman Catholics and their conception of indulgences, says Henri Blocher, "[awaken] horrible doubts as to the genuineness of the agreement."[20] Furthermore, the claim that justification occurs in baptism is disquieting,[21] especially for those of a Baptist persuasion.

Gerald Bray and Paul Gardner in their evaluation of the Declaration note repeatedly that the document is vague.[22] For instance, it is possible that Lutherans will read the word "imparts" simply to mean that God gives righteousness to someone, while Catholics will almost surely interpret it in transformative terms, so that it denotes infused righteousness.[23] On the other hand, many Protestants today agree with the Catholic definition of justification, defining it in Augustinian terms to mean "make righteous." That is their right to agree, of course, as scholars and pastors, but it should be clearly explained in the document that these scholars have veered from the traditional Protestant view.

Bray and Gardner make yet another vital observation.[24] The document fails to articulate clearly the Lutheran view of imputation, nor does it unpack the theology of sin in the Lutheran tradition. One cannot understand the Lutheran view of justification without a clear comprehension of the nature of sin. Again, we see the lack of clarity in the document. By leaving out imputation, one of the main differences between Lutherans and Catholics is glossed over, and the agreement reached is much less substantial than it appears at first glance. Catholics can walk away believing that justification is based on inherent righteousness, while Lutherans can still believe in an

---

20. Blocher, "Lutheran-Catholic Declaration on Justification," 207.
21. Ibid., 208–11.
22. Gerald Bray and Paul Gardner, "The Joint Declaration of Justification," *Churchman* 115 (2001): 110–27.
23. Ibid., 120.
24. Ibid.

imputed righteousness, an alien righteousness. Ecumenical agreements are not significant if major issues are left unaddressed, unless the Lutherans signatories are suggesting that such matters are no longer important. If this is what they are saying, that should be clearly communicated to their readers.

Blocher points out that the Reformers emphasized the need for perfect righteousness to be right with God.[25] Hence, assurance was located in the imputed righteousness of Christ instead of the sanctification and renewal of the human being. But the Joint Declaration is ambiguous on assurance, signaling that a major theme in the dispute between Roman Catholics and Protestants has been intentionally muted.[26]

In my analysis, the Joint Declaration promises more than it delivers — at least to those who are Reformed and evangelical. The Lutheran side seems to concede the Catholic definition of justification so that it refers to being liberated from sin. As such, the forensic character of justification is surrendered, or at the very least it isn't preserved. At the same time, nothing is said about the imputation of righteousness, and thus the document is vague about the ground for justification. The agreement seems more impressive at first blush than it truly is, for the language used is imprecise and both sides are able to interpret it in accord with their tradition. The extent and significance of the agreement, then, is called into question.

Evangelicals and Catholics Together (ECT)

In March 1994 a document called "Evangelicals and Catholics Together: The Christian Mission in the Third Millennium" was issued.[27] It immediately generated a great deal of controversy. The statement does not represent the official position of the Roman Catholic Church, though prominent Roman Catholics participated in framing the document and signed it, including Richard John Neuhaus, Avery Dulles, and George Weigel. On the Protestant side Chuck Colson was the most prominent participant and signatory, though the document was also endorsed by Bill Bright, Os Guinness, Richard Mouw, Thomas Oden, J. I. Packer, and Pat Robertson. Other Catholic signatories included Peter Kreeft, Ralph Martin, Michael Novak, and John Cardinal O'Connor.

The statement promoted cooperation on social issues, particularly on

---

25. Blocher, "Lutheran-Catholic Declaration on Justification," 212.
26. Ibid., 212–15.
27. For the document, see *First Things* 43 (1994): 15–22.

the matter of abortion. But what led to much of the ensuing controversy was the theological agreement trumpeted in the statement, and one of the points of controversy was an alleged common stance on justification. The statement declares, "We affirm together that we are justified by grace through faith because of Christ."[28] Such an affirmation could be misinterpreted, for the differences between the two communions are also acknowledged.[29] In particular, the differing conception of the sacraments is recognized.[30]

Many evangelicals voiced disapproval of the statement, particularly regarding what was said about justification, for the document may give the impression that Roman Catholics have always believed that justification was by grace through faith.[31] Roman Catholics believe that justifying grace is granted in baptism and is sustained through a life of faithful obedience and adherence to the sacraments. For many critics, the absence of the phrase "faith alone" didn't represent an attempt to find consensus between evangelicals and Catholics; rather, it represented a move toward the Catholic position, especially when the statement warns both sides against proselytizing the other.[32] The statement actually makes careful distinctions between proselytizing and evangelizing, acknowledging that there is always a need for evangelism, so that a call to conversion is fitting.

However, critics rightly observe that the statement as a whole could easily be used to discourage evangelicals from spending their time in proclaiming the gospel to Roman Catholics. This is significant, since most evangelicals are convinced that the understanding and articulation of the gospel in Roman Catholicism is weak and attenuated. Many evangelicals believe that Catholic communities still need to hear the witness of the gospel, and their faith is better served in evangelical churches where the gospel is faithfully proclaimed and lived out. This is not to deny, of course, that many evangelical churches have also strayed from the centrality of the gospel. How common it is to hear in evangelical churches a steady diet of sermons on how to be a better wife, husband, child, parent, or business

---

28. I am quoting from the statement, as it is reprinted in *Evangelicals and Catholics Together: Toward a Common Mission* (ed. C. Colson and R. J. Neuhaus; Dallas: Word, 1995). The citation here is from p. xviii. The entire statement along with the signatories is found on pp. xv–xxxiii. It can also be found online at www.firstthings.com/article/1994/05/evangelicals--catholics-together-the-christian-mission-in-the-third-millennium-2.

29. Ibid., xx–xxii.

30. Ibid., xxi.

31. See esp. R. C. Sproul, *Faith Alone: The Evangelical Doctrine of Justification* (Grand Rapids: Baker, 1995).

32. *Evangelicals and Catholics Together: Toward a Common Mission*, xxviii–xxxi.

person without any clear articulation of the gospel of Jesus Christ or any attempt to root moral admonitions in the gospel.

The Gift of Salvation

To clarify the meaning of ECT, a subsequent document called *The Gift of Salvation* was agreed upon by eighteen evangelicals and fifteen Roman Catholics on October 7, 1997.[33] The document is more explicitly evangelical, affirming justification by faith alone and imputed righteousness. In addition, the need to evangelize everyone is emphasized. Nevertheless, it is acknowledged that all the issues relating to justification have not been resolved. The term is not defined, the relationship between imputed and infused righteousness is not unpacked, nor is the status of justification in relationship to other doctrines explicated. Even though the document leans in an evangelical direction, it can also be read in Catholic terms.

We must remember in any case that the document was not ratified officially in Rome. The fundamental weakness of the statement is its ambiguity. One can rejoice in seeing certain Roman Catholics drawing closer to a Reformed position on justification, but we must remember that the agreement is limited to some Roman Catholics, and if I may hazard a guess, probably a minority at that. As with previous agreements, critics of the document lament with some merit that it papers over differences.[34]

The Perspective of J. I. Packer

It is helpful to reflect further on the impact of the original Evangelicals and Catholics Together document by considering the responses of J. I. Packer and Richard John Neuhaus to several criticisms from evangelicals. Packer responded to those who questioned his participation in ECT in an important essay[35] where he states the fundamental objections to ECT well.[36] Packer lists these six objections:

1. Identifying Roman Catholics as fellow believers is disingenuous since they deny the gospel and most are not believers.

---

33. The document is published in *First Things* 79 (1998): 20–23. It is available online at http://www.firstthings.com/article/1998/01/001-the-gift-of-salvation.

34. See Mark Seifrid, "The Gift of Salvation: Its Failure to Address the Crux of Justification," *JETS* 42 (1999): 679–88; R. C. Sproul, *Getting the Gospel Right: The Tie That Binds Evangelicals Together* (Grand Rapids: Baker, 1999), 45–93.

35. J. I. Packer, "Crosscurrents among Evangelicals," in *Evangelicals and Catholics Together: Toward a Common Mission* (ed. C. Colson and R. J. Neuhaus; Dallas: Word, 1995), 147–74.

36. Ibid., 154–56.

2. Affirming that the Scripture is authoritative means something different for Roman Catholics since the magisterium interprets what the Scriptures mean, and hence tradition reigns over the Scriptures.

3. The statement on justification is flawed since it accords with Trent's understanding and leaves out the notion of "faith alone."

4. Conversion is defined in Catholic terms as a life-long process instead of a decisive moment when one believes.

5. The statement wrongly encourages Catholics to remain in their churches, but this is troubling since Catholic teaching does not accord with the gospel.

6. It seems that the statement discourages evangelism among Roman Catholics.

Several months after signing ECT, Packer went on to sign another document, "Resolutions for Roman and Evangelical Dialogue" in August 1994.[37] When this document failed to quell the furor, another statement and clarification was drafted on January 19, 1995 and signed by Packer, Bill Bright, and Chuck Colson among others.[38] The statement affirms in no uncertain terms that justification is *sola fide*, rooted in Christ's substitutionary atonement and imputed righteousness. Packer goes on to explain theologically why he could never become a Roman Catholic.[39] The cooperation called for, he explains, is like the cooperation found in parachurch organizations.

Packer responds to the six criticisms of ECT noted above in various ways.[40] When it comes to justification, Packer doesn't deny disagreement between Protestants and Catholics but argues that a right theology of justification doesn't save us, for it is trust in Jesus that saves. Someone may actually trust in Jesus Christ for the forgiveness of sins but formulate their theology incorrectly. Furthermore, the Tridentine view is fundamentally Augustinian and would anyone want to say that Augustine didn't know the gospel?[41]

What can be said regarding Packer's defense of ECT relative to justification? On the one hand, we can agree that Roman Catholics may be saved if they trust Jesus Christ for their salvation, even if they don't articulate it

---

37. For the statement, see ibid., 157–59.
38. Ibid., 160–61.
39. Ibid., 161–63.
40. Ibid., 168–69.
41. Ibid.

faithfully. Earlier, we read a similar sentiment from John Owen, acknowledging that someone may be justified by faith alone, even though they deny the formulation. In humility, we must acknowledge that this matter is complex, and we can be thankful that God is the final judge on the day of the Lord.

On the other hand, if someone understands what he or she is rejecting in turning away from justification by faith alone, then such a person will not be delivered from the wrath of God. Paul pronounced an anathema on those who proclaimed or received another gospel (Gal 1:8–9), identifying them as false brothers (2:3–5). We should recognize that many in the Roman Catholic communion, even teachers and clergy, may have a poor grasp of such matters and don't fully understand the gospel or the importance of salvation by faith alone. Hence, they may not realize what they are doing in rejecting justification by faith alone. They may personally embrace the gospel even though they reject *sola fide*.

Moreover, Packer surely is right in identifying Augustine as one who believed in and proclaimed the gospel, even though the Lutheran and the Reformed today would say that his understanding of justification was deficient. Roman Catholics who share the faith and sentiment of Augustine belong to the people of God. However, matters today are more complex than they first appear, for we cannot ignore the fact that 1,600 years have passed since Augustine wrote on these matters, and thus there is more clarity on this issue than there was in Augustine's lifetime. In fact, however, as the years have passed the Roman Catholic Church has become less and less Augustinian. Any reader of the *The Catechism of the Catholic Church* knows they espouse a view of free will that fits with Chrysostom more than Augustine. That is to say, the Augustinian view of grace has been chipped away at over the centuries, especially with the increasing role that the sacraments have played in Roman Catholicism.

It is true that Augustine's own writings led to many of these later developments, for his soteriology was a mixture of various elements. Still, the Roman Catholic Church in the centuries since Augustine has moved in a less Augustinian direction. We can think of the suppression of the Jansenists in the sixteenth century, for instance. In many respects, then, it seems that the Roman Catholic Church has significantly lost (though not entirely) the emphasis on grace found in Augustine. So while Packer is technically right about Augustine, the nature of the Roman Catholic Church today is quite different from what it was in Augustine's day. Nor is it satisfying to stop at Augustine, for the nature of justification has been clarified since his day, and teachers of the church are responsible for the hammering out of biblical doctrine that began in earnest during the Reformation.

Finally, I would argue that the fundamental criticism of ECT still stands. The statement as it was first written represents the Roman Catholic view of justification rather than the view of the Reformers. When it is combined with what the document says about proselytizing, the document can easily be interpreted to say that the differences between Roman Catholics and Protestants aren't crucial and fundamental. Omitting the Reformed view of justification suggests that it isn't vital for the proclamation of the gospel and for Christian unity. Packer thankfully explains that this isn't what *he* meant in signing the document, but ECT is susceptible to many interpretations. One can see why many would read the document and conclude that justification by faith alone isn't central to the gospel since Roman Catholics and Protestants can work together without agreeing on this fundamental point. Those of us who agree with the Reformers, however, believe that justification by faith alone is essential to the gospel and can't be dispensed with, and thus the omission of the word "alone" from ECT constitutes a fatal flaw.

The Perspective of Richard John Neuhaus

We turn now to the essay of Richard John Neuhuas, who was a fervent supporter of ECT.[42] Neuhaus converted from Lutheranism to Roman Catholicism and played the leading role on the Catholic side for ECT. Neuhaus responds in his essay to the concerns of those who believe that the Reformation was undermined by ECT. Neuhaus, who is wonderfully learned and fascinating, says many stimulating things in his essay, but my aim is to attend in particular to what he says about justification. Neuhaus acknowledges that the church is *simul iustus et peccator.*[43] When Neuhaus takes up the question of justification by faith alone, he notes that this matter is especially urgent for Lutherans and the Reformed, while Wesleyan, Pentecostal, Arminian, and other evangelical traditions aren't as committed to the formulation.[44] Such a comment confirms what was said above about the development of Roman Catholic theology in the last 1,600 years.

---

42. Richard John Neuhaus, "The Catholic Difference," in *Evangelicals and Catholics Together: Toward a Common Mission* (ed. C. Colson and R. J. Neuhaus; Dallas: Word, 1995), 175–227.

43. Ibid., 190.

44. Ibid., 199.

The theology of the church fits better within an Arminian interpretive tradition, so that the grace of God, articulated in so many wonderful ways by Augustine, is understood in a way that differs substantially from those who hold to a Reformation stance.

Neuhaus goes on to say that justification by faith alone in no way contradicts ECT and "the authentic teaching of the Catholic Church."[45] He protests that the omission of "by faith alone" was intentional and hence should not be construed as deceptive.[46] He defends the omission by saying that "the formula itself is in fact a sixteenth-century theological construct that is not found in the Bible," and the goal of ECT was to affirm "undisputed biblical truth."

Response to Neuhaus

It is understandable why Neuhaus and other Catholics would refrain from saying that justification is by faith alone. But Neuhaus's own words confirm what was said earlier. The statement is minimalist, representing what Catholics and Protestants agree on with respect to justification. Some might think that such an agreement is progress, but this minimalist view actually contradicts the view of the Reformers, for what sets Protestants apart from Catholics is the insistence that justification is by faith *alone*. In other words, the Reformers believed that justification by faith *alone* captures a fundamental element of the gospel, and departing from that standard represents a declension from the gospel.

Neuhaus says that the slogan is a sixteenth-century formulation and does not represent pure biblical truth. I find it fascinating to see a Roman Catholic raise this objection since so much of their theology hails from later developments in the history of the church. Surely, Neuhaus would not make this claim about the doctrine of the Trinity, that it is a fourth-century development and should therefore not have a regulative function. The question is not when the doctrine is formulated but whether the sixteenth-century formulation accords with the scriptural witness. Clearly, Neuhaus would say "no," which is his right, but whether the formula is biblical and fundamental is the real question before us. And that is a question on which Reformed Protestants and Roman Catholics continue to disagree.

Neuhaus doesn't want us to get "bogged down in past disputes."[47] For Neuhaus, healing the breach with Orthodoxy takes precedence over

---

45. Ibid., 200.
46. Ibid.
47. Ibid., 201.

resolving the long-standing division with Protestants, especially since not all Protestants agree that justification is by faith alone.[48] Only a few professional theologians from Lutheran and Reformed traditions think the formulation is still important, according to Neuhaus.[49] But this is just another way of saying that justification by faith alone is not of crucial importance in Neuhaus's opinion, and that the debates and formulations of yesterday shouldn't derail progress today.

But here is the rub. If one actually believes that the Scriptures teach justification by faith alone and if one believes such a truth is fundamental, then you cannot board Neuhaus's train of reconciliation. The reconciliation envisioned is one where justification by faith alone is a train car left back at the station; yet for Reformed Protestants it is a car necessary for the journey, one that cannot be left behind. It enshrines the gospel message that salvation is of the Lord, and that it is entirely his work.

Neuhaus goes on to say that the Catholic Catechism neither rejects or affirms justification by faith alone. It confirms the teaching of the Council of Trent, "which condemned the formula in the sense that it understood the formula at that time."[50] According to Neuhaus, the Catechism confirms human freedom, but it doesn't intend to refight the wars of the past, and those who do so are threatening the unity of the gospel that God desires us to have.[51] Once again we see that Neuhaus's fundamental argument is to say that justification by faith alone isn't that important! In saying that a firm adherence to *sola fide* threatens the unity of the gospel, Neuhaus is saying that justification by faith alone is not essential to the gospel. But that's the very question we are trying to answer! Furthermore, the view of human freedom espoused in the Catechism and by Neuhaus is Tridentine and contrary to the Reformed understanding of God's grace. In that sense, it seems, the judgments of Trent against the Reformation continue to apply, and hence the breach has not been truly healed for those who believe justification is by faith alone.

Neuhaus exhorts us to be broad and charitable in assessing other theological traditions. We must read other formulations with charity and open-mindedness to see if they cohere with our formulations.[52] Here, I believe, Neuhaus's sentiments are right on target. We should be inclined to

---

48. Ibid., 202–3.
49. Ibid., 204.
50. Ibid.
51. Ibid., 204–5.
52. Ibid., 206.

agree where we can agree and slow to condemn. We should seek and pray for unity. Still, that unity must be centered on the truth of the gospel (Gal 2:5, 14). Reformed and Lutheran Protestants would claim that the Roman Catholic understanding of justification is fundamentally incompatible with *sola fide* and in fact contradictory to the gospel since works are part of the basis of justification in the Catholic tradition.

Neuhaus says that those who insist on justification as the article by which the church stands or falls are guilty of sectarianism, for when we read church history, we see that there are many different ways of articulating God's saving work in Jesus Christ.[53] Yet again, in saying that such a doctrine is sectarian, it is another way of saying that it isn't vital. For Neuhaus, justification by faith alone *is* sectarian, and so it is difficult to imagine a wider breach with those who uphold *sola fide*.

A final point should be added here. We have seen that the early church fathers didn't have clarity on justification by faith alone. At the same time, they didn't blatantly deny the truth as Trent did. It is one thing to be fuzzy or inconsistent regarding a truth in the Scriptures, but it is quite another thing to explicitly deny it altogether. Neuhaus essentially argues that justification by faith alone is a matter of indifference, but that's just the question, isn't it? Here is where Reformed Protestants vigorously disagree with him.

Neuhaus worries that proponents of justification by faith alone equate the doctrine with the gospel, and thus land in the uncomfortable position of saying that there is no church where that doctrine is not proclaimed. He goes on to state that this can hardly be the case since many members of the church throughout history didn't endorse the formula.[54] In response, I would say that upholding the centrality of justification by faith alone doesn't mean that all members of the church must trumpet such a statement to be members of the church. God accepts us in his mercy and grace if we trust in Christ for salvation. Thankfully, he doesn't require theological precision. As we have seen in this book, misunderstandings of justification by faith alone may abound. Some may actually believe in justification by faith alone but reject it because they misconstrue what is meant by the phrase. At its heart, the statement emphasizes that salvation is the Lord's work and not our own. We receive and he gives. We are naked, poor, and blind, and he clothes us, makes us rich, and grants us sight.

Such a teaching, though it may be expressed in a variety of ways, is

---

53. Ibid., 206–7.
54. Ibid., 207–8.

central to the gospel proclaimed in the Scriptures. And it is also the case that many in the church, as our study of the early church fathers confirms, taught that salvation was by faith instead of by works. Some of them occasionally spoke of salvation by faith alone, while others did not. We cannot expect our ancestors to have the same precision on a matter, centuries before a sustained and nuanced debate on the issue had occurred.

Neuhaus concludes by saying that in the end matters of theology must be decided by the church.[55] According to Neuhaus, Trent rejected the notion of *sola fide* because those at Trent thought the phrase denied the role of human agency and freedom and promoted antinomianism.[56] Neuhaus believes that the condemnations of Trent need not apply today since Trent likely misunderstood what the Reformers were saying. Hence those who affirm justification by faith alone need not be condemned since they are saying something different from what Trent condemned. Still, Neuhaus believes there is a sense in which the condemnations of Trent, even if they misunderstood what the Reformers were saying, still apply. They still apply in the sense that what Trent condemns is contrary to Scripture.[57]

I find Neuhaus's words here remarkable, for it is difficult for those who are Reformed to see what Trent says as in any way capturing the truth of the Scriptures. Because Neuhaus is Roman Catholic, he has no problem siding with Trent, but it is difficult to see how unity will be obtained if Protestants must, in any sense, say they agree with Trent (even Trent rightly understood). Neuhaus's comments on Trent suggest that things haven't changed dramatically since the Council. Such a judgment fits with our assessment of the Catholic Catechism as well: a natural reading of what is written finds the same basic theology that was present at the Council of Trent.

Near the end of his essay Neuhaus says:

When I come before the judgment throne, I will plead the promise of God in the shed blood of Jesus Christ. I will not plead any work that I have done, although I will thank God that he has enabled me to do some good. I will not plead the merits of Mary or the saints, although I will thank God for their company and their prayers throughout my earthly life. I will not plead that I had faith, for sometimes I was unsure of my faith and in any event that would turn into a meritorious work of my own. I will not plead that I held the correct understanding of

55. Ibid., 208.
56. Ibid., 209.
57. Ibid., 219–20.

"justification by faith alone," although I will thank God that he led me to know ever more fully the great truth that formula was intended to protect. Whatever little growth in holiness I have experienced, whatever strength I have received from the company of the saints, whatever understanding I have attained of God and his ways—these and all other gifts received I will bring gratefully to the throne. But in seeking entry to that heavenly kingdom, I will plead Christ and Christ alone.[58]

Every evangelical Protestant resonates with what Neuhaus confesses here. We find common ground at the foot of the cross, when we contemplate our own hearts and our sins against a holy God. It is wonderful to see Neuhaus articulate these truths, but I fear that these truths will not be preserved if our formal statements of faith undermine or even deny justification by faith alone. Furthermore, even the wonderful words that Neuhaus has written here must be interpreted within his Catholic schema. He may plead Christ's righteousness, and yet may, according to Catholic dogma, fail the test and suffer in hell forever. Or, conversely, he may have to undergo a period of purification in purgatory before entering into eternal life.

A final coda should be added to our discussion here. Despite the comments of Neuhaus and some other Roman Catholics, it is also instructive that other prominent Roman Catholics strongly reject *sola fide*. Scott Hahn attended Gordon Conwell and as a former evangelical knows our theology well, but he and his wife specifically reject the notion that we are justified by faith alone.[59] They appeal to Jas 2:24 to support the notion that works are needed for justification. Along the same lines, Robert Sungenis, who attended a Reformed seminary as well, vigorously rejects the notion that justification is by faith alone.[60] The views of individual Catholics can vary widely and no single individual should be taken as representative of all. That is why we have tried to focus our attention on documents and statements that are broadly representative. In the final analysis, what we find is the continuation of one of the fundamental disputes of the Reformation, that salvation is *sola fide*—by faith alone.

Conclusion

The agreement reached in Evangelicals and Catholics Together spurred controversy on a number of levels, especially over justification.

---

58. Ibid., 212.
59. See Scott and Kimberly Hahn, *Rome Sweet Home: Our Journey to Catholicism* (San Francisco: Ignatius, 1993), 31–32.
60. Sungenis, *Not by Faith Alone.*

The so-called agreement on justification was superficial, and the statement could be interpreted in such a way that both Roman Catholics and evangelicals agreed. We have noted earlier that joint statements from different ecclesial communities often suffer from ambiguity, namely, both sides interpret the statement in a way that concurs with their confessions. Hence, the agreement isn't substantive or profound. The exposition on justification by Neuhaus makes this clear, for it is evident in point after point that justification doesn't play the same vital role for Neuhaus as it does for evangelicals.

Moreover, the definition given to justification isn't the same, for imputed righteousness is bracketed out. Nor is there any indication that the official Roman Catholic stance on justification has changed, and some Roman Catholics, in contrast to Neuhaus, speak polemically against justification by faith alone. Evangelicals and Roman Catholics may continue to cooperate on social issues, but they are far from any concord on justification, though such an agreement would be a cause for great rejoicing.

CHAPTER 18

Frank Beckwith's Return to Rome

"I'm so thankful for the active obedience of Christ; no
hope without it."   *—J. Gresham Machen*

Roman Catholics today often say that the Bible speaks only once about
whether justification is by faith alone—and it specifically rejects the
idea. James 2:24 says, "You see that a person is justified by works and not
by faith alone" (ESV). It is somewhat ironic that Protestants, who proclaim
sola scriptura, are countered by Catholics on the basis of Scripture. To put
it another way: the NT never says that we are justified by faith alone, but
it does clearly say that we are *not* justified by faith alone. So why do those
who claim that justification by faith alone also claim that it is biblical?

This is a good reminder to us that *sola fide* can't be sustained, nor
should it be defended, if we understand it simplistically. Formulas and slogans are often misleading and distorting, and occasionally Protestants have
thrown about the slogan *sola fide* as a mantra, as if the slogan itself captures
the truth of the gospel. As we saw when we unpacked the meaning of
faith in the letter of James, there is a sense in which *sola fide*, understood
unbiblically, is dramatically wrong, for it is flatly contradicted by the words
of Scripture itself.

We might be tempted, at this point, to give the whole thing up.
Protestants, after all, are the ones who trumpet *sola scriptura*, so why
bother holding onto *sola fide* when the Scriptures speak directly against
it? Are we as Protestants guilty of holding onto a tradition which, after
all these centuries, is simply not in accord with what the Bible truly says?

Here we must be careful of treating the matter simplistically again.
The most persuasive advocates of *sola fide* were aware of what James
taught and they never denied the contribution of James.[1] Still, they

---

1. Some in NT scholarship believe Paul and James contradict one another and that they
teach two different ways of justification. Those in the Lutheran tradition who espouse this view
say that we should favor Paul over James. See Jüngel, *Justification*, 19–20; Martin Hengel, "Der
Jakobusbrief als antipaulinische Polemik," 248–65.

believed it was warranted to speak of justification by faith alone to draw a bright red line between faith and works in justification. Drawing that bright red line doesn't mean that faith and works never meet, as if they are foes in the boxing ring. It does mean, however, that faith and works are to be distinguished, and that there is a sense in which it is biblically right, indeed biblically required, to say that we are justified by faith alone. Showing this from Scripture isn't verified by parroting a slogan or by citing proof texts. As I have tried to show in this volume, we need to delve into Scripture, history, and tradition to adjudicate this question wisely.

Too often discussions about justification are marred by accusations of name-calling and heresy hunting, so that those who don't fit one's precise parameters are excluded from being orthodox. To be clear, I am not denying that there is an orthodox teaching or suggesting that heresy isn't a danger. But we should intentionally avoid a sectarian and partisan spirit. In our contemporary context, five hundred years after Luther posted the ninety-five thesis on the door of the church in Wittenberg, we can learn from those who have thought about these issues and from the collective witness of Scripture, history, and theology. Luther himself did not want to split from the Roman Catholic Church. Circumstances and polemics pushed him in a direction he didn't anticipate or plan.

Beckwith's Story

We need to keep all of this in mind when we consider the fascinating case of Frank Beckwith. Beckwith was born in 1960 and raised as a Roman Catholic, but in 1978 as a teenager he was born again and became an evangelical Christian. Beckwith is a well-known philosopher and ethicist, lecturing, debating, and writing to defend a Christian worldview. He was certainly one of the luminaries in evangelical scholarship. As evangelicals we are deeply grateful for his scholarship, especially his work in philosophy and ethics. Why, then, have I dedicated an entire chapter to Beckwith in a volume on *sola fide*?

In 2007, while Beckwith held the position as president of the Evangelical Theological Society, he astonished many of his peers and colleagues by reconverting to Roman Catholicism. He stepped down from his post as president of the ETS and devoted himself afresh and anew to the Roman Catholic Church.

Beckwith defends his latest migration in a book recounting his story where he explains why he returned to the church of his boyhood days.[2] Naturally, his apologia, which is similar in some respects to that of John Henry Newman many years before, touches on a number of issues that divide Roman Catholics from evangelical Protestants. Investigating such matters would be most fascinating, but in keeping with the focus of this book, we want to look at Beckwith's reflections on justification. Beckwith realizes, as one who is fully conversant with evangelicalism, that one of the fundamental attractions of evangelicalism is its teaching on justification by faith alone. Many nurtured in Roman Catholicism have wandered from the waters of the Tiber and have embraced the evangelical gospel, which declares that justification is by faith alone. Many have rejoiced over the freedom that is theirs in Christ as they have realized that their right standing with God does not depend on what they do but on the grace that is given to them through Jesus Christ. Justification, they discovered, is not based on human performance or the works we have done. Instead, it is a gift granted to those who trust in Jesus Christ and him crucified and risen. So, we are not surprised to find that Beckwith devotes more space to justification than to any other issue.[3]

Beckwith's View of Justification

Beckwith acknowledges that his defense of his reintegration into Catholicism isn't technical, and yet anything Beckwith writes is of immense interest and importance since he is well-known for his intellectual acumen. I should say at the outset that Beckwith is unfailingly irenic in the book toward evangelicals and regularly expresses gratefulness for what he has learned from them. He identifies himself as an *evangelical catholic*. Still, the fact remains that he has embraced Roman Catholicism and its view of justification, and we should be eager to find out why.

First, says Beckwith, the view of justification articulated by the Reformers was not shared by the early church fathers. In particular, they did not espouse the imputation of Christ's righteousness. Second, he argues that justification was viewed as a process instead of as a singular event. In other words, justification and sanctification were not rigidly separated into two compartments. Justification was not merely conceived of as the imputation of righteousness but also as the infusion of righteousness. Third, Beckwith believes that the most natural way of reading the

---

2. Francis J. Beckwith, *Return to Rome: Confessions of an Evangelical Catholic* (Grand Rapids: Baker, 2009).

3. Ibid., 84–116.

Scriptures shows significant problems with the Reformed understanding of justification. The NT clearly teaches that people will receive eternal life *based* on what they have done (cf. Matt. 7:21–27; 16:27; 25:31–46; Rev. 22:11–12; etc.).[4] There is no suggestion, says Beckwith, that works are merely an *evidence* for justification. Such a reading strains against what the verses plainly say.

Romans 4:1–8 is often brought in to oppose the Roman Catholic view, and Beckwith agrees that this text teaches that salvation cannot be earned by keeping the Mosaic law.[5] But this text doesn't say that the imputation of righteousness is all there is to justification, for we learn from James that Abraham was also justified later when he sacrificed Isaac (Jas 2:14–26). Plus, Gen 15:6 can't be the moment when Abraham was first justified because he had faith when he obeyed the Lord and moved to Canaan (Gen 12:1–3; Heb 11:8). According to Beckwith, it is wrong-headed to separate infusion from imputation, for we also become a new creation in conversion (Gal 6:15). Indeed, Paul presents justification as past (Rom 5:1–2; 8:24; 1 Cor 6:11), present (1 Cor 1:18; 15:2; 2 Cor 2:15), and future (Rom 2:13; 1 Cor 3:15; 5:5; Gal 5:5; 1 Tim 2:15; 2 Tim 4:8, 18). And Rom 2:6–10, 13 teaches that "works done in faith by God's grace contribute to our inward transformation and eventual justification."[6]

Beckwith also points to texts that demand perseverance for final salvation (Gal 6:8; Phil 2:12–13; Col 1:22–23; 2 Tim 4:7–8) and concludes that there must be inward change in justification.[7] All of this taken together shows that the Reformation distinction between justification and sanctification can't be sustained, for a number of texts *include* sanctification in justification (Rom 6:19–23; 8:3–4; 1 Cor 6:11; 2 Thess 2:13; Titus 3:5–8).[8] And when we add Jas 2:14–26 to the mix, the conclusion seems clear: the Protestant view that justification should be restricted to imputed righteousness does not accord with the Scriptures. Beckwith argues that James isn't talking about our righteousness before people as some of the Reformed say, nor can we deny that works are an instrument of justification here.[9] James fits nicely with the Catholic view that justification includes the notion that we are infused with righteousness.

Beckwith is clear that good works don't earn entrance into heaven, but

---

4. Ibid., 97–99.
5. Ibid., 99–108.
6. Ibid., 102.
7. Ibid., 102–3.
8. Ibid., 103–4.
9. Ibid., 104–5.

we do live out the grace we have received.[10] As he says, good works don't "get you into heaven," but they "get heaven into you."[11] He says that heaven is ours by grace and good works "prepare us for heaven."[12]

Beckwith also wonders whether the differences between the Reformed and Roman Catholicism are really as great as they seem. After all, the Reformed think *"good works are a necessary condition for true justification,"*[13] and is such a contention really that different from the Roman Catholic view? Furthermore, assurance of salvation depends on good works for most Protestants and so practically speaking, they have no more assurance than most Catholics.[14] And where does the Protestant understanding of imputation come from philosophically? Beckwith claims that it hails from *nominalism*, a philosophy that teaches that there aren't essences but only names.[15] Nominalism explains how righteousness is imputed, for it posits no transformation in the sinner contrary to the Catholic view.

Justification, according to Beckwith, represents cooperation between the human will and God's grace. He takes the Catholic view, acknowledging that God's grace takes the initiative,[16] while adding that those who shrink back from any role for the human will make the same mistake as those who think Jesus' assumption of humanity diminished his divinity.

A Brief Response to Beckwith

It isn't my purpose here to set forth a detailed, point-by-point response to Beckwith, for much of the relevant biblical support has already been covered in part 2. Still, there are a few things that should be said in reply. First, we should note that while it can be helpful to take note of the views of the early church fathers and to consult them, ultimately their perspectives aren't determinative. Protestants, after all, believe in *sola scriptura*. The fathers disagreed among themselves far too often (as scholars do today) for them to constitute our final authority. Still, Beckwith's presentation of church history is also too simplistic. There is significant evidence, as we saw earlier in this book, that many of the earliest fathers believed that justification was forensic and not transformative. They lack, as noted earlier, clarity about imputation, but we shouldn't be surprised at this for the matter

---

10. Ibid., 105.
11. Ibid.
12. Ibid.
13. Ibid., 109. Italics his.
14. Ibid., 109–10.
15. Ibid., 110–12.
16. Ibid., 112–13.

wasn't debated during their time. Many of their comments and reflections could be interpreted to support imputation, so the testimony of the church fathers isn't nearly as tidy and simple as Beckwith claims.

Beckwith's analysis also suffers from a failure to make distinctions. Of course believers are a new creation and are sanctified. No reputable Protestant theologian denies such, but Beckwith glides from this to saying that because of this, justification means the infusion of righteousness. Such logic is a serious mistake. Believers are sanctified and justified, but it doesn't follow from this that justification and salvation mean the same thing, or that justification denotes the infusion of righteousness. Such a notion has to be demonstrated from studying the term itself—an enterprise we have undertaken in part 2.

An illustration might help to clarify my point here. When believers are saved, they enjoy both redemption and reconciliation, but it doesn't follow from this that redemption and reconciliation *mean the same things*. Beckwith essentially says that justification must involve transformation since the believer is a new creation, but why should we think that our understanding of the believer as a new creation should provide the definition for justification? The meaning of justification must be demonstrated by examining the term in its own usage and context. Parallel words don't necessarily mean that the terms used are synonyms. No Protestant argues that justification is all there is to salvation. Still, we understand that justification comes from the metaphor of the law court and doesn't signify the infusion of righteousness. Nor is there any evidence that justification is to be understood as a process. Paul says to work out your salvation (Phil 2:12), but such a thing is never said about justification.

Related to this is Beckwith's charge that imputation is nominalism if there is no infusion of righteousness. Yet this accusation is gratuitous. Why? Because Christ's righteousness is truly imputed to believers. We don't have a fictional imputation here. Believers really are counted righteous in Christ. The nominalist charge only works if imputation doesn't truly occur. Beckwith says that imputation isn't real if believers don't become inherently righteous, but why should we believe him when he says that? Such an argument assumes what must be proven. Instead, when we look at the Scriptures, we find that they teach that Christ's righteousness is credited to us when we believe in him, as we saw in chapter 15.

I find Beckwith to be a bit confusing on the role of works. On the one hand, he says salvation is based on works, and on the other hand he says that good works prepare us for heaven. But he needs to be clearer at this vital point. If justification is based on works, then works are one of the bases for our being justified on the last day. Works don't just prepare us for heaven; they function as one of the platforms for entrance into heaven. Evangelical Protestants have maintained that works cannot be a *basis* for our right standing with God, for God demands perfect obedience, and hence our imperfect obedience can't be a ground for justification. It is better, then, to construe our works as evidence of our justification.

Beckwith says that Catholics have no more reasons to lack assurance than Protestants since we both think works are necessary. But the difference between works as a basis and works as evidence is significant. Words matter, and they mean something theologically and practically, and on this point Roman Catholic theology agrees! Catholic theology proclaims that we can't have assurance of salvation unless it is given by special revelation.[17] But Reformed Protestants believe that Scripture teaches that those who are justified can and should have assurance.

There is a long theological tradition where Catholics and Protestants disagree on assurance. I can say as one who was raised a Catholic that there is a practical difference as well. It is understandable why, if our justification is based on our works, Roman Catholics teach that one can't have assurance. At the same time, we can understand why Protestants do have this assurance, for their salvation depends fundamentally on Christ's righteousness and his forgiveness. Our works, since they are imperfect, could never be the basis of our justification, but they do constitute evidence that we are trusting in Jesus Christ. This isn't just a theological debate. When the great Presbyterian NT scholar J. Gresham Machen was dying, he wrote to John Murray and said, "I'm so thankful for the active obedience of Christ; no hope without it."[18] Machen thought of his sins as he was dying, and he realized that he deserved God's judgment. But he faced death joyfully and confidently because he trusted in Christ's righteousness rather than his own.

A word should also be said about Gen 15:6. Beckwith points out that Abraham believed in Genesis 12 when he left his homeland and traveled to Canaan, and hence 15:6 can't be his initial justification, for we know Abraham trusted God in Genesis 12. Hebrews 11:8 confirms that Abraham's obedience in Genesis 12 stemmed from his faith, for we read "by faith Abraham obeyed." Beckwith raises a fascinating issue here, but

---

17. See the Council of Trent 6.12.

18. See Ned Stonehouse, *J. Gresham Machen: A Biographical Memoir* (1954; reprint, Grand Rapids: Eerdmans, 1978), 508.

it isn't clear that the text points to a process of justification. Genesis 15:6 doesn't clearly teach that Abraham continued to be justified every time he exercised faith. Instead, 15:6 clarifies what is implicit in Genesis 12 and brought out by the writer of Hebrews (Heb 11:8). Genesis 15:6 explains that Abraham's faith *counts* as his righteousness. Such a statement doesn't mean that every time someone exercises faith their justification increases. Paul and the writer to the Hebrews teach that a right relationship with God is ours through faith instead of by works. Ongoing acts of faith don't continue a process of justification; they verify the authenticity of the first act of faith.

Conclusion

Frank Beckwith's gifts as a scholar are apparent, and the impact of evangelicalism on his thought is apparent to this day. Still, his understanding of justification isn't convincing. He wrongly maintains that the early church concurs with his notion of justification, but the evidence isn't all that compelling, and there is significant evidence that many of the early fathers understood justification to be forensic. Beckwith also mistakenly merges words together, as if the close association between new creation and justification demonstrates that justification includes the notion of transformation. Finally, he wrongly interprets the biblical evidence to say that justification is on the basis of works. Such comments reveal that he has truly returned to Rome and no longer holds the evangelical notion that our righteousness doesn't lie in ourselves but in Jesus Christ.

CHAPTER 19

N. T. Wright and the
New Perspective on Paul[1]

"The problem Paul addresses in Galatians is not the
question of how precisely someone becomes a Christian,
or attains to a relationship with God.... The problem
he addresses is: should his ex-pagan converts be
circumcised or not?"   —N. T. Wright

As we turn to the New Perspective on Paul, it should be noted that
we cannot investigate the movement in detail, nor can we consider
the nuances that differentiate its advocates. My purpose here is to interact
briefly with its most celebrated adherent—N. T. Wright. The discussion
overlaps to some extent with what has already been said in the book (especially chapters 7 and 15), but it seems best to address some of the issues
again as we turn specifically to the New Perspective.

Perhaps no one in recent years has stirred up the discussion on justification among evangelical Protestants as much as N. T. Wright. Wright is one
of the most well-known NT scholars in the world. He has published scores
of books, is a witty and engaging lecturer and preacher, and has served
as a bishop in the Anglican Church in England. His books on Paul and
Jesus are full of learning and wisdom and are written from an evangelical
standpoint. Many have understood the Scriptures in a deeper and more
profound way because of his scholarship.

Yet Wright is also controversial, for he has been at the forefront of the
movement called "the New Perspective on Paul." The New Perspective
isn't that new anymore, for it was launched by a 1977 book by E. P.

---

1. This chapter and the next one represents my 2010 paper given at the ETS annual meeting
in 2010, which was published subsequently as "Justification: The Saving Righteousness of God"
(*JETS* 54 [2011]: 19–34). It is used by permission and contains some alterations. Note too that
the translations of Scripture in these two chapters are my own.

Sanders titled *Paul and Palestinian Judaism: A Comparison of Patterns of Religion*, published by Fortress Press. A number of scholars picked up Sanders's work, especially James D. G. Dunn and N. T. Wright, though we will focus on Wright because he has been particularly influential among evangelicals.

The New Perspective on Paul questions whether the Reformers read Paul correctly. The idea that the Judaism of Paul's day was legalistic is rejected; those who make that argument are reading Paul through the lenses of the Roman Catholic–Protestant dispute of the sixteenth century. Paul's main concern wasn't legalism but the ethnocentricism, the racial superiority of the Jews. Moreover, New Perspective scholars question the pride of place given to justification and the definition of the term given by the Reformers. Questioning whether the Reformers got Paul right has stirred up, to use the words of Luke, no little discussion. N. T. Wright has been at the forefront of that discussion among evangelicals. We will consider the New Perspective in the next two chapters.

In any case, it is understandable that N. T. Wright provokes strong reactions, for he is a ground-breaking and innovative thinker and one of the premier NT scholars of our generation. I find that two dangers exist in considering his scholarship. Some are inclined toward an uncritical adulation of his scholarship, while others to an uncritical denigration. I for one am thankful for his work and stand in debt to his scholarship. His work on the historical Jesus is creative yet faithful, provocative yet conservative.[2] In my opinion, his book *The Resurrection of the Son of God* is the best and most compelling book on the topic.[3]

Wright has also taught us that we should look at the big picture so we don't just focus on individual exegetical trees and miss the larger forest. Wright has helpfully reminded us of the larger story, of the narrative that unfolds in the Scriptures. Obviously there is always a danger of imposing one's own story onto the biblical text, but there is also a danger where we focus on so many details and end up with interpretations that are full of sound and fury, signifying nothing. Scholars may end up adjusting Wright's narrative account of Scripture here and there, perhaps even making radical adjustments in places, but as evangelicals we should rejoice that there is a voice out there proclaiming the unity of the biblical story. Those of us who

---

2.   But see the recent critique of Richard B. Hays, "Knowing Jesus: Story, History and the Question of Truth," in *Jesus, Paul and the People of God: A Theological Dialogue with N. T. Wright* (ed. Nicholas Perrin and Richard B. Hays; Downers Grove, IL: InterVarsity Press, 2011), 41–61

3.   N. T. Wright, *The Resurrection of the Son of God* (Christian Origins and the Question of God, vol. 3; Minneapolis: Fortress, 2003).

know the history of critical study of the Bible appreciate how radical and refreshing it is to conceive of the Bible as a unified message.

One of Wright's key ideas with which I agree is the notion that the Jews of the NT period saw themselves as still living in exile. Typically, the idea of exile refers to a period of time from captivity in Babylon to the return approximately seventy years later. Wright has shown through Jewish literature that many Jews, including the Pharisees, were not convinced that the exile had ended with that return. He points to this sense of still being in exile as evidence that the Jews of the NT still saw themselves as part of an ongoing, unfolding story, one that still awaited the promises of restoration made in the prophets.

I believe Wright is fundamentally right in what he says about the exile. Jesus came proclaiming the end of exile and the restoration of the people of God, and even if exile is not the right word to use (I don't have any great quarrel with it), the general idea is on target in any case. Israel was under the thumb of the Romans in Jesus' day because of its sin and had not yet experienced the fulfillment of the great promises found in Isaiah and the prophets. God's kingdom dawned in the life, ministry, and death of Jesus Christ. If Wright had merely said that God's kingdom was fulfilled or his saving promises had become a reality in Jesus, it would have been easy to ignore what he wrote. Rhetorically, by speaking of exile, he calls attention to the newness and the fulfillment that arrived in the ministry, life, death, and resurrection of Jesus of Nazareth.

I also want to note at the outset that though I have some problems with what is called the New Perspective (more on that later), I think we can learn from it as well. Wright and others in the New Perspective have reminded us that the boundary markers separating Jews and Gentiles were hot-button issues in the first century. These boundary markers included circumcision, Sabbath, and purity laws. Gentiles were reluctant to follow these regulations because they felt that to do so was to become a Jew ethnically. Here is one of the key teachings of the New Perspective, for they emphasize that Paul proclaimed the unity of Jews and Gentiles in Christ. Gentiles didn't have to observe the boundary markers to become Christians.

The unity of Jews and Gentiles in Christ is a crucial part of Paul's gospel, and Wright correctly trumpets that theme. Paul's theology can be communicated in an abstract individualistic way so that his teaching on the church as the people of God and the promise of a new creation are forgotten. History is going somewhere, and Wright corrects the notion that life in this world is meaningless. The created world matters, and we joyfully await a new creation where righteousness dwells.[4]

Many will concur with Wright that justification has to do with a divine declaration—it is forensic, not transformative.[5] Wright also says that perfect obedience is required to be right with God,[6] and he sees God's wrath as propitiated in Jesus' death,[7] though he may not emphasize these truths sufficiently. Wright is also on target in claiming that justification is eschatological (the end-time verdict has been announced in advance) and has a covenantal dimension, though I would argue that justification is not the same as God's covenant faithfulness but fulfills God's covenant promises.

On the one hand, I think what Wright says about justification by works or judgment according to works could be explained in a more satisfactory way since he occasionally describes good works as the final basis of justification.[8] On the other hand, Wright reminds us of a critical theme often ignored in evangelical circles.[9] Paul does teach that good works are

---

4.   On the other hand, Wright overemphasizes this theme by failing to point out the discontinuity between the present creation and the new creation, for the latter will only become a reality by the unilateral work of God.

5.   He argues, contrary to Augustine, that justification means to declare righteous instead of to make righteous. See N. T. Wright, *Justification*, 91.

6.   He says that "'works of law' will never justify, because what the law does is to reveal sin. Nobody can keep it perfectly" (ibid., 118). Cf. also 119, 195.

7.   N. T. Wright, *The Letter to the Romans: Introduction, Commentary, and Reflections*, in *The New Interpreter's Bible* (Nashville: Abingdon, 2002), 10:476.

8.   He says that "future justification" is "on the *basis* of the entire life" (N. T. Wright, *What Saint Paul Really Said: Was Paul of Tarsus the Real Founder of Christianity?* [Grand Rapids: Eerdmans, 1997], 129). Wright comments in an article on Romans 2, "Future justification, acquittal at the last great Assize, always takes place on the *basis* of the totality of the life lived" (N. T. Wright, "The Law in Romans 2," in *Paul and the Mosaic Law* [ed. James D. G. Dunn; Grand Rapids: Eerdmans, 2001], 144). Wright seems to separate present justification by faith from future justification based on works. He says in his commentary on Romans, "it is present justification, not future, that is closely correlated with faith," but "future" justification "always takes place on the *basis* of the totality of the life lived." And on the same page he remarks, "Justification, at the last, will be on the basis of performance" (*The Letter to the Romans*, 440). And in another essay he remarks, "This declaration, this vindication, occurs twice. It occurs in the future, as we have seen, on the *basis* of the entire life a person has led in the power of the Spirit—that is, it occurs on the *basis* of 'works' in Paul's redefined sense" ("New Perspectives on Paul," in *Justification in Perspective: Historical Developments and Contemporary Challenges* [ed. Bruce L. McCormack; Grand Rapids: Baker, 2006], 260). My thanks to Jason Meyer and Denny Burk for calling to my attention these citations. The italics in the citations are mine.

9.   The issue of what Wright means by "basis" became the subject of intense discussion in the blogosphere after the panel discussion at the ETS on November 19, 2010. Wright's use of the word "basis" confuses people precisely because he rejects the imputation of Christ's righteousness. I think subsequent discussion demonstrated that in using the word Wright does not mean that human works are the ultimate basis of one's right standing with God. Hence, it would be clearer if he continued to speak of justification according to our works instead of on the basis of works.

necessary for justification and for salvation, and Wright rightly says that those texts are not just about rewards. Those who are righteous are also transformed by the Holy Spirit. Only those who are led by the Spirit, walk in the Spirit, march in step with the Spirit, and sow to the Spirit will experience eternal life (Gal 5:16, 25, 28; 6:8–9). Those who practice the works of the flesh and sow to the flesh will face eschatological judgment (5:21; 6:8).

Wright is careful to say that he is not talking about perfection but of God's transforming grace in the lives of believers. He rightly sees that we have too often bracketed out the necessity of good works in evangelicalism. Wright recalls us to what Paul himself teaches on the role of good works, but his formulation would be even more helpful if he avoided the word "basis" in speaking of the necessity of works. That word lacks clarity, for it suggests that our works are part of the foundation for our right standing with God.

Problems with Wright's View of Justification

Even though we have much to learn from Wright, and I give thanks to God for his scholarship, I think his theology of justification veers off course at certain junctures.[10] Wright himself throws down the gauntlet. He says, "The discussions of justification in much of the history of the church, certainly since Augustine, got off on the wrong foot—at least in terms of understanding Paul—and they have stayed there ever since."[11] And, "Briefly and baldly put, if you start with the popular view of justification, you may actually lose sight of the heart of the Pauline gospel."[12] Wright often emphasizes that he follows the reformational principle of *sola scriptura*. Therefore, the theology of the Reformers must be subject to criticism in light of the Scriptures. I think Wright is correct here. As evangelicals we do not grant final authority to tradition. We do not casually or lightly dismiss long-held traditional interpretations, but our traditional beliefs, even our view of justification, must be assessed by the Scriptures.

---

10. For a charitable but perceptive and incisive treatment of Wright's view of justification, see Kevin J. Vanhoozer, "Wrighting the Wrongs of the Reformation? The State of the Union with Christ in St. Paul and Protestant Soteriology," in *Jesus, Paul and the People of God: A Theological Dialogue with N. T. Wright* (ed. Nicholas Perrin and Richard B. Hays; Downers Grove, IL: InterVarsity Press, 2011), 235–59.

11. Wright, *What Saint Paul Really Said*, 115.

12. Ibid., 113. He goes on to say, "This popular view of 'justification by faith,' though not entirely misleading, does not do justice to the richness and precision of Paul's doctrine, and indeed distorts it at various points."

We can be grateful to Wright, therefore, for raising fresh questions about justification. I will argue, however, that his interpretation of justification, though it has some elements that are correct, also stands in need of correction. If I could sum up the problems at the outset, Wright tends to introduce false dichotomies, presenting an either–or when there is a both–and instead. To put it more sharply, even when he sees a both–and, he at times puts the emphasis in the wrong place, seeing the secondary as primary and the primary as secondary.

I see three false polarities in Wright's thought. First, he wrongly says that justification is primarily about ecclesiology instead of soteriology. Second, he often introduces a false polarity when referring to the mission of Israel by saying that Israel's fundamental problem was its failure to bless the world whereas Paul focuses on Israel's inherent sinfulness. Third, he insists that justification is a declaration of God's righteousness but does not include the imputation of God's righteousness.

Ecclesiology or Soteriology?

Let's begin with the first point of discussion, which fits with the idea that justification is more about the church than the individual.[13] Wright mistakenly claims that justification is fundamentally about ecclesiology instead of soteriology. Let's hear it in his own words, "Justification is not how someone *becomes* a Christian. It is the declaration that they *have become* a Christian."[14] And, "What Paul means by justification, in this context, should therefore be clear. It is not 'how you become a Christian,' as much as 'how you can tell who is a member of the covenant family.' "[15] I am not quarreling with the idea that there are ecclesiological dimensions and implications to justification, nor am I saying that the words *sōzō* and *dikaioō* mean the same thing. The word *sōzō* has to do with being delivered or rescued, whereas *dikaioō* and *dikaiosynē* with whether one is declared to be in the right. The issue here should not be narrowed to the issue of word studies. The debate isn't over whether *sōzō* and *dikaioō* have the

---

13. The discussion of points two and three takes place in the next chapter.

14. Wright, *What Saint Paul Really Said*, 129.

15. Ibid., 125. He reiterates this theme elsewhere (*Justification*, 116, 131–32). Wright says that we ought not to detach ecclesiology from soteriology (ibid., 132–33), but he defines justification fundamentally in terms of ecclesiology, not soteriology (ibid., 132–34). In actuality, he enforces a division between soteriology and ecclesiology, despite his protestation here. In my reading, he hasn't changed his fundamental understanding of justification in his most recent work. N. T. Wright, *Paul and the Faithfulness of God* (2 vols.; Christian Origins and the Question of God 4; Minneapolis: Fortress, 2013). See my detailed review, "Paul's Place in the Story: N. T. Wright's Vision of Paul," *Journal for the Study of Paul and His Letters* 4 (2014): 1–26.

same definition. I am addressing the question of soteriology more broadly by asking whether justification belongs primarily in a soteriological or ecclesiological orbit, and I would argue that justification is fundamentally soteriological. Justification has to do with whether one is right before God, whether one is acquitted or condemned, whether one is pardoned or found guilty, and that is a soteriological matter.

Support for the Soteriological Character of Justification

In other words, if we use soteriology in this broader sense, justification *does* explain how one gets saved. The soteriological character of justification is supported by the frequent Pauline claim that we are righteous or justified by faith (Rom 3:22, 26, 28, 30; 5:1; 9:30; 10:6; Gal 2:16; 3:8, 11, 24; Phil 3:9; cf. Rom 4:11, 13; 10:4, 10; Gal 5:5) or that faith is counted to one as righteousness (Rom 4:3, 5, 9, 22, 24; Gal 3:6). Now I am not addressing here whether Paul thinks of faith in Jesus Christ or the faithfulness of Jesus Christ in these texts, though I think "faith in Christ" is the right reading. But even if you take Paul to be speaking of the faithfulness of Jesus Christ, he addresses the issue of *how* one becomes right with God. If one sees a reference to the faithfulness of Jesus Christ, then we become right with God through Christ's faithfulness. If one thinks Paul refers to faith in Jesus Christ, as I do, Paul still addresses *how we* become right with God: through faith in Christ. I conclude that Paul does speak to how we become Christians in using the language of justification. He says we become right through faith in (or through the faithfulness of) Jesus Christ.

The soteriological nature of justification is supported if we look at the same matter from another perspective. Paul also often teaches that we are not justified by works or by works of law or via the law (Rom. 3:20, 21, 28; 4:6, 13; 9:31; 10:3–5; Gal 2:16, 21; 3:11, 21; 5:4; Phil 3:6, 9; cf. Titus 3:5). Once again, the point I am making here is not affected by the definition of works of law, whether one takes it to refer to the whole law or to boundary markers. In either case, Paul explains *how* one is not right with God. We do not stand in the right before God by means of the law, by means of works, or by means of works of law. To say that we are not righteous by works or works of law fundamentally addresses the question of soteriology.

The soteriological thrust of justification is also borne out by the contexts in which justification appears, for justification language is regularly linked with other soteriological terms and expressions. Paul uses a variety of words to describe God's saving work in Christ, for the richness of what God has accomplished in Christ cannot be exhausted by a single term or metaphor. Justification is not the same thing as salvation or redemption or sanctification, but justification regularly appears in soteriological contexts and therefore focuses on how one is saved. For instance, in Rom 1:17 God's saving righteousness is collated with the promise that the righteous one will live by faith, and the word "live" here refers to eschatological life—to soteriology.[16] Similarly, in Rom 2:12–13 justification is contrasted with perishing and the final judgment, which shows that those who are justified will receive the verdict "not guilty" and escape from eschatological ruin.

Redemption in Pauline thinking is surely soteriological, for it features the truth that God has liberated believers from the slavery of sin. In Rom 3:24 justification is closely related to redemption, for we are "justified . . . *through* the redemption that is in Christ Jesus." Believers are right with God by means of the redeeming and liberating work of Christ. Romans 4:6–8 is particularly important, for justification is linked closely with the forgiveness of his sins. "David speaks of the blessing of the person to whom God counts *righteousness* apart from works. Blessed are those whose lawless acts are *forgiven* and whose sins are covered. Blessed is the one whose sin the Lord does not take into account" (4:6–8).[17] Forgiveness of sins and justification are not identical here, but they are closely related and are both fundamentally soteriological. So too, in 4:25 justification is explicated in terms of the forgiveness of our trespasses. Or consider 5:9, where those who are justified will be saved from God's wrath on the final day. It seems clear that justification here has to do with soteriology since it is tied to being delivered from God's wrath on the final day. The close link between justification and reconciliation in the next verse confirms the point (5:10).

In Rom 5:18 Paul refers to the "justification of life." The genitive *zōēs* can be construed in various ways. Is it appositional: justification which is life? Or is it a genitive of source? Justification which comes from life? I think it is a genitive of result: justification *sola fide* leads to or results in life. But however one takes it, justification has to do with eschatological life. Consider also 8:33, "Who will bring a charge against God's elect? God is the one who justifies." The final great courtroom scene is envisioned here, and justification clearly focuses on salvation, on the great declaration that those who belong to Christ will be cleared of all charges of guilt when the final judgment day arrives.

---

16. Paul argues the same way in Gal 3:11.

17. Italics mine to show the close relationship between righteousness and forgiveness.

Salvation and righteousness do not mean the same thing, but they are closely related and they both have to do with soteriology in the broad sense. Paul says in Rom 10:10, "For with the heart one believes resulting in *righteousness*, and with the mouth one confesses resulting in *salvation*."[18] Again, salvation and righteousness should not be equated here, but the parallelism of the phrases shows they are in the same soteriological orbit. The focus in context is not on ecclesiology but soteriology.

Another important text is 1 Cor 1:30. Christ is our "righteousness and sanctification and redemption." The specific contours and meaning of each word must be determined, but all these words are soteriological, focusing on the saving work of Jesus Christ on behalf of his people. Second Corinthians 3:9 points in the same direction, where "the ministry of condemnation" is contrasted with "the ministry of righteousness." The two terms function as antonyms. The Mosaic covenant brings condemnation, but those who belong to Christ are declared to be in the right before God. In 2 Cor 5:21 those who enjoy the gift of "the righteousness of God" are those who are reconciled to God (5:18–20), whose trespasses have not been counted against them (5:19). Titus 3:5–7 confirms this reading. Human beings are not saved according to works done in righteousness. It is those who are justified who enjoy the hope of eternal life.

I have been flying over the top quickly here referring to many different texts, for the thesis defended is not complex. We have seen that justification speaks to *how* we are saved. We are saved *by means of* faith instead of *by means of* works. In addition, justification in the many texts just cited has to do fundamentally with salvation.

Wright's False Dichotomy in Galatians

Wright makes a similar mistake when it comes to his interpretation of Galatians. He says that "the problem Paul addresses in Galatians is not the question of how precisely someone becomes a Christian, or attains to a relationship with God.... The problem he addresses is: should his ex-pagan converts be circumcised or not?"[19] So, justification "has to do

---

18. Italics mine.

19. *What Saint Paul Really Said*, 120. Wright remarks, " 'The gospel' is not an account of how people get saved. It is, as we saw in an earlier chapter, the proclamation of the lordship of Jesus Christ" (ibid., 133). And, "Let us be quite clear. 'The gospel' is the announcement of Jesus' lordship, which works with power to bring people into the family of Abraham, now redefined around Jesus Christ and characterized solely by faith in him. 'Justification' is the doctrine which insists that all those who have this faith belong as full members of this family, on this basis and no other" (ibid.).

quite obviously with the question of how you *define the people of God*: are they to be defined by the badges of Jewish race, or in some other way?"[20] Similarly, "The question at issue in the church at Antioch, to which Paul refers in chapter 2, is not how people came to a relationship with God, but whom one is allowed to eat with."[21]

Wright poses a false dichotomy here, failing to see the soteriological import of the text. According to the OT, circumcision was mandatory to be in covenant with God (e.g., Gen 17:9–14; Lev 12:3). In the Second Temple period the majority Jewish view, as John Nolland and Shaye Cohen rightly argue, is that circumcision was required to enter the people of God.[22] Gentiles who were interested in Judaism but did not submit to circumcision were considered to be God-fearers, not proselytes. The Jewish teachers who came to Galatia almost certainly argued that one must be circumcised to enter into the people of God. Wright says that there was no question about the Galatian Gentiles being Christians since they were baptized and believed in Jesus.[23] But this confuses what *Paul believed* from what the *Jewish false teachers thought*. Paul was convinced that they were Christians, but the false teachers propounded another view, maintaining that circumcision was necessary for the Galatians to enter the people of God.

An illustration might help here. When I was young, I remember running into a person who held to baptismal regeneration, insisting that baptism was only effective if it took place in his church. He told me I was not a Christian but a seeker since I wasn't baptized in his church. I think the false teachers in Galatia said something similar regarding circumcision. They believed the Galatians were seekers but not yet members of the people of God since they had not submitted to circumcision. But Paul assures the Galatians that they truly belong to God since they had received the end-time promise of the Holy Spirit (3:1–5), and warns them that if they submit to circumcision that they will be cut off from Christ forever (5:2–4).

Yes, the issue in Gal 2:11–21 is sociological and ecclesiological—whom Christians can eat with, but the sociological issue also relates fundamentally to soteriology. Paul uses the same verb in rebuking Peter that he uses to describe the false brothers and false teachers who required circumcision

---

20. Ibid., 120.
21. Ibid., 121. Cf. *Justification*, 114.
22. John Nolland, "Uncircumcised Proselytes?" *JSJ* 12 (1981): 173–94; Shaye J. D. Cohen, "Crossing the Boundary and Becoming a Jew," *HTR* 82 (1989): 26–30.
23. *Justification*, 114.

for salvation. The verb is *anankazō*, which means "compel." Both the false brothers in Jerusalem and the false teachers in Galatia were trying to compel Gentiles to get circumcised to obtain salvation (2:3–5; 6:12–13). Paul shocks Peter by saying that his refusal to eat with the Gentiles, whether intended or not, is having the same effect (2:11–14). By not having lunch with the Gentiles, Peter communicated to them inadvertently that they did not belong to the people of God. So, Wright accurately recognizes that there are ecclesiological dimensions to what happened at Antioch, but the ecclesiology is tied to and dependent on soteriology. Peter's actions unintentionally sent the message to the Gentiles in Antioch that they were not saved through faith but had to keep the Mosaic law to be members of the people of God. That explains why Paul immediately plunges into a defense of justification by faith.

Wright Misunderstands "Works of Law"

Here is where Wright's understanding of "works of law" comes in. Like other New Perspective advocates, he sees a focus on the boundary markers that divide Jews from Gentiles.[24] Interestingly, the Reformers and Catholic interpreters disputed this issue as well. Roman Catholic interpreters argued that "works of law" refer to the ceremonial law, while the Reformers emphasized that it encompasses the entire law. The topic is far too large to pursue in detail here, and I have discussed this earlier in this book, but suffice it to say that there are good reasons to conclude that "works of law" refer to the whole law.[25] If Wright is incorrect on works of law, the idea that justification has to do primarily with covenant membership is ruled out. If works of law refer to all the deeds commanded by the law, it follows that Paul teaches that right standing with God is not attained by what one does.

In my view, it makes the most sense to say that works of law refer to the entire law. A reference to the entire law seems to be confirmed by Gal 4:21 because Paul upbraids the Galatians for wanting to be under the law as a whole, not just boundary markers. In 3:10 "works of law" are defined as doing *all* the things commanded in the law, which shows that a general critique of the law is intended.

---

24. Ibid., 116–18.
25. Thomas R. Schreiner, "'Works of Law' in Paul," *NovT* 33 (1991): 217–44; Stephen Westerholm, *Israel's Law and the Church's Faith: Paul and His Recent Interpreters* (Grand Rapids: Eerdmans, 1988), 106–21; Douglas J. Moo, "'Law,' 'Works of the Law,' and Legalism in Paul," *WTJ* (1983): 73–100.

The fundamental sin of the Jews was not the exclusion of the Gentiles from the people of God. The root sin was the failure to obey God and keep his law. When Paul draws his conclusion about the universality of sin in Rom 3:19–20, he argues that no one is justified by works of law. The Jews are not charged with guilt in Romans 2 for excluding Gentiles from the people of God. Paul argues instead that they are guilty before God because they failed to do his will. Indeed, the sins he focuses on are moral infractions: stealing, adultery, and robbing temples (2:21–22). Even when Paul brings up circumcision (2:25–29), his complaint isn't that the Jews are excluding Gentiles from God's people but that they don't keep the rest of the law. They are condemned for being transgressors of the law, not for having bad attitudes toward Gentiles.

That works and works of law refer to the law as a whole is supported by other texts as well. For instance, in Rom 4:6–8 David speaks of the forgiveness granted to those who have transgressed God's will. The sins of David that are in view are almost certainly his adultery with Bathsheba and his murder of Uriah. Nary is a word said about the exclusion of the Gentiles. I am not denying that boundary markers are important to Paul. They are the subject of the next paragraph (4:9–12), but one must not import that issue into 4:1–8. Wright argues that Romans 4 is not about how Abraham was justified but about God's promise to bless the world,[26] rejecting the idea that Abraham is an example of justification by faith.[27] It seems much more likely, however, that we don't have an either–or here. Abraham's faith is an example of how blessing will come to the whole world. That is why Paul speaks of David's forgiveness of sins, and why he emphasizes that righteousness is not given as a debt to one who works for it (4:4). We see in vv. 4–5 a clear polemic against works-righteousness. God's gift of righteousness is given to the ungodly, to those who put their trust in God (4:5), even though they are sinners. Righteousness is not given to those who work to achieve God's favor, to those who expect God to reward them with eschatological life on the basis of their obedience.

Wright contests this view, arguing that Rom 4:1 is not about what Abraham had found before God but instead answers the question, "*In what sense we have found Abraham to be our father.*"[28] Even if this translation is

---

26. *Justification*, 222.
27. Ibid., 216.
28. Ibid., 218 (italics his). He goes on to say, "Grammatically this works very well indeed, a great deal better than the normal translations which have to insert extra words." The point is a technical one, but it is Wright who has added the extra word to make the translation work. He inserts "we" as the subject of the infinitive "found," but the term "we" (*hēmas*) is not present in

correct, and I am doubtful that it is, a contrast between faith and works cannot be washed out of 4:2–8. In other words, even if we accept Wright's translation of 4:1, which builds on Richard Hays's reading, Abraham is only the father of those who trust in God for their righteousness. Those who attempt to secure their righteousness by their works (i.e., those who try to put God in their debt on the basis of their deeds) are not the children of Abraham. Romans 4:1–8 powerfully supports the idea that Paul refers to works in general, teaching that justification comes from believing instead of doing.

We see the same thing when Paul addresses the issue of justification in Rom 9:30–10:13. He does not breathe a word about boundary markers in this context. Nothing is said about circumcision, Sabbath, or food laws. He refers to works in general and argues that one is justified by faith instead of works. If Paul is concerned with boundary markers here, it seems odd that he doesn't mention them at all.

A later Pauline text confirms the idea that "works" in Paul do not highlight boundary markers. Titus 3:5 says that "works done in righteousness" do not save us.[29] Note the addition of the words "in righteousness," which points away from a boundary marker interpretation and focuses on whether the works done are righteous. If Wright is mistaken on works of law and works in Paul—and I think he is—then his claim that justification does not have to do with becoming a Christian is severely undermined. Instead, the old perspective has it right. What Paul explicitly teaches is that right standing with God does not come via what we do.

Wright makes the same mistake in Gal 3:13. When it comes to this verse, he remarks that "Jesus became a curse not so that we could live with God eternally but so the blessing of Abraham might come to the Gentiles."[30] Why the either–or here? Paul even uses the term "life" to denote eschatological life twice in the two verses that immediately precede v. 13. Doesn't the blessing of Abraham include, and even focus on, the promise of salvation? Galatians 3:14 sums up the whole of 3:1–14 and summons the reader back to 3:1–5. The Galatian believers know that they

---

the Greek text. It makes better sense to see "Abraham" functioning as the subject of the infinitive, and no extra word has to be inserted to support this reading. Both Dunn and Jewett rightly reject the suggestion that "we" is the subject of the infinitive "found." See James D. G. Dunn, *Romans 1–8* (WBC; Dallas: Word, 1988), 199; Robert Jewett, *Romans: A Commentary* (Hermeneia; Minneapolis: Fortress, 2007), 307–8.

29. Even if one thinks this text is post-Pauline, it represents the standpoint of one of Paul's earliest disciples and would indicate that this early disciple understood Paul's polemic against works in a way that accords with the old perspective.

30. *Justification*, 124.

belong to the people of God apart from circumcision because they have received the Spirit.

Conclusion

To sum up, there are many things we can learn from N. T. Wright, yet while he helpfully reminds us of the ecclesiological implications of justification, in the process he wrongly downplays the essential and fundamental soteriological dimension of justification that Paul emphasizes in these key texts. Furthermore, it seems clear that Paul often uses justification language to explain *how* we become right with God, so that it is not wrong to say that justification addresses how we become Christians.

CHAPTER 20

New Perspective on Paul: The Sin of Israel and the Rejection of Imputation

"If Paul uses the language of the law court, it makes no sense whatever to say that the judge imputes, imparts, bequeaths, conveys or otherwise transfers his righteousness either to the plaintiff or the defendant."

—*N. T. Wright*

As I said in the last chapter, Wright has powerfully reminded us that we must read the Bible in terms of the overall narrative. However, there are elements of his understanding of justification that are mistaken. Related to this is his discussion about the sin of Israel. He says Romans 2 doesn't teach "that all Jews are sinful. He [Paul] is demonstrating that the boast of Israel, to be the answer to the world's problem, cannot be made good. If the mirror is cracked, it is cracked; for Israel's commission to work, Israel would have to be perfect. It is not. It is pretty much like the other nations."[1] And, "Here we meet exactly the same problem which Paul was addressing in Galatians 3:10–14: not that 'Israel is guilty and so cannot be saved,' but 'Israel is guilty and so cannot bring blessing to the nations, as Abraham's family ought to be doing.'"[2] I agree that the text subverts Israel's claim to be the answer to the world's problem. It is not as clear,

---

1. Wright, *Justification*, 195. See also idem, *The Letter to the Romans*, 445. Wright also says, "The problem with the single-plan-through-Israel-for-the-world was that Israel had failed to deliver. There was nothing wrong with the plan, or with the Torah on which it was based. The problem was in Israel itself. As we shall see later, the problem was that Israel, too, was 'in Adam'" (*Justification*, 196).

2. *Justification*, 195. He says, "God has promised to bless the world through Israel, and Israel has been faithless *to that commission*" (ibid., 67).

however, that the OT itself or Paul emphasizes that Israel was *supposed to be* the answer to the world's problem.

The OT doesn't focus on Israel's call to bless the whole world. Yes, God promises to Abraham that he would bless the world through him and Israel is called to be a kingdom of priests, but when the prophets upbraid Israel for its sin, they do not concentrate on their failure to bless the world or the pagan nations. Instead, they criticize Israel for its violation of covenant stipulations, its failure to be consecrated to the Lord. It seems to me that the main point of the story in the OT is not: Israel failed to bless the nations. That is only occasionally emphasized. The focus is on Israel's idolatry and concomitant failure to do the will of the Lord.[3]

Wright's reading of the role of Israel puts us on a false path. Yes, the point of the narrative is that Israel as a mirror is cracked. But the problem with Israel, according to Paul, isn't fundamentally *instrumental*, that they failed to bless the nations and that they failed to fulfill their commission. The complaint against Israel is primarily *ontological*. Something is inherently wrong with Israel. The people of the Lord are themselves radically evil.[4] They need the same salvation that the Gentiles need, and hence stand under the wrath of God (Rom 1:18; 2:5).

God's Plan for Israel

Contrary to Wright, I think part of God's plan in giving the law to Israel was to reveal to them and to the whole world that the law could not be kept. Wright says that such a reading is "bad theology" and "bad exegesis," for it suggests that God had a plan A (salvation through the law) and then shifted to plan B (salvation through Christ).[5] But Wright misstates the position he disagrees with. It was always God's plan to show that salvation could not come through obedience to the law, and he designed

---

3. Notice that the point being made here is nuanced. I am not trying to resolve here whether or not Israel had a mission to the world. The issue I am addressing is whether in Paul or in the OT the *fundamental* and *main* complaint against Israel is that they failed to bless the Gentiles. I am arguing that Wright's contention that Israel's primary defect was in terms of its mission is not borne out by the textual evidence.

4. Wright's reading in some instances sounds close to what I am saying, but he puts the emphasis on Israel's failure to bless the world. "The point here is that Israel *should* have been—had been called to be—the divine answer to the world's problem; and that, instead, Israel is itself fatally compromised with the same problem. Israel's sinfulness is at the heart of the charge, but the charge itself is that the doctor, instead of healing the sick, has become infected with the disease" (*The Letter to the Romans*, 445, italics his). But later he says, "Paul is not so interested in demonstrating that 'all Jews are sinners' (as we have seen, his argument scarcely proves this point) as in showing up Israel's failure to be the light of the world)" (ibid., 447).

5. *Justification*, 129.

history (particularly the history of Israel) to illustrate that truth. There is no notion here of plan A and a shift to plan B. God's plan all along was to show through Israel's history that the law could not bring salvation. Indeed, Wright's reading could be accused of having a plan A and plan B as well. Plan A: God intended to bless the world through Israel. But plan A didn't work, and so God accomplished his purposes through Jesus in plan B.[6]

The story of Israel, then, is not only or even primarily that they didn't bless the Gentiles. The narrative instead indicates that Israel is as captivated by sin as the Gentiles, and that they need salvation just as much as the Gentiles do. There is something profoundly wrong with Israel. They are rotten trees just like the Gentiles. Like the Gentiles they need to be rescued from sin and the wrath of God. Wright seems to acknowledge this truth to some extent, but he puts the emphasis on Israel's failure to bless the nations.[7]

To sum up, the revelation of Israel's sinfulness was not primarily intended to show that it failed in its mission. We learn from Israel's history that they needed the righteousness of another, and that their own righteousness would not do. That naturally brings us to Wright's third false dichotomy.[8]

Wright's Rejection of Imputation

Wright's rejection of imputation is vigorous and strong. He writes:

> If Paul uses the language of the law court, it makes no sense whatever
> to say that the judge imputes, imparts, bequeaths, conveys or
> otherwise transfers his righteousness either to the plaintiff or the
> defendant.[9]

Here we meet, not for the last time, the confusion that arises

---

6. I understand that Wright would not agree with this restatement of his view, but I think the same criticism applies to his formulation of the view from which he dissents.

7. "But Israel, too, is part of the original problem, which has a double-effect.... Israel itself needs the same rescue-from-sin-and-death that everyone else needs" (*Justification*, 201; cf. 126–27). But he also says in the same book, "This prophetic judgment, echoed by Paul, is thus not about 'proving that all Jews are sinful.' ... The point is that the Old Testament itself declares that things hadn't worked out, that the single-plan-through-Israel-for-the-world had run in the sand" (ibid., 197).

8. See the previous chapter (p. 244) for a listing of the three false dichotomies of Wright.

9. *What Saint Paul Really Said*, 98. He goes on to say, "To imagine the defendant somehow receiving the judge's righteousness is simply a category mistake. That is not how language works" (ibid.).

inevitably when we try to think of the judge transferring by imputation, or any other way, his own attributes to the defendant.[10]
When the judge in the law court justifies someone, he does not
give that person his own particular "righteousness." He *creates*
the status the vindicated defendant now possesses, by an act of
declaration, a "speech-act" in our contemporary jargon.[11]

What are we talking about when we talk about imputation?[12] The
fundamental issue is not the language of active and passive obedience or
whether Paul accords with sixteenth- or seventeenth-century expressions
of the doctrine. Many misunderstand what is meant by active and passive
obedience in any case.[13] The issue is whether God's righteousness is given
to believers in and through Jesus Christ. In other words, does our righteousness ultimately rest in our works (even if Spirit-produced) or in the
work of Jesus Christ? Calvin rightly argued that we enjoy the righteousness
of Christ through union with Christ, and Luther similarly maintained
that we are married to Christ, and therefore, all that is Christ's belongs
to us.[14] According to Wright, there is no sense in which God gives us his
own righteousness.[15] So, the issue is not sixteenth- or seventeenth-century
formulations of the doctrine. Whatever one thinks of those formulations,
my purpose here is to address Wright's contention that God does not give
us his righteousness in and through Jesus Christ.

The Significance of Imputation

Why is imputation important? Why is it vital that we receive God's gift
of righteousness? Because it is our only hope of standing in the right before

---

10. *Justification*, 66. Wright declares, "The judge has not clothed the defendant with his own
'righteousness.' That doesn't come into it. Nor has he given the defendant something called 'the
righteousness of the Messiah'—or, if he has, Paul not even hinted at it. What the judge has done
is to pass judicial sentence on sin, in the faithful death of the Messiah, so that those who belong
to the Messiah, though in themselves 'ungodly' and without virtue or merit, now find themselves
hearing the lawcourt verdict, 'in the right'" (ibid., 206).

11. Ibid., 69. *"But the righteousness they have will not be God's own righteousness.* That makes
no sense at all. God's own righteousness is his covenant faithfulness ... But God's righteousness
remains his own property" (*What Saint Paul Really Said*, 99).

12. For important works supporting imputation, see Vickers, *Jesus' Blood and Righteousness*;
Piper, *Counted Righteous in Christ*; Carson, "The Vindication of Imputation," 46–78.

13. See Murray, *Redemption Accomplished or Applied*, 21–22 (see p. 182, n. 10 for the quote).

14. For Calvin's view, see Craig B. Carpenter, "A Question of Union with Christ? Calvin and
Trent on Justification," *WTJ* 64 (2002): 363–86. For Luther, see Martin Luther, "The Freedom
of a Christian," in *Three Treatises* (trans. W. A. Lambert; rev. ed.; Philadelphia: Fortress, 1970),
286–87.

15. He specifically says in the quote above that there is no way in which God gives us his own
righteousness (*Justification*, 66).

God on the final day. As noted earlier, Wright correctly says that believers must do good works to be justified, but such works are not the basis of our right standing with God since our righteousness is always partial and imperfect. Our right standing with God finally depends on Christ's righteousness. That is why J. Gresham Machen found such comfort in imputation as he lay dying.[16] It is curious that Wright fails to see this since he agrees that God demands perfect obedience. If perfect obedience is required for justification, it seems to follow that we need God's righteousness in Christ to be justified.

Wright's Interpretation of Imputation Texts

I think it is legitimate to read 1 Cor 1:30 as a righteousness from God that is ours through union with Christ. "But of him you are in Christ Jesus, who became to us wisdom from God, righteousness and sanctification and redemption." Wright thinks this verse can't possibly refer to imputation because we don't speak of imputed wisdom, redemption, or sanctification.[17] On the one hand, I agree that we can't read a full doctrine of imputation out of this verse. On the other hand, I don't think it can be waived out of the verse too quickly either. Wright's reading seems to suggest that all the benefits described here must apply to us in exactly the same way, but that doesn't necessarily follow, for the words do not mean the same thing. It seems fair to consider other texts to construe what Paul means by righteousness.

In any case, Paul seems to be arguing that we do not find *in ourselves* wisdom, redemption, sanctification, or righteousness. God's saving work fundamentally stands outside us, and we enjoy what he has done for us as we are united to Christ by faith. Surprisingly, Wright thinks sanctification here refers to "a process."[18] Time and space are lacking, but I think Paul has in mind definitive sanctification here, what is sometimes called positional sanctification—the idea that we are holy before God based on what Christ has done for us.[19] The evidence of the letter shows that the Corinthians had a long way to go in actual holiness, but they were already sanctified in Christ (1 Cor 1:2). If the sanctification of the Corinthians was theirs in Christ, it seems that righteousness could be understood along

---

16. See Stonehouse, *J. Gresham Machen*, 508.
17. *What Saint Paul Really Said*, 123.
18. *Justification*, 156.
19. See especially David Peterson, *Possessed by God: A New Testament Theology of Sanctification and Holiness* (Grand Rapids: Eerdmans, 1995).

the same lines. It would seem to fit the argument well if Paul were claiming that their righteousness is not their own. It is theirs by virtue of their incorporation into Christ.

Against Wright, I think it is clear that 2 Cor 5:21 supports the imputation of Christ's righteousness.[20] The verse says, "The one who knew no sin, he made to be sin for our sake, so that we should become the righteousness of God in him." Notice again the emphasis on incorporation into Christ in the verse. We enjoy God's righteousness by virtue of our union with Jesus, because we are in him. Furthermore, the verse emphasizes Jesus' sinlessness. Partial righteousness will not do. We need Jesus' perfect righteousness to stand in the right before God. Believers are righteous because all of who Jesus is and what he has accomplished, both in his life and his death, belong to us.

Contrary to Wright, I don't think that the first person pronouns in 2 Cor 5:21 restrict what is said here to Paul as an apostle. This is a complex subject, but I would suggest that Paul uses pronouns much more loosely and not in such a technical way. Sometimes in these verses Paul uses the first person plural pronoun to refer to himself, while other times it refers to the Corinthians.[21] Nor does the word *genōmetha* ("we become") in v. 21 rule out imputation, for the word does not necessarily designate the infusion of righteousness.[22] The verb *ginomai* is flexible and doesn't necessarily refer to a process or to the infusion of righteousness. Murray Harris argues that "*ginomai* may be given its most common meaning ('become,' 'be') and points to the change of status that accrues to believers who are 'in Christ.'"[23] Here it signifies that one who was formerly not righteous is now counted as righteous in Christ. Harris concludes that "it is not inappropriate to perceive in this verse a double imputation: sin was reckoned to Christ's account (v. 21a), so that righteousness is reckoned to our account (v. 21b).... As a result of God's imputing to Christ something extrinsic to him, namely sin, believers have something imputed to them that was extrinsic to them, namely righteousness."[24]

---

20. *What Saint Paul Really Said*, 104–5; *Justification*, 159–64. See here Garland, *2 Corinthians*, 300–302; Harris, *The Second Epistle to the Corinthians*, 454–56, and esp. n. 207 on pp. 455–56.

21. Harris, *The Second Epistle to the Corinthians*, 437.

22. Contra Wright, *Justification: God's Plan & Paul's Vision*, 165. Cf. his comments elsewhere on righteousness, "it denotes a *status*, not a moral quality" (ibid., 121).

23. Harris, *The Second Epistle to the Corinthians*, 455.

24. Ibid.

Legal Declaration Versus Moral Character?

Wright leads us astray when he says that because justification is a legal declaration, it is not based on one's moral character.[25] A couple of things need to be untangled here. In one sense, of course, justification is not based on our moral character, for God justifies the ungodly (Rom 4:5). If justification depended on our moral worth, no one would be justified. But Wright fails to state clearly the role that moral character plays in justification, and because he separates moral character from the law court, he fails to see the role that Christ's righteousness plays in imputation. When a judge in Israel declared a person to be innocent or guilty, he did so on the basis of the moral innocence or guilt of the defendant. The biblical text insists that judges render a verdict on the basis of the moral behavior of the defendant. This is evident from Deut 25:1, "If there is a dispute between two people, and they come into court and the judges decide between them, they should acquit the innocent and condemn the guilty." For Wright to say, then, that one's moral behavior has nothing to do with the judge's declaration flies in the face of the biblical evidence. Indeed, the only basis for the legal declaration was one's moral behavior—whether one was innocent or guilty.

What does all of this have to do with imputation? The fundamental question is how God can declare sinners to be righteous. How can a verdict of "not-guilty" be pronounced over those who are in fact ungodly and sinners? For a judge to declare that the wicked are righteous is contrary to the way judges should behave. As Prov 17:15 says, "He who justifies the wicked and he who condemns the righteous are both alike an abomination to the LORD." So how can God be righteous in declaring the wicked to be righteous? The answer of Scripture is that the Father because of his great love sent his Son, who willingly and gladly gave himself for sinners, so that the wrath that sinners deserved was poured out upon the Son (cf. Rom 3:24–26). God can declare sinners to be in the right because they are forgiven by Christ's sacrifice. God vindicates his *moral righteousness* in the justification of sinners since Christ takes upon himself the punishment and wrath sinners deserve. It is clear, then, that moral character plays a vital

---

25. Wright remarks, "'Righteousness,' within the lawcourt setting—and this is something that no good Lutheran or Reformed theologian ought ever to object to—denotes *the status that someone has when the court has found in their favor.* Notice, that it does not *denote*, with that all-important lawcourt context, 'the moral character they are then assumed to have,' or 'the moral behavior they have demonstrated which has earned them the verdict" (*Justification,* 90).

role in justification, for God's own holiness must be satisfied in the cross of Christ for forgiveness to be granted.

The Judge Who Gives His Own Righteousness

Wright insists that no judge in the courtroom can give his righteousness to the defendant. The mistake Wright makes here is surprising, for the significance of the law court or any other metaphor in Scripture cannot be exhausted by its cultural background. In other words, it is true that in human courtrooms the judge does not and cannot give his righteousness to the defendant. But we see the distinctiveness of the biblical text and the wonder and the glory of the gospel precisely here. God is not restricted by the rules of human courtrooms. This is a most unusual courtroom indeed, for the judge delivers up his own Son to pay the penalty. That doesn't happen in human courtrooms! And the judge gives us his own righteousness—a righteousness from God (Phil 3:9).

The biblical text, then, specifically teaches that God, as the divine judge, both vindicates us and gives us his righteousness. When we are united to Christ by faith, all that Christ is belongs to us. Hence, we stand in the right before God because we are in Christ. Our righteousness, then, is not in ourselves. We exult because we enjoy the righteousness of God in Jesus Christ. Once again moral character enters the picture, contrary to Wright. We stand in the right before God because our sins have been forgiven and because we enjoy the righteousness of Jesus Christ.

God's Righteousness in Christ

The imputation of righteousness is also supported by Rom 5:12–19.[26] We don't have time here to linger over the text, but its main point is clear. At least five times we are told in these verses that both death and condemnation are the portion of all people because of Adam's one sin. Adam functions here as the representational head of all human beings. Similarly, those who belong to Jesus Christ are justified (5:16) and righteous (5:17) because of their union with him.[27] Sometimes scholars say that those who defend imputation are importing an abstract and alien notion into the text. But the charge can be reversed, for when believers are united with Christ,

---

26. Wright argues that Jesus was faithful to God's plan, not to the law, and hence there is no "treasury of merit through Torah obedience" here (*The Letter to the Romans*, 529).

27. Wright comes close to saying the same thing here. "That which Israel, or groups within Israel, thought to gain has been appropriately attained by the true Israelite, the Messiah, the obedient one. He now shares this status with all his people" (ibid., 524). But this is still not the same thing as saying we enjoy a gift of righteousness given to us by God in Christ.

they receive all of who Christ is, both in his life and in his death, both in his obedience and in his suffering, both in the precepts he obeyed and in the penalty he endured. Therefore, believers are not just forgiven; they also receive God's righteousness in Christ. All of Christ is theirs, for they belong to him, and thus their righteousness is in him.

Conclusion

Naturally much more could be said about the fundamental importance of justification (see part 2 of this book). The issues here are not merely academic but are crucial for pastoral ministry and the mission of the church and for assurance of salvation. Luther is on target when he says the following about justification by faith,

> This is a very important and pleasant comfort with which to bring wonderful encouragement to minds afflicted and disturbed with a sense of sin and afraid of every flaming dart of the devil ... your righteousness is not visible, and it is not conscious; but it is hoped for as something to be revealed in due time. Therefore you must not judge on the basis of your consciousness of sin, which terrifies and troubles you, but on the basis of the promise and teaching of faith, by which Christ is promised to you as your perfect and eternal righteousness.[28]

In conclusion, I wish to reassert that we can be grateful on so many fronts for the scholarship of N. T. Wright. His innovative scholarship has helped clarify biblical teachings and rectified wrong notions. My hope is that my response to his views on justification in these chapters will be received in the spirit in which it is intended, for like so many I stand in debt to his outstanding scholarship. Nevertheless, in my judgment Wright's view of justification needs to be both clarified and corrected, for our sure hope for eternal life is the righteousness of God that belongs to us through our union with Jesus Christ.

---

28. Luther, *Galatians: 1–4*, 21.

CHAPTER 21

A Concluding Word

"Faith comes from what is heard."
—*Romans 10:17*

I have tried to show in this work that faith isn't merely a mental agreement—an intellectual assent to certain teachings or doctrines. Faith includes mental assent and if such assent is lacking, faith isn't present. Understanding truth is imperative for saving faith, for "faith comes from hearing" (Rom 10:17 NIV), and what must be heard is the gospel of Christ. So, faith is never less than mental assent.

At the same time, saving faith is more than mental assent. Saving faith embraces, leans on, and trusts in all that God has done for us in Jesus Christ. Justification is by faith alone because it relies on and rests on Christ alone for deliverance from God's wrath. Justification is by faith alone, for faith finds its joy in Christ alone, seeing him as the pearl of great price, the one who is more desirable than anything or anyone else. Faith rests in the Beloved, realizing that there is no salvation or peace or joy anywhere else.

Faith, then, recognizes that all the glory belongs to God alone. Faith saves, not because of our faith, but because of the one in whom we trust. The person we trust in saves us, and he is shown to be merciful and mighty, just and loving so that both his judging and saving righteousness are satisfied at the cross. We see from another angle why our faith isn't our righteousness, for such a scenario focuses on our faith instead of the one in whom we trust. This is not to deny for an instant that we must believe and persevere in the faith. Human beings aren't automatons or nonentities. Still, our faith doesn't ultimately save us, for salvation is of the Lord. It is the Lord who justifies us, and it is the Lord who is justified and vindicated in the justification of sinners. God is revealed to be the Holy One of Israel and the loving Savior of his people. The praise, honor, and glory belong to him alone for our salvation.

Finally, justification by faith alone can be considered from another angle. I have tried to show in this book that justification by faith alone is the teaching of the Scriptures and also that such a teaching is deeply rooted in the teaching of the church throughout history. But it is also the case that such a teaching makes sense of Christian experience and Christian history. It makes sense of Christian experience, for we are all conscious of our ongoing sins and flaws. Such an admission doesn't deny the newness of our lives in Christ. We are a new creation in Christ Jesus and have been redeemed from our sins. We live in a new way because of the grace of God, so that we experience love, joy, and peace during our earthly sojourn. By the power of the Spirit we put to death the works of the flesh. We are no longer the old self we were in Adam but are new persons in Jesus Christ, and hence we put off the old person and put on the new. We do and can live in a way that is pleasing to God.

At the same time, we continue to be plagued by sin. Even our best actions are tainted by pride. We aren't entirely free of impatience, anger, bitterness, self-pity, resentment, lust, and so on. Indeed, sometimes these sins manifest themselves in our lives in remarkable ways. Our righteousness, even after we are Christians, can't qualify us to enter the new creation and God's presence, for, despite all the changes in us, we are still defiled by sin. How comforting to know that our righteousness doesn't lie ultimately in ourselves but in Jesus Christ as the crucified and risen one. He is our righteousness, and thus our hope for life isn't anchored to our achievements but to his grace. Faith doesn't save as if it constitutes our righteousness. It saves because it unites us to Jesus Christ, who is our righteousness and our only hope on the day of judgment.

The theology of justification also makes sense of the church of Jesus Christ. On the one hand, God has worked in the church throughout history. By his grace he has changed lives, so the church has been the channel of God's love, mercy, and justice in the world. What stories will be told, stories that are hidden from us now to a large extent, of what the church has accomplished throughout its history. The church has fearlessly, courageously, and lovingly proclaimed the good news about Jesus to the ends of the earth, facing disease, death, and enemies. The church has stood up for truth and justice when the rest of the world has pursued the gods of economic prosperity, material comfort, and sexual pleasure.

On the other hand, the record of the church, just like the record of our own lives, is mixed. The church has also been guilty of horrifying sins. It hasn't always stood for truth and for what is right. In the annals of the church's history, racism, political intrigue, persecution, and sexual abuse are also part of the story. Anyone who doubts such is blind to the history of the church. The church has been changed by the grace of God, but it is also a pilgrim people marked by imperfection.[1] It isn't yet without spot and blemish, and sometimes the blemishes are deeply embarrassing. But the righteousness of the church is found in Jesus Christ. God has washed it clean with the blood of his Son so that we have white robes and can enter the city and partake of the tree of life.

I have worked in churches and Christian institutions of higher learning all my life. What a privilege and joy it has been. My colleagues and students have been a joy to work with, and when I hear stories of the difficulty others have had in their working environment, I give praise to God for the colleagues and students with whom I work. Still, it hasn't been paradise on earth. There is gossip, insensitivity, ambition to get to the top, intellectual pride, and political maneuvering. My interaction with some of the finest Christians I have ever known convinces me of justification by faith alone.

Finally, I know myself, at least to a limited degree. God by his grace has changed me and made me a new person. I have new affections and have lived a totally different life than I would have lived apart from Christ and the transforming work of the Spirit. Yet I still struggle with pride, bitterness, resentment, lust, and so on. The fight with sin is not over, and I have had far too many defeats. Still, "by God's grace I am what I am" (1 Cor 15:10). But my confidence on the last day will not rest on my transformation. I have too far to go to put any confidence in what I have accomplished. Instead, I rest on Jesus Christ. He is my righteousness. He is the guarantor of my salvation (Heb 7:22). I am justified by faith alone, in Christ alone, to the glory of God alone.

---

1. Allen, *Justification and the Gospel*, 153–78.

Select Bibliography

Allen, R. Michael. *Justification and the Gospel: Understanding the Context and Controversies*. Grand Rapids: Baker, 2013.

Arnold, Brian John. "Justification One Hundred Years after Paul." Ph.D. diss., The Southern Baptist Theological Seminary, 2013.

Aune, David A. *Rereading Paul Together: Protestant and Catholic Perspectives on Justification*. Grand Rapids: Baker, 2006.

Beckwith, Francis J. *Return to Rome: Confessions of an Evangelical Catholic*. Grand Rapids: Baker, 2009.

Beilby, James K., and Paul Rhodes Eddy, eds. *Justification: Five Views*. Downers Grove, IL: InterVarsity Press, 2011.

Bird, Michael F. *The Saving Righteousness of God: Studies on Paul, Justification, and the New Perspective*. Paternoster Biblical Monographs. Eugene, OR: Wipf and Stock, 2007.

Bird, Michael F., and Preston Sprinkle, eds. *The Faith of Jesus Christ: Exegetical, Biblical, and Theological Studies*. Peabody, MA: Hendrickson, 2009.

Boersma, Hans. *A Hot Pepper Corn: Richard Baxter's Doctrine of Justification in Its Seventeenth-Century Context of Controversy*. Zoetermeer: Uitgeverij Boekencentrum, 1993.

Bratten, Carl E., and Robert W. Jenson, eds. *Union with Christ: The New Finnish Interpretation of Luther*. Grand Rapids: Eerdmans, 1998.

Buchanan, James. *The Doctrine of Justification: An Outline of Its History in the Church and Its Exposition from Scripture*. Reprint. London: Banner of Truth, 1961.

Calvin, John. *Institutes of the Christian Religion*. Ed. John T. McNeill. Translated and indexed by Ford Lewis Battles. LCC 20. Philadelphia: Westminster, 1960.

Campbell, Douglas A. *The Deliverance of God: An Apocalyptic Rereading of Justification in Paul*. Grand Rapids: Eerdmans, 2009.

Cannon, William Ragsdale. *The Theology of John Wesley: With Special Reference to the Doctrine of Justification*. Lanham: University Press of America, 1974.

Carson, D. A., Mark A. Seifrid, and Peter T. O'Brien, eds. *Justification and Variegated Nomism: Volumes 1–2*. Grand Rapids: Baker, 2001, 2004.

Catechism of the Catholic Church. Rev. ed. New York: Random House, 2012.

Colson, C., and R. J. Neuhaus. *Evangelicals and Catholics Together: Toward a Common Mission*. Dallas: Word, 1995.

Cooper, Tim. *John Owen, Richard Baxter and the Formation of Nonconformity*. Burleigh, VT: Ashgate, 2011.

Davies, W. D. *Paul and Rabbinic Judaism: Some Rabbinic Elements in Pauline Theology.* 4th ed. Philadelphia: Fortress, 1980.

Dunn, James D. G. *The New Perspective on Paul.* Rev. ed. Grand Rapids: Eerdmans, 2008.

Dunn, James D. G., ed. *Paul and the Mosaic Law.* Tübingen: Mohr Siebeck, 1996.

Edwards, Jonathan. "Justification by Faith Alone." Pages 147–242 in *The Works of Jonathan Edwards:* Vol. 19, *Sermons and Discourses, 1734–1738,* Ed. M. X. Lesser. New Haven, CT: Yale University Press, 2001.

Elliott, Mark W., Scott J. Hafemann, N. T. Wright, and John Frederick, eds. *Galatians and Christian Theology: Justification, the Gospel, and Ethics in Paul's Letter.* Grand Rapids: Baker, 2014.

Fesko, J. V. *Beyond Calvin: Union with Christ and Justification in Early Modern Reformed Theology, 1517–1700.* Reformed Historical Theology 20. Göttingen: Vandenhoeck & Ruprecht, 2012.

Gaffin, Richard B. *The Centrality of the Resurrection: A Study in Paul's Soteriology.* Grand Rapids: Baker, 1978.

———. *"By Faith, Not By Sight": Paul and the Order of Salvation.* Waynesboro, GA: Paternoster, 2006.

George, Timothy. *Theology of the Reformers.* Rev. ed. Nashville: B & H Academic, 2013.

Gorman, Michael J. *Inhabiting the Cruciform God: Kenosis, Justification, and Theosis in Paul's Narrative Soteriology.* Grand Rapids: Eerdmans, 2009.

Hahn, Scott and Kimberly. *Rome Sweet Home: Our Journey to Catholicism.* San Francisco: Ignatius, 1993.

Husbands, M. A., and D. J. Trier, eds. *"Justification": What's at Stake in the Current Debates.* Downers Grove, IL: InterVarsity Press, 2004.

Jüngel, Eberhard. *Justification: The Heart of the Christian Faith: A Theological Study with an Ecumenical Purpose.* Trans. Jeffrey F. Cayzer. Edinburgh: T&T Clark, 2001.

Kärkkäinen, Veli-Matti. *One with God: Salvation as Justification and Deification.* Collegeville, MN: Liturgical Press, 2004.

Kertelge, Karl. *Rechtfertigung bei Paulus: Studien zur Struktur und zum Bedeutungsgehalt des paulinischen Rechtfertigungbegriffs.* 2nd ed. NTAbh 3. Münster: Aschendorff, 1967.

Lane, Anthony N. S. *Justification by Faith in Catholic-Protestant Dialogue: An Evangelical Assessment.* London T&T Clark, 2002.

Luther, Martin. *Lectures on Galatians, 1535. Chapters 1–4.* Vol. 26 of *Luther's Works.* Ed. Jaroslav Pelikan. St. Louis: Concordia, 1964.

———. *Lectures on Galatians, 1535. Chapters 5–6.* Vol. 27 of *Luther's Works.* Ed. Jaroslav Pelikan. St. Louis: Concordia, 1964.

———. *Martin Luther: Selections from His Writings.* Ed. John Dillenberger. Garden City, NJ: Doubleday, 1961.

———. *Three Treatises.* Trans. W. A. Lambert and Rev. Harold J. Grimm. Philadelphia: Fortress, 1970.

Macchia, Frank D. *Justified in the Spirit: Creation, Redemption, and the Triune God.* Grand Rapids: Eerdmans, 2010.

Mannermaa, Tuomo. *Christ Present in Faith: Luther's View of Justification.* Ed. and intro. by K. Stjerna. Minneapolis: Fortress, 2005.

Mattes, Mark C. *The Role of Justification in Contemporary Theology.* Lutheran Quarterly Books. Grand Rapids: Eerdmans, 2004.

McClymond, Michael J., and Gerald P. McDermott. *The Theology of Jonathan Edwards.* Oxford: Oxford University Press, 2012.

McCormack, Bruce L., ed. *Justification in Perspective: Historical Developments and Contemporary Challenges.* Grand Rapids: Baker, 2006.

McGrath, Alister E. *Iustitia Dei: A History of the Christian Doctrine of Justification.* Vol. 1. *From the Beginnings to 1500.* Cambridge: Cambridge University; Press, 1986.

———. *Iustitia Dei: A History of the Christian Doctrine of Justfication.* Vol. 2. *From the 1500s to the Present Day.* Cambridge: Cambridge University Press, 1986.

Moody, J., ed. *Jonathan Edwards and Justification.* Wheaton, IL: Crossway, 2012.

Oden, Thomas C. *John Wesley's Scriptural Christianity: A Plain Exposition of His Teaching on Christian Doctrine.* Grand Rapids: Zondervan, 1994.

———. *The Justification Reader.* Grand Rapids: Eerdmans, 2002.

Owen, John. *The Doctrine of Justification by Faith through the Imputation of the Righteousness of Christ; Explained, Confirmed, and Vindicated.* In *The Works of John Owen.* Vol. 5. Ed. William H. Goold. Carlisle, PA: Banner of Truth, 1965.

Piper, John. *Counted Righteous in Christ: Should We Abandon the Imputation of Christ's Righteousness?* Wheaton, IL: Crossway, 2002.

———. *The Future of Justification: A Response to N. T. Wright.* Wheaton: Cross, 2007.

Rainbow, Paul A. *The Way of Salvation: The Role of Christian Obedience in Justification.* Waynesboro, GA: Paternoster, 2005.

Reumann, John H. P. *Righteousness in the New Testament: Justification in the United States Lutheran-Roman Catholic Dialogue, with Responses by Joseph A. Fitzmyer and Jerome D. Quinn.* Philadelphia: Fortress, 1982.

Rupp, Gordon. *The Righteousness of God: Luther Studies.* London: Hodder and Stoughton, 1953.

Sanders, E. P. *Paul and Palestinian Judaism: A Comparison of Patterns of Religion.* Philadelphia: Fortress, 1977.

Schreiner, Thomas R. *The Law and Its Fulfillment: A Pauline Theology of Law.* Grand Rapids: Baker, 1993.

———. *Forty Questions about Christians and Biblical Law.* Grand Rapids: Kregel, 2010.

Schumacher, William W. *Who Do I Say That You Are? Anthropology and the Theology of Theosis in the Finnish School of Tuomo Mannermaa.* Eugene, OR: Wipf & Stock, 2010.

Seifrid, Mark A. *Christ, Our Righteousness: Paul's Theology of Justification.* NSBT 9. Downers Grove, IL: InterVarsity Press, 2000.

Sproul, R. C. *Faith Alone: The Evangelical Doctrine of Justification*. Grand Rapids: Baker, 1995.

———. *Getting the Gospel Right: The Tie that Binds Evangelicals Together*. Grand Rapids: Baker, 1999.

Stendahl, Krister. *Paul among Jews and Gentiles and Other Essays*. Philadelphia: Fortress, 1977.

Stuhlmacher, Peter. *Gerechtigkeit Gottes bei Paulus*. FRLANT 87. Göttingen: Vandenhoeck & Ruprecht, 1965.

Sungenis, Robert A. *"Not by Faith Alone": The Biblical Evidence for the Catholic Doctrine of Justification*. Santa Barbara, CA: Queenship Publishing, 1997.

Thompson, Virgil, ed. *Justification Is for Preaching: Essays by Oswald Bayer, Gerhard O. Forde, and Others*. Eugene, OR: Pickwick, 2012.

Torrance, Thomas F. *The Doctrine of Grace in the Apostolic Fathers*. Grand Rapids: Eerdmans, 1948.

Vanhoozer, Kevin J. "Wrighting the Wrongs of the Reformation? The State of the Union with Christ in St. Paul and Protestant Soteriology." Pages 234–59 in *Jesus, Paul and the People of God: A Theological Dialogue with N. T. Wright*. Ed. Nicholas Perrin and Richard B. Hays. Downers Grove, IL: InterVarsity Press, 2011.

Vickers, Brian. *Jesus' Blood and Righteousness: Paul's Theology of Imputation*. Wheaton, IL: Crossway, 2006.

———. *Justification by Grace through Faith: Finding Freedom from Legalism, Lawlessness, Pride, and Despair*. Phillipsburg, NJ: Presbyterian & Reformed, 2013.

Wengert, Timothy J. *Defending Faith: Lutheran Responses to Andreas Osiander's Doctrine of Justification 1551–1559*. Studies in the Late Middle Ages, Humanism, and the Reformation 65. Tübingen: Mohr Siebeck, 2012.

Wesley, John. "On the Wedding Garment." Pages 140–48 in *The Works of John Wesley*. Vol. 4. Ed. Albert Outler. Nashville: Abingdon, 1987.

———. *Sermon I, "Salvation by Faith"* (1738). Pages 7–52 in *Wesley's Standard Sermons*. Ed. Edward H. Sugden. Vol. 1. London: Epworth, 1951.

Westerholm, Stephen. *Justification Reconsidered: Rethinking a Pauline Theme*. Grand Rapids: Eerdmans, 2013.

Wright, N. T. *What Saint Paul Really Said: Was Paul of Tarsus the Real Founder of Christianity?* Grand Rapids: Eerdmans, 1997.

———. *Justification: God's Plan and Paul's Vision*. Downers Grove, IL: InterVarsity Press, 2009.

———. *Paul and the Faithfulness of God*. 2 vols. Christian Origins and the Question of God 4. Minneapolis: Fortress, 2013.

Scripture Index

Subject Index